Most people have emotions they can't handle, so they 'screen them off', hiding them from others and even themselves. They often choose partners with the same inhibitions, which are then passed on to their children . . . from generation to generation.

Using the most modern experiences of family therapy this book shows how understanding can lead to progress, the taboos can be broken down, and development of healthy relationships and families can take place.

The subject is vital to us all, and the authors deal with it lucidly and incisively, with a lightness of touch that is brilliantly served by Bud Handelsman's cartoons.

Robin Skynner has been a pioneer in group and family techniques of treatment and one of the founders of both the Institute of Group Analysis and Institute of Family Therapy, where he continues to teach. He is the author of the text book *One Flesh: Separate Persons; Principles of Family and Marital Psychotherapy*.

John Cleese is best known as a comic. He was born in Weston-super-Mare in 1939, got 'A' levels in science at the Clifton College Sports Academy, taught for two years and then studied Law at Cambridge, where he joined the Footlights.

FAMILIES
and how to survive them

Robin Skynner/John Cleese

Cartoons by
Bud Handelsman

METHUEN LONDON

A Methuen Paperback

First published in Great Britain 1983
First paperback edition published 1984
by Methuen London Ltd
11 New Fetter Lane, London EC4P 4EE
© 1983 Robin Skynner and John Cleese
© Illustrations 1983 Methuen London Ltd
Designed by Behram Kapadia

Printed and bound in Great Britain by
Hazell Watson & Viney Limited,
Member of the BPCC Group,
Aylesbury, Bucks

ISBN 0 413 56520 3

Contents

Acknowledgements

We would like to thank the following friends and colleagues for sparing time to read and comment on parts of the manuscript, or for providing information and advice; however, responsibility for the views expressed, and for any errors and omissions, remains, of course, entirely our own:

Jane Abercrombie, Susan Barrows, Ruth Berkowitz, Dennis Brown, Arnon Bentovim, John Bowlby, John Byng-Hall, Douglas Connor, Chris Dare, Shirley Dare, Ronald Eyre, Lionel Kreeger, Marianne Kreeger, Malcolm Pines, Denis Robinson, Margaret Robinson, Meg Sharpe, David Skynner, Prue Skynner, Katrin Stroh and Barbara Trentham.

We would particularly like to acknowledge the quite exceptional editorial contributions of Christopher Falkus and Ann Mansbridge, and we are also most grateful to Daphne Day, Dee Edwards, Joan Pakenham-Walsh, Briar Silich and Joan Snell for their sterling work in typing the many drafts.

Author's Note

We have used 'he' throughout this book when referring to the baby or child, not for any sexist reason, but because we felt it enabled us to refer clearly to 'he' and 'she' in our frequent discussions about the baby and the mother.

To Prue and Barbara

Introduction

Why we wrote this book

John Ten years ago, I went into group therapy. I did this for two reasons. First, I had suffered for at least two years from low-grade 'flu symptoms which my doctor wasn't able to cure. Eventually, after three full check-ups, he advised me that the cause was probably psychosomatic, and suggested that a psychological approach to the problem might prove fruitful. At about the same time I was having problems connected with my first marriage and had come to the conclusion that I was too confused to sort them out without outside help – in fact, I remember thinking at that time that I lacked the intellectual tools to understand what was going on. I now realise that I also lacked then certain emotional experiences that I needed to go through in the group if I was to solve the problems that were bothering me.

Of course, I didn't enter the Wonderful World of Shrinks very enthusiastically because I had all the usual British reservations about the Whole Psychiatry Business. Nevertheless, despite my scepticism – I might almost say mistrust – I began to attend a therapy group. It was run by Robin Skynner and his wife Prue, who worked together as co-therapists. There were seven other people in the group, including several couples. And so, for an hour and a half late every Thursday afternoon, the ten of us sat in a circle and just talked, for the next three and a half years! The people in the group changed over this period, of course; as some felt ready to leave, they were replaced by new recruits.

After about a year, I began to feel I was undergoing the most interesting experience of my adult life. For a start, once we'd all lowered our barriers a bit, I was able to see my fellow group members behaving in a freer, more open way than you can ever hope to observe in normal social life, except perhaps with your two or three most intimate friends. Without wishing to trivialize what was happening in the group, I remember thinking that it made most film and TV drama seem pale, artificial and unconvincing by comparison. But such a thought may imply that I was trying to distance myself from the group's proceedings. I wasn't. I was very thoroughly involved, in a sense that as the months progressed I went through a very wide range of moods and emotions, some of them quite new and difficult to handle. But apart from these emotional experiences, and also certain discoveries I made about myself – which didn't quite fit my image of myself at that time! – the most startling realisation was that some of my deepest ingrained attitudes were being questioned for the first time – especially some of my basic assumptions about man/woman relationships. These were being exposed to scrutiny in an entirely new way, so that I was beginning to wonder if the ideas that I'd grown up with in Weston-super-Mare really worked for me.

Today, more than five years after I finally left therapy, I can say without any reservation that what I learnt from the group has helped me enormously. Since that time, I've led a much more enjoyable life. My experiences in the group certainly freed me from all the physical symptoms I'd been suffering, and also reduced substantially my physical tension; I think the group has helped me to empathize better with other people, even perhaps on occasion to be able to help friends more effectively than I might have done before; the therapy has also helped me professionally, by allowing me better insights into 'character'; and it's opened my mind up to a whole new way of looking at people's behaviour in the social and political sphere, which seems to me to make sense of things I previously couldn't understand at all. But the greatest benefit, the single thing that has freed me most to enjoy life more, is that any problems I now experience are much milder and more manageable – almost an echo of their former selves – while the methods of handling them that I learned in the group allow me to deal with them much more easily and efficiently when they do arise.

For all these reasons I feel a considerable debt of gratitude not only, naturally, to Robin and Prue Skynner, but also towards all the ideas, attitudes and methods of modern Group and Family Therapy, which have been developed in recent years in the mental health profession.

Furthermore, I believe that these new ways of thinking will fascinate a lot of people. But most, of course, will have neither the need, the time nor the inclination to bother with therapy itself. And yet I have never seen them satisfactorily expressed in a non-technical book. So a couple of years ago I suggested to Robin that we should try to make them available to the layman.

And yet today, having just finished the book, I suddenly find myself wondering how new or startling these ideas are! And I really don't know. For example, it now seems quite obvious to me that most of our attitudes and characteristics are grounded in our original family experience and relationships. But I know that *some* people are very surprised – even astounded – by this. Similarly, I now accept that many of our 'problems' are really childhood difficulties that we failed to resolve when we were young, and consequently carry around with us in our adult lives. But is this obvious to you, or is it a revelation? Perhaps I'll have to rely on the comforting thought that even the oldest joke is new to the person who hears it for the first time. But let me say this: even if these ideas are only one-hundredth as intriguing to you as they were to me, I shall still get the royalties.

Robin On my side, the thought of a book like this first entered my head in 1976, during a conversation with my Uncle Fred. My professional text, *One Flesh: Separate Persons*, had just appeared, and complimentary copies had been sent to all my relatives. I had expected these just to gather dust on family bookshelves in the normal way, and was agreeably surprised when Uncle Fred, a man with no special interest in, or education for, such a subject, who had run a small business most of his life in the Cornish fishing village he and my mother grew up in, told me that he had not only read it but had found it both interesting and helpful to him in understanding and coming to terms with difficult experiences he had undergone in his early family life. He added that he hoped I would not be upset by what he was going to say next, and continued, in his lilting Cornish accent: 'You wouldn't think of it yourself unless you saw it written down there in front of you, like you've done in that book of yours, but once you *do* see it written down like that, d'you know, *'tis all common sense.'*

Though the book received very favourable reviews, no other

comment gave me as much pleasure as this. And as he talked, I became aware that what he had understood of the ideas presented there had transformed his views of his life in some positive way. Painful experiences which he had felt to be due to some fault of himself, or to undeserved harshness from others, or to some meaningless stroke of fate, had come to be seen more as a simple consequence of family history over which no one had any control. This not only seemed to free him to some extent from feeling responsible and at fault where he was not, but also to help him to accept responsibility in another family relationship where mutual blame was preventing a reconciliation he really desired. I later heard, before he died, that he had taken steps toward putting this right.

For years I had taught my students that, though we could help others with our professional knowledge and skills, we should not hope to help our own families with psychological problems because we were too involved ourselves to be unbiased and objective. Yet if even a professional book containing such ideas could help one's own family, I remember wondering, as we spoke, what one specifically written for the general public might accomplish.

But why had I written that earlier book? Why had I entered the profession in the first place, and been drawn towards the study of the family? On this visit to Cornwall I had been interested to learn more about my family history. In common with family therapists all over the world, the small group of colleagues I had brought together to teach the subject in London (which later developed into the Institute of Family Therapy) were at that time sharing our experiences of exploring our own family histories, to help us in understanding families which came to us for professional help. Uncle Fred was known as the family historian, full of amusing anecdotes about everyone's past. Another thing he told me on this particular evening was something my mother had said about me when I was a child: 'I really don't know what to make of Rob; either he's going to be a genius, or he's going to end up in Bodmin Asylum [the local mental hospital].' I realised with hindsight that, lacking the talents to fulfil her first option, I had spent much of my life trying to avoid the second, ultimately compromising by entering a different mental hospital through the staff entrance.

But why had this been necessary at all? And why me, rather than one of my four brothers? Looking back with the knowledge gained about my own family from Uncle Fred and others, and the knowledge of families in general derived from my profession, I see that I was the focus of very powerful emotional cross-currents in my family which disturbed and confused me as a child, and that much of my adult life was spent in trying to escape the consequences of these. My parents were decent, kindly, well-intentioned people, respected and liked in our community, doing the best they knew. They could not understand how they had produced a child who was full of fears, unable to cope with reality, who escaped into dreams and solitary interests.

I now realise that they were as confused as I was. But at the time I was only aware of concealing my problems to avoid disappointing them, and can remember my longing for some kind of map or chart or compass to help me to understand myself better, and to find a solution.

Not finding this in my family, I searched outside it, without success. Eventually, while on active service as a pilot in the Royal Air Force in World War II, I decided to take up medicine and psychiatry. I later saw that this was as much to help myself as to be of use to others, and that I was trying to find out 'which way was up' – that is, what it meant to be 'normal' or 'healthy' and how to progress towards that direction myself. But when, having qualified as a doctor, I finally arrived at the Institute of Psychiatry to begin my training in psychological medicine, and searched the extensive library for writings on normality, I found only three short papers. Two of them were useless and the third was interesting but anecdotal.

Realising that even here, as in my family, I would have to find out for myself, I became a psychotherapist studying individuals, groups and families, while at the same time undergoing a therapeutic group experience involving personal self-exploration in order to find answers to my questions: what did mental health really mean, and how could families bring it about?

Over twenty years later, I put what I had learned into the book that my Uncle Fred, when he 'saw it all written down there', realised was 'common sense'. By that time, studies of healthy families were at last beginning to appear, and the first study of exceptional mental health – 'optimal' health – was published in the same month, by the same publisher, as the American edition of my own book. Both these books were sent to me together, and reading about this work, at the Timberlawn Research Foundation in Dallas, Texas, I was excited to find out how similar their findings were to my own conclusions based on clinical experience. Before I had finished their book, I received a letter from the leader of this research team (who, unknown to me, had been reading *my* book) also commenting on the similarities of our findings.

It seemed, therefore, that I had at last got certain things right, and also made them understandable to ordinary people, even in the textbook intended for professionals.

So, when it was suggested to me by John Cleese that we might attempt a popular presentation together, I eagerly accepted, after hesitating briefly at the scale of the task of trying to condense and clarify so much knowledge. If our book succeeds in conveying to the general public some of the interest, excitement and usefulness of recent discoveries about the way families work, and how they may be helped to work better, this owes as much to John's lively, original mind and clarity of thought as it does to the knowledge I bring to it from my profession. I hope that the conversations we have distilled here will be as helpful to others as they have been to each of us and to our families, and that some of the very great enjoyment I have experienced in working with him will be conveyed as well.

1 Why Did I Have to Marry <u>You</u>?

John Let's start with an easy one . . . Why do people decide to marry each other?

Robin Because they're in love.

John Oh, come on.

Robin No, I'm being serious.

John Well, perhaps, but this falling in love routine is very bizarre. You find perfectly ordinary, rational people like computer programmers and chartered accountants, and there they are, happily computing and chartering away, and suddenly they see someone across a crowded room and think, 'Ah, that person is made for me, so I suppose I'd better spend the rest of my life with them.' It borders on the occult.

Robin Perhaps you'd have preferred it three hundred years ago when parents arranged all the marriages for sensible reasons like land and money and social climbing. They all regarded 'falling in love' as the worst possible basis for marriage – a recipe for disaster.

John Yes, Samuel Johnson said that all marriages should be arranged by the Lord Chancellor without reference to the wishes of the parties involved.

Robin So the point I'm making is that nowadays we are free to marry the person we love, the one who can really make us happy.

John And of course we have the highest divorce rate in history.

Robin Since you and I have both made a contribution to those statistics, we'd better not sound too critical.

John I'm sorry if I did. Actually, I think divorce is underrated. It gives you insights into some of the trickier aspects of marriage, the more delicate nuances as it were, that couples who've been happy together for thirty years wouldn't begin to grasp. But nevertheless, divorced or not, here we are, millions upon millions of us, all blithely pairing off, thinking, 'This is the one for me.' So what's going on, Doctor?

Robin What do you think falling in love is about?

John It's obviously a great deal more than sexual attraction. And a serious lover is more than a friend you happen to fancy, too. But what the extra element is I've no idea. I've never heard it explained. People smile knowingly, say 'chemistry', and change the subject. So what is it?

Robin Well I think the reason that we're attracted to someone at this very deep level is that basically they are _like_ us – in a psychological sense.

John But the wise saw tells us 'opposites attract'.

Robin They don't. Or if they do, it's because they _seem_ to be opposites. But what really draws people together is their similarities, and moreover a similarity in one of the most fundamental aspects of all – that of their family backgrounds.

John You mean all those people who used to get married – and still do – to escape from their families are in some way taking their families with them, psychologically speaking.

Robin Exactly.

John But hang on. I didn't know much about, for example, my first wife's family until long after we'd fallen in love.

Robin Did you tell her about _yours_?

John I don't think I did, no.

Robin Maybe that's something you had in common.

John I don't understand.

Robin Maybe the reason you didn't talk about your families much was that your parents, both sets, didn't talk about *their* families much. In other words, perhaps your family backgrounds were similar in that way.

John That's too clever to be convincing. In any case, you get the 'buzz' from someone *before* you ever start exchanging that sort of family information.

Robin That's true.

John You agree?

Robin Let me explain. I should say this whole idea was perhaps the most startling discovery I encountered in years and years of working with families, and I only gradually came to accept it as true. But the most dramatic piece of evidence for it is called the Family Systems Exercise. The first time I saw this was in 1973, when some visiting American family therapists demonstrated it to us. We've now incorporated it into our training methods at the Institute of Family Therapy.

John What's the exercise for?

Robin Its purpose is to show what lies behind the way that couples pick each other out across a crowded room! And it demonstrated to me more clearly than I'd ever realised how unconscious attractions work, and what they're about.

John You mean it shows how we pick each other without knowing anything about each other?

Robin Yes. The trainees do this exercise very early on – in fact ideally when they're still complete strangers. They're put together in a group and asked to choose another person from the group who either makes them think of someone in their family or, alternatively, gives them the feeling that they would have filled a 'gap' in their family. And – here's the interesting bit – they're not allowed to speak at all while they're choosing. They just stand up and wander around looking at all the others. When they've all chosen someone, that is when they're in pairs, they are told to talk together for a time, to see if they can find out what made them pick each other. They're encouraged to compare their family backgrounds. Next, each couple is asked to choose another couple, in order to make foursomes. And then, each foursome is asked to form itself into a family of some kind, agreeing with each other what role in the family each person will take. Then they talk together about what it was in their family backgrounds that led to their decisions. And finally, they report to the whole group what they've discovered.

John Which is what?

Robin That they've somehow, each one of them, picked out three people whose families functioned in very similar ways to their own.

John How do you mean 'functioned in very similar ways'?

Robin Well, they'll find that all four of them are from families where there was difficulty in sharing affection; or perhaps in expressing anger, or envy; or where there had been a lot of near-incestuous relationships; or where people had always been expected to be optimistic and cheerful. Or they might discover that all four of them had fathers who were away from home during the years when that mattered a lot to them; or that all their families had suffered some big loss or change of a similar kind when they were all at similar ages.

John Couldn't this just be because they are looking for things they have in common?

Robin That's not really a good enough explanation for the *number* of *connected* similarities they always find. I know it may sound unconvincing to anyone who hasn't actually tried it, but it's quite uncanny when you experience it for yourself.

John But what about all the 'wall-flowers'? How do you explain the ones who don't get chosen?

Robin Well, funnily enough, it was the 'wall-flowers' that clinched the argument for me – finally convinced me that there was something extraordinary going on. The very first time that I was in charge of putting about twenty trainee family therapists through this exercise, I suddenly got worried that the ones who came together last would feel they were all rejects. So, when I asked the groups to report on their experiences – the family similarities they'd discovered – I put off asking the 'wall-flower' group till last, as I was rather dreading what their reaction would be. But they were just as fascinated as the rest of the trainees. They had discovered that they had all been fostered, or adopted, or brought up in children's homes. They had *all* felt rejected early in their lives, and had somehow, in this exercise, unerringly picked each other out!

John So every time this exercise is staged, you find the trainees choose each other because of the remarkable number of similarities in their family backgrounds – in their family histories, and in their families' attitudes.

Robin Right.

John So how are the reasons why *they* choose each other related to the reasons why *we* fall in love with each other?

Robin Fundamentally. You see, there are lots of reasons for a couple getting together, but most of them are easy to understand. One of the pioneers of marital therapy in the fifties – Henry Dicks – boiled them down to three main categories. First, social pressures like class, religion and money; second, conscious personal reasons like good looks, shared interests, things you *know* you're picking someone for; and third, these unconscious attractions that everybody calls 'chemistry'.

John So the exercise is demonstrating this third group, the unconscious attractions; and it tells us that people unconsciously choose each other because of similarities in the way their families functioned?

Robin Right. Remember that our trainees are actually looking for someone who made them think of a person in their own family, or who would have filled an important gap in their own family. Yet they are all strangers – there's *no inherited* likeness in appearance or personality. And the astonishing thing is that nevertheless, just by *looking*, they choose people who have astonishing similarities in childhood experiences and specific family problems, too.

John In other words, we're carrying around our families with us, somewhere inside us, and we're giving off signals which enable others with similar backgrounds to recognise us?

Robin And by getting together with such people, we're recreating our own families again, in a sense. It's a bit startling, isn't it?

John ... I think you could safely say that, yes. I know that you, as a psychiatrist, are used to the idea of the influence that unconscious forces have on people's behaviour but it's a bit of a shock for a layman like me to realise, quite suddenly, how much we're doing things for reasons we're not aware of. For example, just take the immense amount of information we must be picking up from each other the whole time, quite unconsciously.

Robin It is quite extraordinary how many signals we're receiving from people which tell us about their characters, and hence, their families.

John Can you explain more about these signals?

Signals ......

Robin We're all giving off information the whole time about what sort of people we are. It's conveyed by our facial expressions and the way we use our bodies – all that 'body language' stuff we've heard a lot about recently.

John Posture, dress, the ways we move, gestures ...

Robin And not just which movements we make, but also how we make them, and how often, and so on.

John All right, but I don't see how these signals can indicate the person's family background.

Robin We can all guess how people are feeling at any given moment, can't we? We can tell that they're friendly or hostile, cheerful or miserable, and so on. Well, over and above these constantly changing emotions that we're experiencing all the time, everyone tends to have certain *habitual* emotions or attitudes.

John Which come from their basic personality, you mean? They're usually gloomy, or skittish, or a bit of a martyr, or whatever.

Robin Right. And these habitual emotions will show themselves in posture, facial expressions and the typical way they move. Take a depressive person. He'll tend to slump and slouch and move apathetically. And by virtue of having his face in a depressed expression over the years, he'll develop certain facial lines which we recognise immediately. The same applies to a cheerful fellow who smiles a lot – he'll get laugh lines, and will usually move in a more positive, eager, upright kind of way; somebody a bit manic will move jerkily and seem tense and tend to have rather staring eyes.

John Well, I'm very aware of *that* look. It's exactly how I get when I'm under pressure, and it's also something I consciously use a lot in my acting. The eyes bulge slightly, and the muscles round the temple and forehead and jaws get rather tight.

Robin Have you noticed my eyes often look like that?

John . . . I never have. Do you know, I'd never realised that.

Robin Well the funny thing is, when I did the Family Systems Exercise, I paired up with someone, and then we chose another couple . . . before *any* of us realised that *all four* of us had eyes like this!

John Do you think the two of us get on well because our staring eyes indicate we've got similar family backgrounds?

Robin It's very likely. We'll keep an eye open for similarities as we go along.

John Come to think of it, I now remember that a few years ago I noticed I was often attracted to girls with eyes like this – though oddly enough, once I was aware of it, the attraction didn't operate so strongly any more. And certainly one person in my family had eyes like this. Actually that brings me to the next point I don't understand. You're saying that a person's personality, or habitual emotions as you put it, will indicate what his family was like. Why? What's the connection?

Robin Well you see, each family tends to have a particular way of handling emotions. They'll all tend to think some emotions are 'good' and some 'bad'. So they'll be open about expressing the 'good' ones and very guarded about the 'bad' ones. Or they may keep a stiff upper lip about emotions in general, or a completely floppy one. The result is that each family develops a characteristic set of emotional attitudes, so the members of that family will all share the same emotional habits.

John So they'll all tend to give off the same kinds of signals and to look a bit similar?

Robin Yes, it's not just heredity that makes families look alike. Even adopted children will grow to look like others in the family in some respects.

John Is that why dogs tend to look like their owners?

Robin Yes, there's a lot of truth in that. The pets get treated according to the family attitudes. So families which believe in self-control will have obedient dogs and families which don't and have rather wild children will excite their dogs to behave in the same way.

John So to sum up ... we signal, by our expressions, postures and ways of moving, certain habitual emotional attitudes we have, which we share with other members of our family. And people from similar families will pick them up and respond to them.

Robin Exactly. That's what the Family Systems Exercise shows.

John All right, but there is something I still don't understand. You said that people who choose each other in the exercise often find they've experienced, at the same kind of age, the same kind of event – you instanced an absent father, or a death in the family. How does that fit in to what you're saying?

Robin Well, let's express what we learn from the Family Systems Exercise another way. Let's say that someone who's had trouble coping with a certain stage in their development will be attracted to a person who's also had trouble at that stage.

John That doesn't sound like another way of looking at it so much as a completely new and unrelated idea.

Robin No, it's closely connected with what I've been saying. Just trust me for a few minutes and I'll show you how.

John What did you say about 'trouble at a certain stage of development'?

Robin Well, if someone missed out on a stage in their development, then a person that they're attracted to, with a similar family history, will probably have missed out on that *same* stage too.

John I'm trying not to panic ... perhaps you could start by explaining what you mean by 'a stage of development'. Then I might be able to understand how you could miss it out.

Stages of development ......

Robin You can look at life as a series of stages we have to pass through. And as we go through each stage, we learn certain lessons. In fact, we may need to learn the lessons of one stage before we can pass on properly to the next.

John Give me examples of some of the earlier stages.

Robin Well, we all need to have consistent, reliable love and care when we're children. The mother usually plays the most important part in this when we're very young, of course.

John And what do we learn from that?

Robin Well, if our mothers haven't been able to care for us properly, we haven't learned how to take care of others.

John Really?

Robin Yes, if they haven't filled us with good, loving feelings, we won't have so many to hand on to other people.

John I see. But it seems a strange use of the word 'learned'.

Robin A lot of learning isn't conscious, you know. Especially in childhood, when most learning is copying, modelling yourself on people, particularly the parents, of course. So if they don't give you an experience, it's harder later for you to provide it for others, harder to know if you're getting it right.

John What's the next stage?

Robin Well, as we begin to develop some independence and willpower, we need some loving firmness and control from our parents. The father's contribution becomes especially important at this stage.

John From which we learn ...?

Robin Self-discipline. Without that, we'll never get a good relationship with authority. We won't be able to accept it easily, we'll resent it, and even the *need* for it. Also, if we're ever placed in a position where we have to *exert* authority, we'll find it difficult. We'll tend to vacillate between being too weak and indecisive and suddenly acting arbitrarily and being too rigid, to show we really are strong.

John You mean a politician who's been a rebel all his life might find it difficult to be sufficiently firm if he ever got put in a position of power?

Robin Either that, or else he'd become very authoritarian but *pretend* that all his decisions were really being made democratically, on behalf of the silent majority perhaps, or the proletariat.

John Whereas if the parents have exercised authority lovingly and firmly . . . ?

Robin Then, when that person's grown up, they'll be able to consult everyone fully and then take a decision and stick to it; although they'll also be able to change their mind if it becomes apparent they've made a mistake.

John We're getting side-tracked. Give me another stage of development.

Robin Well, next we need brothers and sisters or friends to play with in order to learn to share also; to cope with the rough-and-tumble of life – teasing, being left out sometimes, how to stand up for ourselves, and so on. 'Only' children, or eldest children who don't have any competition for several years, often don't learn these lessons so well and so have trouble later.

John Yes, I was an only child and certainly missed out on this stage because I didn't have many friends of my age. So when I went to a bigger school at the age of eight, I was very bad at mixing and got bullied a lot. Still, that stopped eventually.

Robin So you learned the lessons, even if you did it a bit late. Then there's the stage of learning about the opposite sex. Children who miss out on that experience, like a girl with no father or brothers, or a boy who spends his adolescence in an all-boys boarding school, will be unsure how to deal with them later on.

John This is becoming autobiographical. I went through the English public-school system and, at the age of eighteen, discovered that girls were from another galaxy. It took me several years to get over that painful public-school awkwardness – you know, sitting there at dinner, trying to impress them by explaining how the stock market worked while persistently putting my elbow in the butter.

Robin Yes, and that lack of contact with the opposite sex while growing up not only makes people anxious and awkward, it can also give them unrealistic expectations, so that they get disappointed a lot when they embark on relationships. Then the next stage is becoming independent of your parents; and it's hard to learn that unless you join in a crowd of your own age in your teens. People who've never had the chance to do that tend to cling to their parents. Or even if they do get married, they turn their husbands or wives into parents and cling to them, instead of having a circle of friends of their own sex to get support from too.

John Right. I think I now understand what you mean by 'stages of development'. And I see there are lessons to be learned at each one. So what happens if you miss out on a stage? You have a problem in those circumstances for the rest of your life?

Robin Not necessarily. If you miss a stage, you can always go through it later and learn the lessons then. As, for example, you learned to 'mix in' better and to stand up for yourself when you did get to a bigger school. Similarly, someone whose father dies when they're young will tend to look for replacements – an uncle, a teacher, a youth club leader, a boss – who will take a personal interest and give them something of that fatherly experience. Or a young person, whose parents have kept him close to the family and discouraged him from mixing with other children in case they are unsuitable, may catch up when he has to mix with others when he starts work or goes to college.

John At that later stage, the support of the peer group will enable him to become more independent.

Robin Yes. So you see, if we miss out on a stage, we can always pick it up later by seeking out a substitute experience.

John But people don't really 'seek out' a substitute experience deliberately, do they?

Robin No, I agree it's not usually something that people think out and plan – especially when they're young. It tends to happen because they're drawn towards it – they sense a need for it, just as we're drawn towards food when we're hungry. So when the substitute experience becomes available, they make more use of it than others might. But I do remember that when I was eleven, I did make a real, deliberate effort to mix in better when I changed school because I hadn't done that at the previous one.

John What other steps do you think you missed out?

Robin One thing was that my father was never firm enough with me because he didn't get on with *his* father when *he* was a boy. That gave me a problem with authority, but later on I was helped with that a lot by the discipline in the RAF during the war.

John My father was actually too kind with me, so I never had the experience of someone being really tough or angry with me, and when it happened later on it rather scared me.

Robin Do you think you were able to pick the lessons up later?

John Only to a very limited extent. Funnily enough, I think there was a kind of discipline in making TV shows, because if they weren't finished on time, there was a blank screen. And researching management training films changed my attitudes a lot – for example, one film on decision-making forced me to revise all my ideas about authority. But these are pathetic substitutes for the real experience. Still, maybe I've learned *something* because I've been able deliberately to be tough and angry with my daughter sometimes, so that she wouldn't be frightened by it as I was. Consequently she's learned to handle it – it doesn't *panic* her. I think because of that she's turning out much tougher than I was at her age.

Robin Do you regret missing National Service?

John I do actually, but that's because I'm safe now. But I suppose you'd recommend a few weeks in the SAS for me, really?

Robin It's never too late for a substitute experience, my boy.

John Well if it isn't, answer me this. If we're *drawn* to substitute experiences, which will let us catch up on and learn lessons that we've missed, why do *any* of us have any real problems?

Hiding a missing stage . . . . . .

Robin If we miss out a stage, we can catch up on the lessons by seeking a substitute experience, right?

John Right.

Robin Now there's something that can stop us making up the lost ground. And that is *pretending that we haven't missed the stage* – hiding the fact that we've failed to grow up in some way.

John Because we're embarrassed about it?

Robin Yes. As we grow up, we become ashamed that we've missed an earlier stage. And the older we get, of course, the more ashamed we feel about showing that we haven't coped with something basic – something that would make us feel silly and childish if it was revealed.

John So we try to hide it from other people.

Robin Well, we start off by hiding it from others, but after a time that becomes such a habit that we end up hiding it *from ourselves*.

John From ourselves? You mean we now don't even realise that the problem's there?

Robin Yes. And once you deny to yourself that you've missed out on some basic experience, you're *not* going to look for a substitute experience. Which is, of course, what you need to solve the problem.

John Yes, but I don't understand how hiding the problem from other people causes us to finish up being unaware of it ourselves.

Robin The feeling embarrasses us, right?

John Yes.

Robin We'd rather not have it. Well, in the world outside us, we can pay attention to something or ignore it as we choose. We can do the *same* thing *inside our head*, with our thoughts or feelings. We can avoid certain kinds of ideas or emotions, and learn to look away quickly if we glimpse them. If we do this often enough, the habit of avoiding noticing some kind of feeling becomes so firmly established, so instinctive, that we hardly know we're doing it. It's a process that the American psychiatrist Harry Stack Sullivan called 'selective inattention'.

John So if we hardly know we're avoiding noticing a particular feeling . . .

Robin The next step is that we succeed in forgetting it's there *at all*. It's as though we've pulled a blind down inside our heads to screen off the emotion that we don't want to look at, the one we feel we should hide.

John Because it feels shameful – like a weakness.

Robin Yes, and also because it makes us feel bad.

John Bad in what sense? Morally?

Robin Well, it will come to feel morally bad eventually. But much more important it gives us very bad, painful and uncomfortable feelings, as if we are unacceptable, unlovable.

John The emotion makes us feel 'bad' even if it's only revealed to ourselves. So we screen it off.

Robin Right.

John Can you take a specific emotion – say, anger – and show how a child learns to put it behind the screen?

Robin Well, in a healthy, normal family, everyone will get angry at times and that won't be regarded as a hanging offence. The child will be expected to control it within reason, but the parents won't make a federal case out of it each time. The child will see that this is a normal emotion; that it can be expressed; that it is *not* destructive and deadly. If his parents have this relaxed attitude to anger, he can feel safe to experience his own and, through being supported and helped to cope with it, he learns to exercise the normal control over it that's required socially.

John So how does all that go wrong?

Robin Actually, there are *two* ways it can happen. First, let's take the traditional explanation that Freud and the early analysts originally came up with. They said that a feeling got screened off – repressed – because of a 'trauma'.

John One isolated but very painful event.

Robin That's right. Take the example of a toddler who has become abnormally frightened of anger. The single bad experience might be that his mother had to disappear into hospital for treatment just at a time when he's having a lot of temper tantrums. He's too young to understand the true explanation for his mother going to hospital, so he may think she's left him because he's been so angry – so 'bad'. So, instead of out-growing the tantrums, learning to control his anger, and being able to feel secure and loved even when he's cross, he'll now get very frightened whenever he feels angry. Also, any similar traumatic experience which occurs later will have an exaggerated effect and make the fear even stronger. For example, he might get into a fight with another boy who gets badly injured quite accidentally, but he will think it was all his fault again, so his anger will become even more terrifying to him. Eventually anger feels so 'bad' that he tries to pretend it's not there at all – he screens it off.

John So that's the Freudian explanation. But I've also heard you refer to that as a Hollywood story.

Robin Well, it makes a good drama! But nowadays we realise the same screening-off can happen in a much less obvious and dramatic way. It can be a much more gradual process arising from fear or awkwardness about that particular emotion on the part of the child's family. So our toddler will gradually pick up the idea that anger is 'bad', because all the rest of his *family* are very uneasy and uncomfortable and embarrassed about anger.

John The *whole* family feels 'bad' about it?

Robin Yes. So the child gets the message over and over and over again. He sees too how greatly anger upsets his parents, how they just can't cope with it, and how they ignore him or isolate him or even attack him whenever *he* tries to express it. Pretty soon, he's feeling very bad about anger too. He sees that they can't love him when he's cross, and since all children want to be loved by their parents and to love them in return and make them happy, he tries to hide any feelings of anger from them.

John So he's associated anger with fears of rejection by his parents, which must be the worst possible threat for a child.

Robin Yes, that's what I was talking about just now when I said how *bad* one feels. Of course, the child now feels *deceitful* too, because he can't be his true self. He'll feel rather cut off from his parents because he's not *fully* accepted – he has to pretend he doesn't feel anger. But feeling deceitful isn't as bad as the threat of total rejection, so he'll probably choose to be false and loved, rather than be his true self and get rejected.

John So from now on, when something happens that would make a normal child angry, this child will bottle his anger up.

Robin To hide it from his parents. But next, he learns to hide it from himself, as that's the only way he can feel he's *lovable*. Anger is *so* 'bad', he mustn't admit to having any, even to himself. So he acquires the habit of not noticing his own – he learns to screen it off – and finishes up by thinking that it isn't even there.

John Well I can see how he learns to do that, but I'm still struggling with the idea that whole families screen off the *same* things.

Robin They *tend* to, yes. You find that in each family some emotions are regarded as 'good' and some as 'bad'. The bad ones get put behind the screen and the entire family has a kind of unspoken but very powerful agreement that the feelings behind the screen mustn't be noticed. Everyone in the family pretends they're not there. So each new child learns to put the same things behind the screen too. The habit of screening them off gets passed on, like the measles, quite unintentionally, without anyone knowing that it's happening.

John I have no problem seeing how the children follow the family pattern. But I don't see how the pattern gets established in the first place. Why should the *parents* be screening off the same things? After all, *they're* not from the same family.

Robin You're right. But do you remember my saying that people were attracted to each other because they had missed out at the same stage of development?

John Yes. In fact, I have the feeling that all this present chat is part of the explanation of why that's so.

Robin That's right. This is why a husband and wife will tend to screen off the same things. But I can't explain that yet because there are some missing pieces of the jigsaw that I'm going to give you in a moment. So will you just take it on trust for the time being and shut up.

John ... This wouldn't wash with Sir Robin Day.

Robin I agree. Fortunately he was too busy.

John Thank you. Well ... if the parents do tend to screen off the same things, then I can see why the children will learn to do that too. With the result that the whole family will screen off the same thing. They'll all have the same blind spot.

Robin Or blind spots. There may be more than one emotion screened off.

John All right. And different families have different blind spots?

Robin Yes. Each family will screen off different emotions, or a different combination of emotions.

John How can a therapist tell which emotions a family has screened off? How do you recognise a blind spot?

Robin One simple give-away is that they'll all *deny* having the feeling that they've screened off. If they say, 'Oh, we're never jealous in *our* family', then you know jealousy's a family problem – that with them, jealousy's *taboo*.

John It's that simple?

Robin That's the best single clue. But there will be many others. The therapist soon begins to see how the family avoids the blind spot, skipping over it, changing the subject – just not noticing it. And what's fascinating about the blind spot, the taboo, is that it gets passed on from generation to generation to generation.

John Without anyone knowing?

Robin Yes, because if they *knew*, whatever it is that's behind the screen wouldn't be behind the screen, would it?

John How do you know it gets passed on?

Robin Family therapists see it again and again when we explore patients' backgrounds to understand what their families were like, or when we see several generations of the same family together, or begin to look more closely at our own families. There's also research supporting this.

John All right. Let me see if I've got this so far. As we grow, we go through various stages of development and learn different lessons at each stage. The lessons are fundamentally to do with handling emotions. For example, we learn how to handle those aroused by dealing with authority; or we learn how to cope with the feelings aroused by the opposite sex; or we learn how to cope with emotions that come from being more independent and separate from our parents.

However, we may miss out a stage. But if we do so, we can still pick up the lessons later on by seeking out a substitute experience. That will enable us to get back on schedule, as it were.

But something can go wrong. If we miss out a stage and don't go through a substitute experience, the emotions that we haven't learned to handle will feel very awkward to us. So we're likely to start by trying to hide them from others, and end up by concealing them even from ourselves. We 'screen them off' and then we don't even realise they're there.

Now, there are two main reasons why we fail to learn how to handle an emotion and are forced to stick it behind the screen. The first is that we suffer a sudden trauma – a single, dramatic, very painful event. The second, and the more common, is that we gradually learn to put the emotion behind the screen because there's a taboo on it in our family.

Every family regards some emotions as bad and screens those off. The child learns to follow suit, because he risks parental rejection if he displays the taboo emotions; they feel 'bad'. So the pattern gets handed on down the family.

Robin And from generation to generation, too. Don't forget that. Because if the children haven't learned to handle an emotion, they won't be able to help *their* children to handle it either.

John Right. So what's wrong with this taboo business?

Robin ... What do you mean?

John Well, if you've got a nasty emotion that you haven't learned to handle and which makes you feel very bad, why *not* stick it safely behind the screen and get rid of it?

Robin Ah! Because the screen *doesn't work very well*, and often ends up producing more problems than it solves.

The faulty screen ......

John In what way does the screen not work?

Robin In several ways. First, it slips up now and again, and lets the forbidden feelings out for a bit. Second, trying to keep the screen firmly in place takes up a lot of energy. And third, well, you can't just cut off a bit of human personality without unbalancing the whole system – the whole human being.

John Very glib, Doctor. Could we take them one at a time, please? The screen can *slip*?

Robin Yes, especially if we're tired or ill or have a bit too much to drink. Then the emotion can escape. And because we're out of touch with it, it takes us by surprise and isn't easily controlled if it does. So we might suddenly say or do something very nasty, something that seems 'not like us'.

John Yes, I'll never forget that happening to me once in the group you ran. It was as though someone else had said the words, someone not connected with me. And I was quite shocked when I realised that *I'd* said it. I can recall how ashamed I felt, because it contradicted the image I had of myself as someone who wasn't snide.

Robin That's exactly what I mean. Because it's behind the screen normally, it doesn't feel like 'you'. And sometimes the feeling will suddenly erupt over something very trivial – it's been building up behind the screen for some time and suddenly bursts out. But because the cause is so petty, the eruption seems ridiculous, so we're ashamed and embarrassed and there's even more reason to cram it back behind the screen again. Or the feeling can escape in much more disguised forms. If we resent someone, but have screened that off, we might forget their name, or their birthday, or drop an 'accidental' brick. Or we might have a destructive fantasy about them. Or even disguise *that* as a worry about them.

John A worry?

Robin Oh yes. If a wife's angry with her husband for being late for dinner and not 'phoning, she may imagine him in a motorway pile-up, as a way of expressing her natural disguised anger at him. But at the same time, the way she's imagining ringing the ambulance to get there in time expresses her positive

> Thank heaven you're home! I pictured you horribly mangled — it was lovely.

feelings too. But the repressed feeling can escape in all these forms because we're not in touch with it. So it operates a bit like a bandit, something out of our control.

John Next, you said it takes up our energy trying to keep the screen firmly in place?

Robin Yes, because of the danger we somehow sense that the feelings behind it – anger, jealousy, fear, or whatever – *may* slip out if we're not on guard. So a bit of you is always keeping a sharp look-out for an enemy you can't see. Even though you don't know why, you can never completely relax, and that makes you tense and tired. The feelings are *always* lurking there behind the screen and the effort to keep them out of sight, out of mind, is connected with all kinds of psychosomatic illnesses – headaches, stomach-aches and indigestion, high blood pressure, some kinds of rheumatism, and so on.

John Well, I first went into therapy because my doctor simply couldn't find a physical explanation of why I was suffering low-grade 'flu symptoms a lot of the time, and also because I couldn't understand why I carried so much tension.

Robin Do you remember what happened?

John The 'flu symptoms disappeared quite rapidly and never returned. The tension level dropped steadily, but really quite slowly. I think it took about three years to get to about the normal level. Even so, it's fascinating, isn't it, to talk to physio-therapists and masseurs and to realise what a high degree of tension is regarded generally as 'normal'.

Robin And it's common for families to have quite a lot behind the screen, as I said.

John Now, what about the third reason you gave why the screen didn't work – that it 'upsets the balance of the person-ality'?

Robin Well, all our feelings have a useful function.

John *All* of them?

Robin Yes, even the ones we sometimes think of as negative, *provided* that we've got some control over them. So in a healthy person all these feelings are balancing each other out. But if we screen off some emotion, then our overall balance will be affected. To put it another way, that screened-off emotion isn't *available* to us when we *need* it.

John Well I see that in a way, but I find it very hard to imagine how anger, envy, cruelty, and so on, can be useful.

Robin If they're screened off, they're not. Then we're not in touch with them and we never learn to handle them anyway. So when they break out, they're out of control and destructive. But if we _haven't_ screened them off, if we're _aware_ of them and reasonably comfortable with them, we're then able to get some control over them.

John I can see they're not so destructive then, but how can they be _useful_? Take anger.

Robin You'd use that to stand up for yourself if someone tried to push you around or take advantage of you. Without it you can't defend yourself when you need to. So someone who's put it all behind the screen will seem passive and timid and will get bossed around a lot, because his anger's _not_ available to him. He won't be able to stand up for himself.

John He'll be too nice for his own good?

Robin And 'too good to be true' as well. People won't quite trust it, because they'll sense the anger is there somewhere. As of course it is, behind the screen.

John All right. But how can envy be useful?

Robin Envy is all right if we're aware of it, and it's therefore under control and balanced by the other emotions. Then it can be positive, because we can use it to compete in work or games, and try to emulate someone we admire.

John ... Yes, actually that's true, isn't it? I'm envious of Tom Stoppard's work, and Michael Frayn's and Alan Ayckbourn's, but in the sense that I'd like to do something as good one day. But envy can easily turn nasty, can't it? Then you just sit around resenting everyone's success.

Robin Envy only gets nasty when you want something very badly, but the gap between what you've got and what the other person's got is so great there seems no hope of reducing it and eventually sharing in the good thing yourself.

John That's exactly why I can't stand Mother Teresa. Anybody that much saintlier than the rest of us ought to be taken down a peg or two. I wish the gossip columnists would get after her.

Robin They'd be wasting their time.

John That wouldn't stop them. Which brings us to cruelty. Can that be useful?

Robin Yes, because sometimes we have to hurt someone for their own good. That's necessary even with the people you love

most. Or perhaps especially with them. For example, parents
need to help their children gradually to become more independent. But that always entails a certain unhappiness on the
part of the child, since his first taste of independence usually
makes him feel rather anxious and frightened. However, if the
parents get it right, they can allow the child to suffer a little
more discomfort each time so that he can learn, bit by bit, to
face and overcome his fear, and grow in confidence.

John They have to be 'cruel to be kind', in other words.

Robin And if they'd screened cruelty off, they couldn't do that
and the child could never achieve real independence. Then what
about a surgeon who has to cut human flesh? He couldn't do it
if he was too squeamish. And, as a psychiatrist, I sometimes
have to put people through very painful experiences if they are
to face their problems and get over them – and *I* can't use an
anaesthetic. I used to find that much more difficult than I do
now because I didn't like being thought cruel by others, or
feeling I was being cruel.

John You mean you had cruelty behind the screen to some
extent, but becoming more aware of that helped you to become
a more effective therapist?

Robin I think that's right. If a patient really needs to face up to
something painful, I'm less likely now to shrink away from
getting them to do so. But, of course, if anyone defines cruelty
as the desire deliberately to inflict pain for its own sake, that
could never be right.

John How about anxiety?

Robin That's *vital*.

John How?

Robin You wait till you get into a car driven by someone who
doesn't have any, then you'll see!

John Yes, all right. So all our feelings are useful if we're aware
of them and reasonably comfortable with them, because then we
can handle them. But if we screen them off, first, they're not
available when we need them; and second, when the screen
slips up and they escape, they may do damage because we've
got no control over them.

Robin That's about it.

John Now you say we've all got all these emotions in us.

Robin Yes, I think human nature's pretty much the same everywhere, in the sense that all human beings are made up of the same range of feelings, just as our bodies are composed of the same range of chemicals. We've all got affection, jealousy, courage, sadness, determination, joy, cowardice, kindness, cruelty, sexiness, shyness, and so on and so on.

John And we've all got some of them behind the screen. *All* of us.

Robin Yes. To some extent, anyway. Different combinations of emotions are screened off in different people.

John Well, does that mean you think that it's the way that we each learn to screen off our emotions that helps to give us our particular personalities?

Robin Exactly. So someone who's got rid of affection looks unfriendly. Someone who's screened off anger is too good to be true; a loss of courage makes us timid; the loss of envy means we can't compete; the loss of sexiness makes us up-tight; the loss of sadness makes us a bit manic; and the loss of anxiety can make us terribly dangerous!

NO AFFECTION   NO ANGER   NO COURAGE

NO SEX PLEASE   NO SADNESS   NO ANXIETY

John One last question. Is this screening-off what Freud calls 'repression', and is the stuff behind the screen 'the unconscious'?

Robin More or less. We're expressing the same ideas in a different way.

John Why different?

Robin Well I'm trying to link up not just Freud's ideas, but also those of other analysts and psychologists with a lot of new ideas from family therapy and behaviour therapy. They're only very rough images but I think they convey the idea that keeping part of ourselves out of our awareness is a very *active* process; that it usually begins as a deliberate *hiding* of some feeling from our family; that it's only later that we lose sight of it ourselves; and that the feeling's nevertheless always there, threatening to appear again at any moment.

John And that the screen – repression – doesn't work.

Attraction ......

Robin I think we now have enough ideas to go back to the original question of why couples who are attracted to each other have similar family backgrounds – that is, tend to have missed out on the same developmental stage.

John Well, if they've both missed out on the same stage, they'll both have problems with the same emotions, won't they? That is, with the feelings that they *should* have learned to handle at the missing stage – but *didn't*.

Robin Right. And if they've both had trouble with the same feelings ...

John ... they've put the same ones behind their screens?

Robin Eureka. *That's* why they're attracted to each other. Because they've got the same things behind their screens, and the same things in front.

John Why the same in front? Human nature *minus* what's been screened off, you mean?

Robin That's right. So they see each other and ... it's a perfect match. They're made for each other! It's quite amazing how much they have in common. And they *have*. They've divided up to fit each other beautifully. The perfect mate!

John But hang on a minute. They're not attracted by what's behind the screen, are they? They'd be *repelled* by that – that's the taboo bit.

Robin No, you're right. It's the *front* that attracts them – the shop window. But the front's the way it is because of what's *behind*.

John I see. So they're attracted by what they're allowed to see in front of the screen.

Robin Yes, because they see there all the qualities, the emotional attitudes, that they've been brought up to approve and admire. And better than that, because their partner so obviously *hasn't* got the kinds of feelings that are screened off in their families and themselves. Best of all, the partner thoroughly disapproves of such feelings, too!

John Whereas, so far as the screened-off parts are concerned . . . well, they've been taught by their families *not* to notice them! So they can't see each other's faults.

Robin That's how it works. But there's something else going on too. You see, people usually have a bit of *fascination* – a mixture of interest and horror – for the kinds of feelings that have gone behind the screens. If it's cruelty, they might be drawn to re-read a story in the papers about torture, while feeling bad about doing so and hiding from the partner the fact that they're drawn to that kind of report. If lusty sexual feelings are behind the screen, they might read the *News of the World* carefully to agree with each other how disgusting it is that a paper prints terrible stuff like that. Don't expect to understand it logically – it's not about thinking, but about emotion, and all feelings can be contradictory.

John So you mean, if they just sense for a moment what's behind the partner's screen, it can *add* to their fascination?

Robin Provided it's only a *hint* of the feelings back there, it can be exciting, a bit of a 'turn on'. If it was more than a hint, it would repel. Just as a little whiff of a bad smell has a different effect from a really powerful dose of it. But it's hard to really understand what's going on because it's 'double-think' – trying not to let your left hand know what your right hand's doing.

John Nevertheless ... why should a whiff of the taboo be so enticing?

Robin Well ... although we all want to be loved by our families and not display feelings that upset them, we also have a keen hunger to be whole, to be complete. When we sense, and are drawn to, the denied parts behind the screen in our partner, we're really hoping, deep down, to get back the missing parts of ourselves again.

John Poetry's loss has been psychiatry's gain, Robin. So we have the young couple in love with each other, ardently admiring the goods in their respective shop windows, valiantly turning a blind eye to their screened-off faults, and slightly aroused by just a whiff of the forbidden. But why doesn't this idyllic state ever last?

Robin Because we can't keep the screens firmly enough down. We can all keep the screens tightly in place for an evening or a weekend, but when we start living together, the screened-off parts start showing through. Gradually our partner can seem less and less like the one we married.

John So, Doctor ... is it a *good* thing that we fall in love with people who have screened off the same things that we have? Or should we go back three hundred years and let our parents pick our spouses?

Robin Well the good part is that we've both got the same weaknesses, through no fault of our own, so we *can* be more understanding of each other.

John That's why someone we're in love with seems to 'have our number' and why we can feel so vulnerable with them, and yet trust them?

Robin Yes, they seem to understand us, to be aware of our weaknesses, and *yet* they seem to accept us. They don't attack us as we're frightened they may do if we reveal our most intimate feelings. And we sense, without ever really knowing why, that this is the person who can instinctively understand us, help us, and perhaps make us more whole.

John Well that all adds up. But, and this is the cruncher ...

how can we possibly help each other if we have the *same* blind spots?

Robin That's the catch! The extraordinary paradox is that your partner is *exactly* the one you can best grow with ... but *also* the one you can get most stuck with. Even ... the one you can end up hating most of all.

John Here's the $64,000 question then, pundit. What's going to determine which way it goes?

Robin It all depends on *how much* the couple are willing to admit to, and to look at, what is behind their own screens. The more willing people are to do that and the more courageous they are about accepting the discomfort of finding they're different from the idea they have of themselves, the better chance the couple has of working things out, if problems arise.

John ... Why do you qualify that by saying 'if problems arise'?

Robin Because there's a middle range of marriages which are quite stable, even if not very exciting, where the partners can rub along reasonably well without either of them needing to look behind his or her screen.

Types of marriages ......

John Can we move on now and look at different kinds of marriages? Is there any way you can relate the happiness or success of a marriage to the *amount* the partners have behind their screens?

Robin Yes, but not only to that. Their attitude to what is behind the screen is very important too; it's not just a matter of the amount there.

John So how would you describe the happiest marriages?

Robin Well, both partners are more tolerant of what's behind the screens – their own and their partner's. They're more prepared to look behind their screens and to go through the temporary discomfort that will bring. Consequently they're freer; they lead less restricted lives, have more fun, avoid getting in a rut, and so grow and develop more as people.

John And at the other end of the spectrum?

Robin At the least happy extreme, both partners have a lot
behind their screens and absolutely refuse to admit there's anything wrong with them. In fact they're very touchy about the
slightest criticism, the very subtlest mention of their faults.

John So there's a lot of conflict?

Robin They fight a lot. Cat and dog.

John And between these two extremes?

Robin Well in the middle-range marriages, as we call them, the
partners are in a reasonably happy and stable relationship. But
they don't care to look behind the screens much. In fact they
rather back each other up in keeping all that stuff hidden away.
So the marriages are quite secure but the price that the partners
pay is that they get in a bit of a rut. Their options are rather
limited. In fact, you could say that they defend each other too
much against criticism which might be helpful in freeing them
from any ruts they do get in.

John I'd like to know more specifically how some of these
relationships work.

Robin Well, let's look at typical ones from each part of the
spectrum. What do you want, the good news or the bad news?

John Let's get the bad news over first.

Who's Afraid of Virginia Woolf? ......

Robin To give you a real feeling of what one of these least
successful marriages is like, I suggest you read this extract from
Edward Albee's play, *Who's Afraid of Virginia Woolf?* George and
Martha are a middle-aged couple who are almost permanently
locked in a bitter and vicious verbal fight.

> *Martha* Uh ... you make me puke!
> *George* That wasn't a very nice thing to say, Martha.
> *Martha* That wasn't *what*?
> *George* ... a very nice thing to say.
> *Martha* I like your anger. I think that's what I like about you
> most ... your anger. You're such a ... such a simp! You don't
> even have the ... the what? ...
> *George* ... guts? ...
> *Martha* Phrasemaker! Hey, put some more ice in my drink,

will you? You never put any ice in my drink. Why is that, hunh?

George I always put ice in your drink. You eat it, that's all. It's that habit you have ... chewing your ice cubes ... like a cocker spaniel. You'll crack your big teeth.

Martha They're my big teeth!

George Some of them ... some of them.

Martha I've got more teeth than you've got.

George Two more.

Martha Well, two more's a lot more.

George I suppose it is. I suppose it's pretty remarkable ... considering how old you are.

Martha You cut that out! You're not so young yourself.

George I'm six years younger than you are ... I always have been and I always will be.

Martha Well ... you're going bald.

George So are you. (Pause ... They both laugh) Hello, honey.

Martha Hello. C'mon over here and give your Mommy a big sloppy kiss.

George Oh ... now ...

Martha I want a big sloppy kiss!

George I don't *want* to kiss you, Martha. Where *are* these people? Where are these people you invited over?

Martha They stayed on to talk to Daddy ... They'll be here ... *Why* don't you want to kiss me?

George Well, dear, if I kissed you I'd get all excited ... I'd get beside myself, and I'd take you, by force, right here on the living-room rug, and then our little guests would walk in, and ... well, just think what your father would say about *that*.

Martha You pig!

George Oink! Oink!

Martha Ha, ha, ha, HA! Make me another drink ... lover.

George My God, you can swill it down, can't you?

Martha (Imitating a child) I'm firsty.

George Jesus!

Martha Look sweetheart, I can drink you under any goddam table you want ... so don't worry about me!

George Martha, I gave you the prize years ago ... there isn't an abomination award going that you ...

Martha I swear ... if you existed I'd divorce you ...

George Well, just stay on your feet, that's all ... These people are your guests, you know, and ...

Martha I can't even see you ... I haven't been able to see you for years ...

George ... if you pass out, or throw up, or something ...

Martha ... I mean, you're a blank, a cipher ...

George ... and try to keep your clothes on, too. There aren't many more sickening sights than you with a couple of drinks in you and your skirt up over your head, you know ...
Martha ... a zero ...
George ... your *heads*, I should say ...

John Well, there are a couple of little truces, moments of affection when they laugh together, but most of the time they're trying to wipe each other out, aren't they?

Robin Yes. It's not just a brilliant play, it's practically a textbook example for us.

John Do you often see marriages as destructive as this?

Robin Oh yes. And sometimes a lot worse too, though the feelings can be more hidden and the attacks more devious – though not less vicious.

John So what do you think is actually going on between them?

Robin Well, George and Martha are both enormously vulnerable. Each of them has an almost child-like longing for affection. But they've put that longing behind the screen. They deny it completely; they're quite unaware of it now, and they've covered it up with a sophisticated façade.

John Which is very brittle. Perhaps because their child-like sides never get the affection they crave?

Robin That's it. So the 'child' part of themselves is always frustrated, angry and resentful. That anger builds up until the point is reached when the 'furious child' bursts out from behind the screen. So they spend half their lives in infantile rages with each other.

John Because they never realise what the cause of their rage is – that they're not getting the love they so desperately need?

Robin Right. And one reason they never get that love is that they deny their need for it so completely that they can never ask for that love in a simple, open way.

John Martha has to say, 'Give your Mommy a kiss'. Saying, 'Give me a kiss' would make her too vulnerable?

Robin Yes.

John So what attracted them to each other in the first place?

Robin The similarity of the stuff *in front of* their screens – the goods in the shop window. They would have seen each other as sophisticated, intelligent, witty, very grown up, competent, worldly people. And, of course, they would *also* have sensed intuitively what was behind each other's screens, caught a glimpse, as it were, of the desperate, violent child there – horrifying, but strangely enticing and fascinating, and familiar.

John *Familiar* in the literal sense that they'd experienced it in their own families.

Robin Exactly. So in the way they'd been taught by their families, they immediately looked away from this horrifying shadowy figure – which must seem like the devil to them. They didn't notice it. But then, as they started living together, the devils began to burst out more and more and couldn't be ignored any more. So, when one devil did appear, the partner became horrified and attacked that devil furiously.

John Wait a moment, we're talking about a 'devil'. It's not a devil, is it? It's a desperately unhappy child having a tantrum.

Robin Of course, but that looks like a devil to the other partner. And it's so familiar and frightening for them both because it must have lurked in their parents, who therefore couldn't give George, or Martha, enough reliable love. That's what has created the raging child in each of *them*.

John And the parents must have *denied* the child in themselves too, so that the blind spot was passed on to George and Martha.

Robin So when one of them sees the other's 'devil', they attack it – with their own devil! Hence the terrible fighting.

John But we've nearly all had bad rows like this at some time of our lives, haven't we? To put it another way, if we've all got stuff behind the screen, don't these *Virginia Woolf* scenes occur in all marriages?

Robin To a point, yes, even if they're in milder or more disguised forms. But with this kind of couple, there's *so much* behind the screen, and the *fear of it is so great*, that there's no compromise. They've no tolerance at all for each other, which makes for a vicious circle of increasing hate and bitterness between them. Often it will end in quite serious physical violence too. But in most cases the escalating violence stops short of murder because they run out of energy. They literally become exhausted. Then, after a time, the pressure builds up and it starts all over again.

John But if there's so much conflict, why don't they get divorced?

Robin It may be hard to understand, but a couple like this finds it very difficult to separate. The relationship looks terrible to everyone else but, despite all the mayhem, the partners in this kind of marriage function better in *some* ways together than they would be able to do apart.

John Is that because as long as they're fighting the devil in their partner, they're distracted from noticing the devil in themselves?

Robin Exactly. That lets them feel better about themselves – more 'angelic' if you like. And there's another pay-off in this kind of marriage. Because they have the excuse of their partner's dreadful devilish behaviour, the forbidden side of themselves can escape and get expressed without them feeling guilty about it. Each one can say it was the other's fault because 'they started it'.

John 'All I said was . . .'

Robin 'I'm a patient man but there are limits . . .' So each can believe that he or she is *not really like that*. They can believe their own devil is only a *reaction* to the partner, that it's not *really* there, and that with *someone else* everything would be different.

John And, of course, if they're feeling aggrieved with each other all the time, they're justified in not offering the partner love and affection.

Robin Right, so they can stay where they are and neither of them has to acknowledge what's behind their screens.

John What happens if they *do* separate? Or if one of them dies?

Robin Well, then they may be at risk, because now they can't blame their bad feelings, their 'devil', on the partner. So they often have some kind of mental breakdown, sometimes even commit suicide.

John I know of an old couple who were supposed not to have spoken to each other for ten years. They lived in the same house, but they had separated it up, and even put a partition at the front door. Eventually the old woman killed herself. Within four days, the old man did so too.

Robin That's why these marriages are very enduring. They may break up repeatedly for short periods, but then they both feel worse again, and have to get back together.

John Wait a moment, though. George and Martha, for example, in between the fighting, have moments of very sentimental, baby-talk behaviour.

Robin What I've missed out is the changing moods. Sometimes the desperate, raging child will be more frustrated and closer to breaking through the screen; in other moods it may be quieter, more easily hidden. So sometimes one 'devil' leaps out from behind the screen and the other springs out for battle too. At other times both 'angels' – the fronts of the screens – take over. When these coincide, the partners will feel, and seem to others, even closer and more absorbed in each other than normal couples who get on pretty well. In this phase, they make up and they say they'll never do it again, and they *really* believe it. Indeed, the bitter fight of the day before seems just like a bad dream. They can't understand why it happened and they really believe they will never do it again.

John Because the problem is back behind the screen. So it's hidden again, and they therefore can't really believe it's there once they're feeling better. So the marriage is really out of control, isn't it, because the partners are so out of touch with reality . . .

Robin Yes. About the only positive attitude you can take to it is what was said about Carlyle, the writer, and his wife, that at least they were married to each other and not making two other people miserable. But we should remember that these are just a tiny proportion of marriages, right up at the bad end of the spectrum.

John Even so, I can recall rows that echo this kind of conflict.

Robin Few people can't! But the fact you *can* see that means it isn't behind your screen. If it was, you *wouldn't* recognise *anything* of yourself in this couple! So anyone who can see they've taken part in a scene like this is immediately many, many miles better off. And because the problem isn't behind the screen, they'll be on the way to solving it, even if they haven't done so already.

John All right. So what about the more normal relationships – the 'middle-range' marriages?

The 'Doll's House' and the hen-pecked husband ......

Robin Well, there are more kinds of middle-range marriages than there are types of trees, so we'll just have to select one or two as examples. A very common one is a type we call a 'Doll's House' marriage, after the play by Ibsen. Here the couple have taken on very stereotyped male and female roles. He appears the big, strong man, very grown up and parental; and she's the poor, helpless little woman, very childish and dependent.

John Remind me about the story. The husband gets ill and the wife saves his life by taking him abroad ...

Robin And she has to make sacrifices to get the money for the trip. But the point of the story is that she has to keep those sacrifices hidden from her husband because she believes it would destroy him – that is, it would dent his male pride too hopelessly – if he ever discovered how much he owes to her. In other words, if he sees how dependent *he* really is on *her*.

John So a 'Doll's House' marriage is one where it's obvious that the wife is emotionally dependent on the husband; but he's dependent on her too, but doesn't know it. And they both behave as though he isn't.

Robin Right. He has been taught that males must be strong and independent. They never cry, they never need looking after. But he's been forced to grow up too quickly. Therefore he's had to suppress, rather than *grow out of*, childish needs to be looked after. So there's a hidden, unsatisfied baby in him – though it's not so starved of care as to be desperate and vicious, as it is in the *Who's Afraid of Virginia Woolf* type of couple.

John So he's got a baby behind his screen, which needs love and attention; but he can't admit that and *ask* for it.

Robin No. He's got to get that emotional support in a disguised way. And the commonest way is to get ill; because when you're ill, even if you're a 'big, strong man', you have to be looked after and made a fuss of.

John You get a kind of nurturing, a kind of love and attention, without admitting that it's what you're really after?

Robin Yes. And if you need even more complete looking after, you might have a 'nervous breakdown'. The point is that, either way, the 'big, strong man' gets looked after, but at the same time can feel that it's his illness and not *him* that's being cared for.

John He can believe it's just a chance physical illness, and *not* a psychological need – which he would see as a weakness.

Robin Absolutely.

John So what's happening on the *wife's* side in a 'Doll's House' marriage?

Robin Well, she's been taught that girls are sugar and spice and all things nice. She's allowed to be affectionate and spontaneous and sensitive, or to cry, and it's quite permissible for her to operate on feelings rather than logical thought; but she's also learned that she must never be assertive or aggressive or, worst of all, make men feel inadequate by outdoing them.

John So she's hanging on to childish behaviour. Instead of a baby behind the screen, she's got her . . . more *adult* side there?

Robin Yes, she's screened off her strong, grown-up, capable side.

John Especially, I suppose, any aggressive feelings she has.

Robin Oh yes, especially those. So if she does express her assertiveness or strength or aggression, it will have to be in disguised ways. If she accomplishes something, she'll have to pretend she *really* didn't know *how* she managed to do it. Or if she feels aggressive towards her husband, it might come out in the form of destructive fantasies.

John Like worrying he's had an accident.

Robin Splattered all the way across the road, yes. Or, she might start vacuuming the floor unnecessarily under his feet while he's trying to read the Sunday papers.

John Or she might recite a long list of complaints about shop assistants and Mother and the weather and the children and the shape of the earth, until the husband somehow begins to get the idea that it's all supposed to be his fault?

Robin That's another. But the point is, she doesn't realise she's angry; *or* that she's capable of being strong and taking charge. It's all screened off.

John All right. So what was the attraction when they originally met?

Robin Well, they discovered they fitted together beautifully, like a jigsaw. At a conscious level, they're a good match because she's the kind of woman his family taught him to admire, and he's the kind of man her family approved of. At the same time, they fit equally well on an unconscious level where a trade-off happens. She accepts his 'baby' and, in return, he handles her tougher, more adult side.

John What do you mean by 'she accepts his baby'?

Robin Well, they both have an immature, childish side. But she can pretend to carry *all* this childishness – she's childish for *both* of them. While at the same time, he pretends to carry all their more *adult* sides, all the decisiveness and competence and assertiveness. So they function quite well together because the bits behind their screens are no longer so likely to cause trouble by expressing themselves in disguised ways. The couple in some ways work better than they did as separate individuals.

John 'In *some* ways'. So what's the catch?

Robin The catch is that she is now, as it were, carrying two lots of childishness, and he's carrying all the responsibility, so they're likely to get *locked into* the 'Me Tarzan, You Jane' set-up in a more and more extreme way. So he finds it becomes harder and harder to be spontaneous, to play, to relax and have fun; and at some level, he may feel resentment about this, though he won't be aware of the reason.

John Whereas she stays more and more in the home, and becomes apprehensive about taking on any outside activity?

Robin Yes, she spends all her time making jam and building sand-castles with the children. Part of her wants to do more grown-up things, but she gets progressively less confident about even trying them.

John But the arrangement works to some extent, even if they're both rather restricted.

Robin Oh yes. After all, it's the system that won the West and built the British Empire. And it still seems to work in *Dallas*!

John So what can go really wrong with it?

Robin If one of the partners becomes dissatisfied with being 'Jane' or 'Tarzan' – and that dissatisfaction may be largely unconscious – then the moment he or she starts trying to change the balance, the other partner resists it furiously. And because it's terribly difficult for just one partner to break the mould, the original Tarzan–Jane balance usually gets restored.

John What exactly *happens* if one of them tries to change?

Robin Let's take big, strong hubby – Tarzan – first. Suppose he gets more stress at work than he can cope with. His baby behind the screen becomes fretful and needs some nurturing; so some helpless, childish feelings, usually hidden behind the screen, begin to break through and trouble him. Now he may start to get depressed, become less responsible and lean on his wife. But this is outside the 'Me Tarzan, You Jane' script, so it makes her anxious.

John Because if she responded, she'd have to become more responsible – which involves letting out the stuff behind her screen.

Robin Yes, it alters the whole deal they entered into when they chose each other in the first place. That's very frightening to them both. He feels bad about revealing his needs, about being 'weak'; she's scared about taking more control. So she tries to restore the balance by resisting the change.

   She might get even more depressed or ill than he is. Very often, despite the fact that her husband was the one who had

the stress and began getting depressed first, she's the one who comes to the doctor in these circumstances. And the doctor, of course, wonders why his pills won't work.

John What's happening to the husband?

Robin She's forcing him back into the big, strong man role by becoming even more helpless and making him worry about *her*. So in this subtle way, without even realising what she's doing, she keeps him going. He *has* to be 'strong' to stay on his feet to look after *her*! Just as an exhausted soldier carrying a wounded comrade will push himself past the point where he would give up if he were just looking after himself, or if there were someone to carry *him*.

John Yes, but what happens to his depression or his illness? Why doesn't it go on indefinitely?

Robin Oh, the stress will end, or he'll find a way of coping with it, or he'll change his job, or whatever. So sooner or later, his 'baby' settles down quietly again behind the screen, and stops threatening their whole marital arrangement.

John And then *she* can get better?

Robin Yes, because the purpose of the illness has been fulfilled. And then, perhaps, her doctor is very relieved that the other pills did work!

John So, in a 'Doll's House' marriage, even though each partner may get dissatisfied at times, the other will always resist change – helped perhaps by the fact that the one who's trying to change may feel bad about it anyway.

Robin Yes. So it's quite stable, but a bit stifling.

John Well, supposing one of them becomes *determined* to change. The wife joins the women's movement or the husband refuses to stay in the rat race?

Robin Well, this will create the kind of stresses in the relationship that are likely to lead to a split.

John They're *not* likely to be able to resolve that?

Robin No, not unless the partner who doesn't want to change can get some outside help to learn how to do so.

John All right. Now what about a 'Doll's House' marriage where the roles are reversed – where the woman's playing the strong, grown-up role? 'Me John, You Tarzan.'

Robin Well, the most famous example is the hen-pecked husband, the old seaside postcard joke. Just like the 'Doll's House' wife, he won't take responsibility, stand up for himself, and look after his wife properly. In fact, he's behaving just like a child. But someone in the family has to be the grown-up and see that things get done, so the wife ends up doing that. She becomes his mother, in fact. But a part of her will resent it and that's where the hen-pecking comes in.

John She's carrying the assertiveness, the aggressiveness for both of them, because he won't take his share. As she's now got a double load, some of it spills over in his direction?

Robin Yes.

John Well this is something I've noticed in my relationships with women. If I get too passive, it seems to make the woman more aggressive. If I then deliberately take up a more aggressive stance, the woman becomes less so; it's as though a natural balance has been restored.

Robin I see that kind of seesaw in every couple that comes to see me professionally, and I certainly experienced it in my own marriage. I think it's universal – if one partner doesn't take his or her fair share of assertiveness and aggression, it forces the other partner to turn up the volume instead.

John So in this kind of marriage, why has the woman become Tarzan?

Robin She has usually had a family experience which made her frightened of being vulnerable and dependent. So her more child-like, needy part has been screened off; in this kind of marriage it can stay that way because she's chosen a man who carried all that for her.

John So he's the one with the adult side screened off; he's scared of being assertive and taking control, and she does that for him.

> Siegfried, Liebchen, I am a Valkyrie.

> I am a Virgo with Aquarius rising. Be gentle with me.

> On second thought, be violent.

Robin It's an exact reverse of the 'Doll's House'. So the marriage is again quite stable, but they'll feel a bit stifled sometimes by being locked into their roles. And again it's very difficult for either of them to change.

John Well, supposing one lovely spring morning, the man wakes up feeling a bit more assertive and grown up. What happens?

Robin Well, of course, she's always criticising him for being unreliable. But if his more responsible side *does* start to show, she'll immediately sense that this might induce her to be more vulnerable and dependent on him. So she'll pull her own screen down even harder.

John She'll deny even more than usual that she needs any support or affection.

Robin And to protect her familiar role even more strongly, she'll undermine his more grown-up mood by telling him it's no good, he couldn't look after her even if he tried, it would never work.

John She feels she's been through it all before and, let's face it, he's hopeless.

Robin And since the poor so-and-so is pretty short on confidence anyway, he'll soon give up, pull his screen down too, and shove his grown-up side back where it's safe. That's one scenario. Now, at another time, *she* may suddenly expose a little of her vulnerability – opening up to him and showing that she really needs him, wants some affection and support . . . which *terrifies* him. He feels he can't meet the challenge.

John So he pulls down his screen even tighter, and becomes more ineffectual?

Robin *And* he now undermines her by saying, 'What are *you* up to? Oh yes, it's all right if you're in the mood, isn't it?' And as her ability to open up is pretty limited, she gives up and thinks, 'Oh, what's the use, I knew it wouldn't be any good.'

John So they're safely back where they were. Even if it isn't particularly satisfactory, at least they feel at home there.

Robin Exactly. Because that's what home was like, remember? That's why they married each other in the first place.

John It has an enormous, enveloping, mad logic about it all, doesn't it? But look, one thing's struck me as very inconsistent. In the bad, *Virginia Woolf* marriage, the partners have got the same things in the shop window – the angels – and the same behind the screens – the devils. But with the 'Doll's House' and the hen-pecked husband, one's got the baby *behind* the screen and the other's got the baby *in front*. The screen's in the same place, they're divided up the same way, *but* they complement each other instead of being identical. So doesn't this mean that some couples are attracted because they had the same kind of family experience, and others because they were different?

Robin Fair enough. You've spotted that the explanation I've given you so far is a bit too simple. A little complication I now have to add, therefore, is that the first screening off of a bit of the personality can later lead to problems with *other* feelings, which then have to be screened off in turn. Take the example of the person who has screened off anger to please his family, and now can't stick up for himself properly. That will lead him to lack confidence and fear confrontation, so his family may now criticise him for being a cissy. The next thing that may happen is that he hides his natural fear, and need for support, from others, and then from himself. So now *that's* behind the screen too. A therapist may sometimes have to help a patient to raise a number of screens, one after another, to get back to the most fundamental family taboo.

John So if a person hides emotion x and then hides his *fear* of emotion x, he may look, *on the surface*, as though he's comfortable with it. But how does this fit in with what you were saying about couples choosing to marry each other?

Robin It explains why there's some truth in the saying that 'opposites attract', although that seems to contradict the idea that couples tend to choose each other on the basis of *similarities* in the way their families dealt with feelings. To give you an example, a typical 'Doll's House' couple were referred for treatment because the wife was always complaining of feeling ill. She was timid and fearful, while her husband was confident and apparently strong. But it soon emerged that they had *both* suffered similarly through the deaths of their fathers when they were each six years old. At a deeper level they were similar, and in both of them feelings of sadness had been shut away behind the screen. She dealt with saddening events by feeling ill, while he dealt with them by being 'strong' and concentrating on looking after *her*.

John So the superficial *differences* between the partners in a marriage like that are possible because the partners can play different roles to handle similar hidden problems. But is there a basic difference between the really destructive relationships and the mid-range ones?

Robin If there's a massive amount hidden behind the screen, and a great pressure for it to burst through – as you're liable to get with the more unhealthy couples – the partners are more likely to be in conflict and competition with each other. That's *less* likely where the partners complement each other and play opposite roles. This allows them to divide the territory up according to their differences, and so to get along better. But, of course, it's all a question of degree.

John Now a lot of middle-range marriages – ordinary, normal marriages – will show 'Doll's House' or hen-pecked-husband characteristics, will they?

Robin Yes. They'll usually show quite a lot, though perhaps very mildly so.

John Well I'm glad that's normal, because I recognise several.

Robin Such as?

John Well, when I first came to your group, I was very much in the 'Tarzan' role. I saw myself as 'strong', not really needing support and affection. I reckoned I could do without it, really!! And I remember your gently pointing out that I did need it and how difficult – how very difficult – it was for me to admit that. But once it's been pointed out to you a few thousand times ... well, first you begin to accept that it's *possible* ... and then you start *seeing* it for yourself. You also begin to see how you look away from it when you do notice it.

Robin It's very surprising at the start, isn't it? But you get more and more curious about it.

John Yes, you start 'catching yourself doing it'. And then you seem to change, bit by bit. Is that *just* because you're seeing it more clearly?

Robin Yes, once you really notice the bit that's hitherto been hidden, you can start taking it on board and achieve a better balance of your whole personality.

John The other thing I remember is that the process of discovery was quite uncomfortable. Admitting to myself that I needed affection or, worse still, asking for it in an open, undisguised way, felt somehow shameful, almost a sign of weakness or inadequacy.

Robin It was probably because you associated asking for affection with those 'bad' feelings that put the need for affection behind the screen in the first place. And as it emerged, the shameful feelings originally associated with it had to be experienced too, for a time. This is why treatment takes time – it actually feels wrong to get better!

John And when you're changing, it's an odd feeling, isn't it? You suddenly sense you've never been where you are now; it feels very unfamiliar, rather disorientating and risky.

Robin That's why happiness needs a lot of practice!

John Anyway, we've seen two examples of middle-range marriages. What about the ones right up at the healthiest end of the spectrum?

The healthiest marriages ......

Robin The most curious thing about really healthy marriages is that mental-health professionals have shown almost no interest in them. So up to ten years ago, there wasn't any information about them at all. And now that we have some research at last, the findings are still being ignored. It's very strange.

John Yes, I've asked shrinks about this sort of research, but they've never heard of any. Perhaps they're hushing it up because it would make them feel insecure. Anyway, what are the main findings?

Robin Well to boil it down to one sentence, I'd say that the less the partners have behind their screens, and the more they're prepared to look behind them if the other does point something out, then the more they can grow as individuals and the richer their relationship becomes.

John They're not limited by the need to hold the screens firmly down, you mean. And they don't have to worry about keeping the balance of the relationship as it's always been.

Robin So each gets more space to grow, to explore more possibilities and become more fulfilled. So, of course, they have more to give back to each other. And they're more interesting as people, so they enjoy each other more. They're on an upward spiral.

John Do they have any key characteristics?

Robin An absolutely fundamental finding of the research is that they can accept *change* very easily.

John Again, presumably, because they're not frightened by the idea that there are things behind the screen that might emerge if changes occur?

Robin That's one reason, certainly. In fact, they actually *help each other* to bring feelings out into the open. In other words, they both accept the need to take criticism from each other, although that criticism is usually made in a constructive and supportive way – and at the right time.

John All criticism is slightly painful, isn't it, provided that there's some truth in it?

Robin Only if it touches upon something that's behind the screen.

John Really?

Robin Because then our self-image is dented. That's what's painful.

John You mean if we're aware of the fault, it doesn't hurt if it's pointed out.

Robin Not if we've become aware of *all* its aspects. At least, that's my experience.

John So are these 'healthiest' couples so healthy because there wasn't much behind their screens to start with; or because they've both been very willing to look at what was back there?

Robin It could be either. Some people are more 'together' right from the beginning because they come from really happy families – which is the best luck anyone can have. Others have less perfect starts, so they begin more divided – but they've been lucky enough to find a partner who makes them feel less frightened of what's behind their screens; so they've had the support, the love, which they needed to let them go through the discomfort of getting in touch with the hidden parts of themselves and bringing them out in the open. Doing that has enabled them to change and to move up towards the healthiest end of the spectrum.

Moving up/getting it together ......

John So are you suggesting that it's an ideal for us all to try to get everything out from behind the screen?

Robin Well I suppose it's an ideal, a star to steer by, but I don't imagine anyone achieves it, and it's certainly not necessary.

John But we can all succeed to some extent.

Robin Certainly. I think a lot of people become more aware of themselves without even particularly trying to. Others get interested and work at it a bit, and therefore may make faster progress than they otherwise would.

John Could that happen with the *Virginia Woolf* couple, George and Martha?

Robin Really destructive relationships like that don't usually change. There's *so much* behind the screens, and it's *so* terrifying that they usually simply try to keep the screens down as tightly as they can. It feels safer to stay that way and just go on fighting.

John Is change possible *at all*?

Robin Only if the couple get help from outside the marriage. They couldn't surmount the taboos and fears on their own.

John Supposing they saw a shrink, then?

Robin Well *if* they did ... there's a limit to what you can do for a relationship as bad as this. You can help a bit in crises sometimes, but a lot of the time you feel it's right for them to keep their screens down.

John What would happen if you tried to raise the screens a bit?

Robin It would just be too painful for them to bear. If you tried to force them into it, they would just defend themselves by ganging-up on the therapist and they wouldn't come back for any more therapy. You would have put them through a lot of discomfort for nothing; you wouldn't get another chance to help them yourself, and they'd be less likely to trust anyone else they consulted in the future. So it would be bad practice to try to force the issue.

John All right. Let's move on to middle-range marriages. The couples in this kind of relationship might change, might get stuff out from behind the screens, and move up towards the healthiest end of the spectrum?

Robin Yes, they might. It all depends on their attitude to the screens. They may prefer to let sleeping dogs lie, and avoid the discomfort that looking behind the screens always brings. Remember, these marriages can be quite stable, even if the partners occasionally feel a little restricted.

John Supposing they started having problems and came to a shrink?

Robin Well, with middle-range marriages we can make progress, we can help them look behind the screens; *if* they want to!

John So what might happen if a 'Doll's House' couple came for help?

Robin Let's imagine that they're coming because the husband has come under unusual stress and really needs support, but as his more childish part is securely hidden behind his screen, he can't ask for it. As a result, it's becoming more and more restive and fretting louder and louder and some of the fretting is beginning to escape through the screen and show itself in subtle ways.

John So the wife will be getting frightened that she'll have to be more responsible because she's screened off her more adult side. So I think you said she responds by getting *even more* depressed and fretful than he is.

Robin That's right. *Now* . . . if a therapist spots this happening, he can reassure the husband that it's natural, normal and, in fact, positively healthy to express this more needy, child-like side at times – indeed, that it's amazing, even a bit worrying, that it's not getting expressed more. This eases the husband's fear, so that bit by bit he can allow himself to become aware of these needs and let his wife support him *too* sometimes. *At the same time*, the wife is shown that she could help most in the long run by *accepting* what's behind his screen rather than protecting him from facing it, and that it's also all right for her to express some of her screened-off assertiveness – the bit of her that's capable and able to take charge.

John So, basically, by conveying the feeling that what is behind the screen is *all right*, the shrink can encourage them to help each other grow, instead of keeping each other stuck.

Robin Yes, and the great thing is that, after a certain point, they can carry on doing it on their own.

John So applying the same principles to the hen-pecked-husband marriage, the shrink will need to allow the hen to see how frightened she is of trusting her husband to be responsible.

Robin And while you're helping her to see that, you're giving her enough emotional support to carry her through the unpleasant feelings she'll experience while she's realising how scared she is of him letting her down. And if, at the same time, you can show the husband that he's scared of taking responsibility . . . and *also* help him to see the vulnerable little girl hidden behind her screen, as well as to realise that the bossy mother figure only appears because he doesn't look after that vulnerable little girl . . . you can get their relationship to start changing in the right direction.

John In doing this, you're really explaining to them how they're caught in this system of helping each other to conceal the truth, aren't you?

Robin Yes. But it's most effective of all if you just point out the *positive* side of it – how Jane sacrifices herself by staying helpless to keep Tarzan strong. Or how the hen-pecked husband protects his wife from feeling weak and vulnerable by allowing her to take all the responsibility. Once they begin to see a *bit* of the pattern and start to look at it together, they can't help seeing the rest too and wanting to change it.

John So at one end of the marriage spectrum we've got the Georges and the Marthas desperately holding down their screens because there's so much crammed behind. At the other, we've got couples who keep lifting the screens up, who haven't got much there and are always reducing the amount anyway. And in the middle, the rest of us.

Robin Yes, only remember that the two extremes are statistically pretty small proportions of the population. The majority of us will be in the middle range. Just as most of us are near average height rather than 4′ 8″ or 6′ 6″.

John So I'm obviously mid-range, and up at the very healthiest end, of course, are all you shrinks.

Robin Pull the other leg for a change, John!

John Well, I mean, everybody knows psychiatrists are crazy – I've seen more mad psychiatrist sketches than I've had hot dinners – but you don't believe that, do you?

Robin I'm not suggesting we're crazy. But I think most of us are around mid-range.

John Really? But how can you help people, then?

Robin Well, look at it this way. If you've never had any serious problems, never had to go through this painful experience of getting things out from behind the screen, I don't think you'd be very good at helping other people to do it. You'd never really know what it felt like. It would be very difficult to apply your intuition, your understanding, to an experience you were completely lacking. Also, I'd be very surprised if a really healthy

person would be interested in doing this kind of work. I mean, they might be friendly and helpful, but they probably wouldn't want to make a career out of it.

John This is slightly unexpected.

Robin Well, try it another way. If you're trying to climb a mountain, the guide who's most helpful is the one who's just above you and can guide your next step. The chap who's ten thousand feet further up isn't much use.

John I remember thinking that once while listening to Krishnamurti. You know, I suddenly realised that I feel rather envious of these people who are right up the healthiest end – even if they would make hopeless therapists.

Robin Of course. So do I.

John Well ... I can't help wondering whether this research showing that there are really healthy people has been *ignored* by *shrinks* because *they* feel jealous of these really healthy people too, and would prefer not to acknowledge them. Because it rubs in the fact to the shrinks, and the other mental-health professionals, that most of us are mid-range and maybe *not so far apart*.

Robin Maybe. And if we *are* mid-range, we're obviously going to have the usual mid-range faults, like jealousy, just as other people do, aren't we? Why should we be any different?

John But look ... if becoming more healthy is just a matter of getting stuff out from behind the screen, why aren't we all doing it more?

Robin It's the *pain*, remember? Taking stuff out from behind the screen is painful. And worse than that, it actually feels *wrong*. I said earlier that we screen things off because it was a pattern in our family to do so, a pattern that got passed on, because if anyone in the family started to show the forbidden emotion, the taboo ... then the rest of the family would feel threatened.

John So the family would attack them.

Robin Or, just as bad, ignore them. Ostracise them. *Reject* them. And that rejection by the family is a deeply frightening experience, particularly for a small child.

John So bringing these feelings back out from behind the screen arouses all the old feelings of fear?

Robin Yes. It feels as though we're going against the disapproval of the whole family, as if we're going to lose all their love and support. And *that's* why we need someone to help us.

John A shrink, you mean.

Robin Perhaps in the more serious cases, yes. Although it can always help people to get started even if they don't have serious problems. But, for the long haul, the ideal person is someone from a different family – so that they haven't got exactly the same blind spots – but from a family which is also very similar in many ways, so they can understand us.

John I can hear Mantovani striking up. You're about to say that our partners can be our best shrinks.

Robin They can be. But shrink means what it says.

John How do you mean?

Robin If we're wishing to hear the truth, it hurts and makes us feel smaller. But it's only our swollen heads that are getting smaller. Remember, shrink is short for head-shrinker, isn't it?

John Oh, I like it.

Robin And as our swollen heads get smaller ... as people we grow.

2 I'm God, and Let's Leave it Like That

Changes are good – and bad . . . . . .

John I'd like to know more about these 'really healthy families' that research has been done on. What is it that distinguishes them from other families?

Robin Several things. But the basic principle is that they handle *change* so well.

John Nasty changes?

Robin No, all kinds of change.

John Well, what's so clever about handling pleasant changes?

Robin It may be surprising, but scientists have found that *any* kind of change produces stress. Look at this chart.

LIFE EVENT	STRESS VALUE
Death of spouse	100
Divorce	73
Marital separation	65
Prison term	63
Death of close family member	63
Personal injury or illness	53
Marriage	50
Fired at work	47
Marital reconciliation	45
Retirement	45
Change in health of family member	44
Pregnancy	40
Sex difficulties	39
Gain of new family member	39
Business readjustment	39
Change in financial state	38
Death of close friend	37

Change to different line of work	36
Change in number of arguments with spouse	35
Mortgage over $10,000 [now about £20,000]	31
Foreclosure of mortgage or loan	30
Change in responsibilities at work	29
Son or daughter leaving home	29
Trouble with in-laws	29
Outstanding personal achievement	28
Wife begins or stops work	26
Begin or end school	26
Change in living conditions	25
Revision of personal habits	24
Trouble with boss	23
Change in work hours or conditions	20
Change in residence	20
Change in schools	20
Change in recreation	19
Change in church activities	19
Change in social activities	18
Mortgage or loan less than $10,000 [now about £20,000]	17
Change in sleeping habits	16
Change in number of family get-togethers	15
Change in eating habits	15
Holiday	13
Christmas	12
Minor violations of the law	11

* This table is reproduced, with minor adjustments to make it more applicable to a British reader in the 1980s, from Thomas H. Holmes and Richard H. Rahe's social readjustment rating scale, *Journal of Psychosomatic Research*, Vol. 11 (Pergamon Press, 1967).

As you see, the death of a spouse is rated as the greatest stress. That's 100. The more units you rack up in a given period of time, the greater the likelihood that you'll suffer some kind of illness.

John Well you'd predict that getting pregnant or having a kid has got a stressful as well as a nice side, but isn't it extraordinary that getting reconciled with your spouse after a period of living separately costs you as much as 45 points. And I'm amazed that a *reduction* in the number of rows you normally have with your wife can put you 35 points down. I suppose if my life suddenly became perfect, I'd have a crack-up. How can this be, Doctor?

Robin When there's a change in our external circumstances, good or bad, we have to adjust to it.

John Yes, but what's actually *happening* to us when we 'adjust'? What's going on in us, in our heads?

Robin OK. I have to introduce a new idea to explain that.

John Feel free.

Robin We'll keep coming back to it, incidentally. We all have in our heads a record or picture of our world as we know it, a mental map which corresponds to our external circumstances. Just as a map of Britain corresponds to Britain. And we use our map to guide our behaviour.

John Everything to do with our life is on it? Our spouse, kids, parents, friends, house, neighbourhood, office . . .

Robin Everything that touches our lives is mapped there, to guide us in coping with our lives.

John We only look at one part of it at a time, but it's all available.

Robin Right. So if your spouse dies, you have to go from a mental map where the spouse figures very large indeed, bigger than anything else in fact, to a map on which the spouse no longer appears. And that process of changing from one map to another is what I mean by 'adjusting'.

John It's a kind of re-wiring of our mental circuits.

Robin Yes. And the point of all this is that the readjustment, including this redrawing of the map . . . takes *energy*.

John Even if the change is 'nice'. OK. But we're going through changes *all the time*. In fact back in Weston-super-Mare we say that a change is as good as a rest, my dear.

Robin Yes, the world's always changing. In fact we need a certain level of change, of stimulation. If we get too little, we feel bored and only half alive. Change is harmful only when it goes beyond the ability of our system to cope with it – as when there's a big sudden change or too many small changes in a row that don't allow us time to recover our equilibrium.

John Like a house being made untidy faster than we can tidy it up. So if there is too much change over any given period, we get stressed. So what helps us to cope?

Robin First, we need to be relieved of some of the usual demands on our energy so it can go towards dealing with the changes.

John Doctors call this 'rest', I believe.

Robin Yes, though I should tell you that when doctors do nothing, we call it 'masterly inactivity'. Rest usually means someone shielding us from most of the usual demands. And then, because we usually have some anxiety about changes, any information that we can be given that will reassure us that we will be able to cope, and show us *how* to cope, is very helpful too.

John The energy we might waste on worrying can also go towards handling the changes.

Robin Yes.

John But there's something else too, isn't there? Sometimes just being with someone we like and trust helps us in a way that's slightly different from either rest or reassurance.

Robin I think that's right. It's easy to remember to do the shopping for people under stress, to take round some food, or share experience, but sometimes we forget that just sticking around, just 'being there' also helps enormously. Even though it doesn't feel as though we're doing much.

John Well what *are* we doing?

Robin By just being there? It's very hard to say, isn't it, although we've all experienced how important it is. Let's just call it 'emotional support' for the moment.

John So just to summarize, to handle change we need: one, to be shielded from usual demands so we can rest; two, information to reassure anxieties and help us to cope; and three, 'emotional support'.

Robin Right.

John So now let's talk about all this in relation to families. We've discussed why a couple choose each other. Now they get married. That'll cost them 50 points, because they have to re-draw their maps to include each other on a more permanent basis. Now, in the honeymoon period they're still admiring the goods in each other's front windows, so to speak. Then as they start living together, some of the stuff behind their screens will start coming out.

Robin It starts becoming a more real relationship. That's more change.

John A bit of redrawing there, now and again.

Robin Helped by the fact that most of the time they're giving each other a lot of love and support, more perhaps than they've ever had before.

John So what's the next big change?

Robin That moment when they become a real family, the arrival of the first baby.

John 39 points off, folks.

Robin Only 11 points better than getting married in the first place.

John This is obviously why we're supposed to keep the events separate.

Robin Especially round Christmas.

John . . . Quip, quip we go but it's suddenly all sounding terribly negative.

Robin It's negative only in the sense that it's a huge adjustment they have to make, a big jump forward to being more respons-ible, more grown-up. So it is a big stress for a time. Once they've made it, once they're through that barrier, they'll get a lot of joy and happiness from the child.

John But for the moment, they've lost more than just their freedom.

Robin Yes, the new baby's needing so much attention and love that they both have that much less – a *lot* less – to give to each other. And that can be painful for them both.

John So this first baby's a Comparatively Happy Event.

Robin Yes, it's hard not to get the feeling that society's conspired to romanticise it all. Of course it's a wonderful moment and a wonderful experience, but one oughtn't to forget how tough it frequently is at first. *Especially* if the couple didn't quite know what to expect. And remember that the change and stress of going from 'no baby' to 'one baby' is usually much bigger than going from 'one' to 'two' or more.

The parental emergency......

John All right. The baby's arrived. What should the couple expect?

Robin Well let's look first at just how drastically the balance of the family changes. Before the baby arrives, they're both free to give each other their full supply of emotional support, but after the baby arrives, he needs an enormous amount of this nurture from the mother. This puts considerable demands on her and means she needs even more love and support than she usually gets from the husband. But she's giving so much to the baby that she often has very little left over to give back to her husband. So he's deprived of *his* usual emotional support at the time when the *mother* needs more emotional support from him than she's ever needed before.

Robin So if he can't cope with a lot less support than he's been used to, she can end up feeling very isolated and deprived indeed.

John Which coming so soon after the euphoria of the actual birth could be a very nasty jolt.

Robin Yes. Up to then, the mother's been the focus of attention. She's been looked after, cherished, perhaps as never before. Then, suddenly, there's this tiny, incredibly vulnerable baby which she feels totally responsible for 24 hours of the day and night.

John They're so helpless, you feel they could snuff it at any moment, don't you?

Robin I remember not quite believing ours would go on breathing without help. And I'd served my time on an obstetrics ward! So it's not surprising how terrifying that responsibility seems to the new mother. My wife, Prue, runs a support group for ordinary mothers of first children and they nearly all complain that no one had prepared them for such a huge change.

John The mother feels responsible for keeping the baby alive and she's *never done it before*!

Robin And she's exhausted a lot of the time, so sometimes she's going to feel she can't cope. She may feel guilty about that because she thinks she isn't a 'good Mum'. So she has to hide her feelings of inadequacy from people, and *that's* a strain. Of course the big problem is that nowadays, without the extended family, she often *does* have to cope with very little support. It's sometimes fine for the first couple of weeks. Her mother might move in, or his mother, and the husband generally takes a week off. But after that, she often feels terribly inexperienced and abandoned.

John Well, she's certainly being deprived of all the support that she used to get from her friends, but the father's in there helping to some extent, isn't he?

Robin At the start, yes, but after a time, he often begins to feel rather left out.

John Yes, I remember feeling I was nothing to do with what was going on!

Robin Well, that's very common. Actually Prue sometimes feels a bit sorry for the father because at least the mother has got the tremendous satisfaction of the intimate relationship with the baby. That's giving her some wonderful deep new feelings even if it is so exhausting. But Dad's supposed to give his wife much more care.

John Things could get a bit tense.

Robin Well, he gets back tired from work – he probably went to work tired, because of the disturbed nights – his wife's had nothing but the baby all day, the baby's probably getting colic just about then and howling, Father's sitting there feeling neglected and wanting his dinner, and Mother's feeling terrible. 'Split in two' is how they describe it.

John Stop! This is terrible. It sounds like something out of Strindberg. Or Billy Connolly.

Robin Well, remember these are the really tough moments with the first child. But it gets better.

John What helps?

Robin Just time. It all starts feeling less desperate. The mother becomes more confident, less frightened.

John She's beginning to adjust to all the changes.

Robin Right. And she's getting more rest – the feeding times are getting spaced out. Then she starts to visit the Child Health Clinic regularly and gets to talk with other mothers and that's a terrific source of support. And all the time she's feeling more confident about looking after the child.

John Still, hearing all this reminds me there's an American psychologist called Guttman who calls the arrival of children 'the parental emergency'.

Robin Yes, he believes that the psychological differences between men and women arise mainly from the struggle to cope with bringing up babies. He thinks that, after the birth, we take up the male and female roles a bit like soldiers taking up battle stations. Of course society trains us for it from the very beginning but until the baby arrives it's as though we're in the 'reserve', still able to play around with bits of both roles if we want to . . .

John When baby comes we're 'called up'.

Robin And we find ourselves polarising into warm, nurturing Mums and tough, responsible Dads. Because that's how we've been programmed.

John Is there research to show that when the kids grow up and leave home the mothers and fathers become human beings again?

Robin Interestingly, there's evidence that a compensation then takes place with the men becoming softer, less driven, more keen to relax and enjoy the good things in life, while the women often start becoming more active, organizing things, becoming more assertive, and generally making up for lost time. In fact I believe that it's only after the kids have left that we can begin to understand what the 'battle' was all about.

John What do you think about the different roles we play while the children are still with us?

Robin Well, more and more people claim that either parent can do the mother's job. Certainly fathers *can* do it, and some can do it better than some mothers. I'm sure it's good for the child if they share it to some extent. But, if male and female bodies are built so differently to make a baby, it seems most unlikely to me that there aren't some inborn, psychological differences which make women better at doing *some* things that children need and men better at doing others. In general. But it isn't settled yet.

Is there a telephone here? It's eight o'clock, and if I know my husband he'll forget to breast-feed the baby.

John Anyway, for new parents the question of whether the differences are genetic or conditioned is a bit sterile, isn't it? Even if it isn't genetic, the conditioning has taken place.

Robin No, I don't agree with that. Quite profound changes in these roles are taking place at the moment, and I'm sure they'll continue. Both men and women are becoming less 'locked in' to the old stereotypes and are much richer and more interesting for the greater freedom and understanding this has brought with it. It has certainly affected me and I'm very grateful to be living in such an interesting time.

John Do you know the Chinese blessing, 'May you live in uninteresting times'? It means, 'May you have a peaceful life'. Anyway, we've heard enough about the parents' problems with the 'emergency'. What about it from the baby's point of view? Being born brings a distinct change in one's life-style, doesn't it?

Robin It must be shattering. Up to then, many things are being done for the baby by the mother, like breathing and digesting food. Now he has to do all these himself. And inside the mother's body he was completely safe, protected, warm, dark, quiet – now he's suddenly vulnerable, unprotected, every single

*I've finally mastered the foetal position, and **I'm not leaving**.*

element in his environment is new and strange. And anything new and strange is *frightening*. In addition, his rate of growth is tremendous relative to his size.

John Looking back to our stress chart, I notice that being born hasn't been included on the list.

Robin It would probably be right off the top of the scale, if you could measure it.

John It would be worth about sixteen reconciliations and a car accident, I'd guess. Which is why the baby needs all the care he does. That is, rest, protection from all unnecessary additional stress; love or emotional support; and . . . ah, but of course he can't get the other – reassuring information.

Robin And that's one of the problems with a new-born baby. If something is making him uncomfortable, he has no conception that he will feel better again later on. Which explains how distressed he gets.

John So until he begins to get the idea that discomforts are more or less temporary, he's going to need that much more emotional support and rest.

Robin Yes, the parents have to shield him almost completely from outside disturbance, keeping him warm and comfortable, seeing he doesn't get too hungry, protecting him from too much noise and upset. They'll give him little bits of change, of course, but they'll be careful to keep them simple and gentle, enough to stimulate the baby but not more than he can comfortably manage. He's completely dependent, and fortunately nature has programmed us, and all other animals too, so that mother and child instinctively stay together and search for each other if separated.

John Is this what's called attachment behaviour?

Robin That's right. It simply means that a foal, for example, despite the fact that it can stand up within a few minutes of being born, will still instinctively stay close to its mother for years. I remember trying to get between a foal and its mother in our field in Wales and how uncomfortable it made them both. In fact, I never succeeded. This attachment behaviour has obviously got an evolutionary advantage, since it makes sure that the young are protected while they're most vulnerable to predators. We've all seen on nature films how the isolated young animal is the one that the predators attack.

John I appreciate that, but isn't there more than protection going on with this attachment behaviour? What about the need for love?

Robin A lot of experts would quarrel with you about that way of putting it, though I'm not sure the two things we're saying are really all that different. I'm talking about what this attachment behaviour seems to be achieving, for the individual and the species, looked at *from outside*. You're talking about what it *feels* like to be involved in it.

John From the inside. Let's talk more about that. About emotional support as you've put it. I mean, when we talk about a mother loving her baby, I suddenly wonder what is it that the baby's actually *getting*?

The baby and mother-love ......

John So, Doctor, what's mother-love as seen from the baby's point of view?

Robin Let me tell you about some fascinating research by a psychologist called Harlow. He reared monkeys in a number of different ways: some with their mothers in the usual way; others in bare cages separated from their mothers; a third lot in similar cages with a wire frame in the shape of a mother which was fitted with little teats in the places where the mother's nipples would normally be, from which the baby could get food; and a fourth lot with a similar mother-shaped wire dummy, but which was covered in *furry cloth*.

John One 'normal' group; one 'no-mothers', one 'wire-mothers'; one 'cloth-mothers'.

Robin Right. Now the 'normal' monkey babies alternated between exploring the world nearby, then going back to cling to mother, then going off exploring again, and so on. But Harlow found that the second group, the monkeys reared apart from their mothers in the bare cages, were very withdrawn and inhibited. They didn't play and explore but just crouched in a corner looking terrified. And when they grew up they seemed unable to cope with social situations; they usually couldn't mate; and even if they succeeded in having babies they weren't interested in parenting them.

John And the ones with the 'wire-mothers'?

Robin They were very similar to the 'no-mother' group. *But* the ones with the cloth-mothers were *better off*, healthier.

John So the furry cloth-mother actually had the effect of lessening the harm caused by the real mother's absence.

Robin Yes! The little monkeys would spend a lot of time clinging to it, as they normally do to their mothers' bodies, and this somehow made them able to explore and play, in between the clinging. Also, when they were adult, they were a bit more able to mix normally with others.

John So the physical contact, even just with the 'cloth-mother', gave the baby *something*. But *what*?

Robin Harlow called it 'courage'. I prefer the word 'confidence', which stands for the same idea but means literally 'with faith', that is, acting on the expectation that things are going to be all right. Maybe even the comfort provided by the 'cloth-mother' soothes the baby, calms its agitation when it has been away exploring and has experienced more change than it can cope with.

John It gives the baby an interlude of stability, an oasis of calm to help it regain its balance?

Robin That's what it looks like. Scientists would probably call it 'negentropy', a reduction of disorder. Of course, a little cloth dummy won't do a *lot* towards that, but it helps.

John And you think that's what 'mother-love' is!!

Robin Well, I do say it's the *effect* it has for the baby. Giving 'love' means being able to bring that effect about in another person when it's needed.

John And without this love the baby will be too scared to venture out?

Robin Yes. He can grow up – which almost by definition means becoming more independent – only if he's got the confidence that comes from this reliable comfort and security.

John Kids at a playground can forget all about Mum . . . until they fall over! The shock of that sends them back for another injection of love and confidence.

Robin You can put it like that if you like but, as I said, what they're getting is a chance to get steady again after too much change, rather than something passing into them from the mother as if there's a kind of refuelling going on.

John I see. And obviously as we grow up this attachment behaviour diminishes.

Robin That's right. As we get more confident and learn more about the world and how to handle it, we can cope with more and more stress before having to go back for support. But the potential need for it continues *all our lives*. *All* of us in suficiently stressful situations will need looking after. And that 'looking after' very much corresponds to what babies and children get – mothering.

John Yes, after a natural disaster, earthquakes, volcanic eruptions, bombing, and so forth, the instinctive reaction of all survivors is to look for other people.

Robin It's an automatic reaction, built-in; we're programmed to

seek support from others when it's needed, and to respond when it's required of us.

John Getting back to the baby, how does the mother know what he needs? How can she understand the tiny creature's signals?

Robin Well, a normal mother senses what he's feeling and needing by getting in touch with her own baby feelings – that is, by reliving her own babyhood and childhood.

John You mean she'll just drift back in her memory . . .

Robin . . . In a receptive, intuitive, way. She'll really enjoy doing that and that's how she'll tune in and find the empathy to communicate with this tiny creature, by picking up signals and responding appropriately. And as she does so, the baby slowly gains more confidence and it's that confidence that allows him to explore the outside world.

The baby begins his maps . . . . . .

John So the mother's giving the baby the confidence he needs to start exploring this bright, noisy, new world he's arrived in. But he's practically helpless, so what can he do?

Robin Well, one of the main things is to start learning what the world is like.

John You mean he begins drawing his own *mental map* of the world?

Robin Yes. And that world, of course, includes *himself*.

John So how does he go about mapping himself?

Robin Well, what's the first thing you do when you draw a map of Britain?

John The outline.

Robin Exactly. You'd start with an *outline* – where it begins and ends – not the details. The baby has to draw an outline of himself too. He has to discover what's inside himself and what's outside himself. In other words, he has to find out what's himself and what isn't. And to start with, for all practical purposes 'what isn't' is his Mum.

John This is a bit rum.

Robin Well, look at it from the baby's point of view. The brain of a new-born baby is getting messages from outside and inside his body, but at the beginning there's no reason for him to understand that the inside messages belong to him and the outside ones don't. For all he knows, they could *all* be about him.

John You mean he thinks he's everything. Or that everything's him.

Robin Well, there's no reason for him to believe otherwise. And until something happens to change that view, his mother must seem like an extension of himself. A sort of unusually busy limb.

John So what causes the truth to dawn?

Robin The very gradual discovery that the outside can't be controlled as easily as the inside.

John I don't think I've got this yet.

Robin You see, I know these are *my* fingers because I can move them. So I know they are part of me. But if I try to move *your* fingers they don't move, so I know they're *not* part of me. They must be outside my edges. So I'm learning where my edges are – where I end and other people begin. Babies learn the same way.

John But that means that the baby learns about his boundaries only when the mother doesn't do what he wants.

Robin Right.

John So if she could be a perfect mother who never failed to meet the baby's needs completely, the baby wouldn't know the difference between himself and her?

Robin Yes. He would stay muddled, completely mixed-up in his mind with her. So it would be hard to grow up and get free.

John But are you now saying that frustration is *good* for the baby?

Robin Yes and no. For the first year at least, and to a lessening degree after that, the baby's ability to cope with the strong feelings aroused by change and stress is pretty well stretched to the limit, even when the parents are doing everything they can to meet his needs. Even when they are trying to provide as much stability and security as they can, there will be more than enough frustration without trying to create it deliberately – ordinary human failure will see to that. Whether it's because she doesn't wake immediately the baby cries, or the phone rings, or there's someone at the door, the mother won't *always* appear immediately the baby wants her. So the baby will gradually get the message that his mother is separate, outside the boundary, part of the 'not me' rather than the 'me'.

John So if the baby is to draw his map, there has to be a right balance between, on the one hand, the frustration that gives him new information about the world, and, on the other hand, the emotional support that allows him to cope with this frustration?

Robin Yes, and he needs so much support because the frustration is very painful, for the following reason. As we saw, at the start of his life, before the experience of failure and frustration begins to define his edges, the baby has every reason

to suppose that he is 'everything', 'everywhere', 'omnipotent'.
Now, each time he discovers *another* bit that is 'not me' that's
. . . well . . . a bit of a blow to this massive God-like idea he has
of himself.

John   You mean just as no one *really* likes criticism because it
shrinks our ego a bit, the poor old baby has to learn not just
that he isn't God, but that he's just tiny and helpless. And a
deflation of that scale is pretty painful. Like Mussolini discovering he's a budgerigar.

Robin   Yes. So while there needs to be a steady, gradual increase
in the mother's *failure* of the child as time goes on, to give
him the chance to take over responsibility for himself gradually,
at this early stage the mother will have her work cut out to keep
frustrations to a minimum. The accidental frustrations will be
quite sufficient.

John   Right. But I'm not finding it easy to get the feel of all this.

Robin   Don't worry. That's natural. Everyone experiences the
same kind of difficulty in imagining what it must be like for the
baby, when they try to *feel* what it might be like rather than just
thinking about it in a detached, logical way. I always find it
extraordinarily difficult to think about this stage of development
no matter how many times I do so or how much I read. I think
it's because the baby's world *is* very confusing at this stage for
the reasons we're talking about, and if we try to put ourselves
back into that world, we get very confused too.

John   Yet this is exactly what you say the mother has to do – to
feel her way back into what the baby is going through so that
she can tune in to his needs and provide the right emotional
support to help him cope with the stress. So how does she do
that?

Robin A healthy mother who's had a good experience when she was a baby herself will tune in to the baby's feelings naturally, automatically. She won't have to 'think'. She will 'sense' whether she is meeting his needs or doing something he doesn't like.

John So he will get fed when he's hungry, but she'll stop if he isn't. She'll pick him up when he wants the stimulation or soothing, but won't bother him when he wants to sleep. So there'll be a minimum of frustration for the baby.

Robin Yes, but there's more to this than just getting the baby's *physical* needs right. There's the social contact, the *emotional* interplay. The 'tuned-in' mother really enjoys this. You know the way a mother and a baby gaze at each other and play a kind of game with their eyes, an 'eye-dance'. Baby gazes at Mother and makes a face. Mother will respond, will want to make a face back, and in fact will tend to imitate the expression, to mirror what the baby's doing. And the baby makes a new face, and so on . . .

John How important is this for the baby?

Robin In some ways, it looks as if it can be just as important as the physical needs. It's hard to convey how disturbed a baby becomes if the mother doesn't respond and join in that game. In fact, a psychologist once asked a group of mothers to *avoid* reacting to their babies in this way, as an experiment, for *just three minutes*, but the distress this produced in the babies was so great that the mothers couldn't bear to complete the experiment.

John So what would be the result if the mother, for some reason, couldn't join in the 'eye-dance' with her baby? If she *couldn't* establish this kind of emotional contact?

If Mother can't respond . . . . . .

Robin If this close emotional contact between mother and baby is *not* established in the early stages, in other words if they get *really* badly out of synch – and I'm talking here of a *very severe* mismatch of responses, which is extremely unlikely with an ordinary mother who is following her instincts – you can get what I'll call a 'tuned-out' baby. The problem may begin on either side – the baby or the mother. On the mother's side, remember that she gets her empathy working by allowing herself to reach back into her own babyhood and childhood and

to experience the feelings she had then. Well, suppose the mother had an unhappy babyhood herself . . .

John You mean reaching back will be painful.

Robin Exactly. If she was handled badly as a baby and toddler herself, any attempt to recall those feelings will hurt. So if she *stops* reaching back into her memories, she'll be able to avoid these distressing feelings.

John But since she's *not* now consulting her own baby-like feelings, she won't be able to be so empathetic with her child; she can't establish such a close rapport.

Robin And, of course, at some deep level, the child will sense this.

John He'll feel he's not in full communication with his mother, that something is being held back.

Robin Yes. And you remember the experiment where the mothers withheld communication for the first three minutes and the pain that caused? Well, you can imagine what it must be like if the mother *can't* respond *at all*, and doesn't even *know* she *should* be responding. The baby may find it so painful that he cuts off and gives up trying, and of course that will make things worse because the mother will feel rejected, and that will make it even more difficult for her to open up and be natural, and put things right.

John And I suppose the same process could start because

there's something wrong with the *baby*, which therefore doesn't do the right things to turn the mother on, even if her instinctive reactions *are* working and she's ready and waiting for the cue? I've read that normal babies are programmed to smile at the mother's face from very early on, before they can have any idea what they're smiling at, and that the baby's smiling engages the mother's feelings so she enjoys and loves the baby more.

Robin Correct. An abnormal baby may fail to switch on the mother, so her maternal instincts don't get the go-ahead. Then she has to do everything from her head, from books, whether she wants to or not.

John So the problem can start on either side?

Robin Yes. Some experts think it's *always* the baby, but all the evidence I've seen suggests that there's a range, from one extreme where the parents do seem to be very cut off from their feelings, to the other where it's very hard to understand how they could have ended up with such a tuned-out, abnormal child. And, of course, remember that however this starts it can become a vicious circle – if the baby doesn't thrive, the mother gets discouraged and depressed, which means the baby gets even less empathy, even less sensitive responses, and so on.

John If that vicious circle develops, the baby will feel less and less supported, so in a sense, he's been frustrated too soon?

Robin And much too severely. If the mother can't tune in, for *whatever* reason, the baby has to try to make a massive adjustment to her, instead of the other way round. He has to grow up instantly to adjust to Mother's grown-up attitudes, instead of at the very gradual pace he needs.

John But surely he can't do that.

Robin Of course not. All he can do is to *give up* and cut off – turn his back on the world and deny it exists – at least those parts of the world which cause him so much pain and distress. He'll behave as though a lot of the world isn't there.

John So what kind of a mental map of the world will he be constructing then?

Robin One with no other people marked on it. And the child behaves as though there's no one else around – as if his map says the world is a 'desert island'.

John You mean so far as other people are concerned, the child's keeping his map the way it is for a baby right at the start?

Robin Yes, he's occupying the whole space. He's the only one. It's hard to express, it's so crazy.

John It is craziness.

Robin One kind anyway. The most extreme examples of 'tuned-out' children are called 'autistic'. Kanner, a child psychiatrist who first described them, found that a high proportion of the parents were highly educated, super-sensible people who tended to live in their heads, in ideas and abstractions, and were less interested in feelings. People, that is, who would find it more difficult than others to bear the emotional confusion that arises when they try to share the baby's world. Nowadays it's widely believed that there's some kind of abnormality in the *child* which interferes with his ability to *respond* to the parents' care. Where the truth lies is still uncertain. But luckily the condition is extremely rare. Although, in fact, we once had a little epidemic of cases very similar to these, some children of recent immigrants. The children, both of whose parents had to work, had been left with baby-minders who fed them but gave them no attention.

John What do autistic children look like? How do they behave?

Robin The most striking thing is their complete failure to engage in the kind of social to-and-fro we're talking about. People will describe them as 'cut off', 'in a shell', 'living in a world of their own'. In their presence you're very aware of being shut out, even wiped out in their minds as if you don't exist.

John But they're *really* aware that you're there with them?

Robin Oh yes. They'll walk round you, or use you to get some-thing they want, but it's as if you're a bit of furniture. It shows

particularly in the way they avoid contact with another person's eyes. In fact you usually spot them immediately by the way their gaze repeatedly slides away whenever you think you're about to catch it. They give the feeling that they are intensely aware of your presence, yet wiping you off the map at the same time. It's very strange.

John As if they're 'cutting you dead'?

Robin That gives the feeling of it, but it's much more extreme.

John And they do this with their parents?

Robin Yes. They show none of the usual attachment behaviour. They don't want to be touched or cuddled, and they don't display clinging when their parents leave, or pleasure when they return. Which is terribly distressing for the parents, of course.

John Can they get support from other sources?

Robin They often show an intense attachment to particular objects – a stone, for instance, or a particular item of clothing. Or later, the same kind of intense involvement with information like train timetables, maps, bus routes. There's a need for sameness, routine, too, so they can't bear it if the furniture is changed around or certain things aren't done in the same order every time.

John Well, that all makes sense, doesn't it. They can't bear change because the automatic support system with the mother has broken down. So they have to keep the change in the world around them to a minimum to reduce the stress and get what little support they can by attaching themselves to inanimate objects. How am I doing, Doctor?

Robin It's certainly how it seems to me, and a lot of others, though I should tell you that a great number of specialists in the subject don't see it like that. They'd regard what you say as pretty meaningless.

John Never mind. Now you said real autism was very rare – how rare?

Robin Only around one in 2,000.

John So why are you banging on about it?

Robin Because these extreme cases illustrate so clearly what happens if a baby finds life so stressful and disturbing that he just has to tune out and live alone in his own world.

John And because the extreme cases help us to understand the more ordinary, much milder examples of the problem we're likely actually to meet?

Robin That's true. I'd see these autistic cases as the extreme end of a spectrum ranging right up to almost normal people.

John Almost?

Robin Yes, people we'd regard as normal but who are very detached, distant, withdrawn, who are extremely awkward in company, who give their main attention to hobbies, who basically 'tune other people out and live in their own world'.

John That sounds like a cue for a song. But if the mother and child are in close communication, as they are in 1,999 cases out of 2,000, the baby will have no need to cut himself off.

Robin No. The ordinary mother will be able to tune in with her own babyhood feelings and just do what comes naturally. Because she's on the baby's wavelength she can just let the baby *affect* her. She'll know his feelings and needs instinctively. And she'll find that wonderfully enjoyable.

The boundaries get clearer . . . . . .

John So if Mother's 'tuning in', the baby's getting the deep emotional contact he needs. And this is vital to help him cope with his 'shock, horror' discovery that he's not omnipotent; and to support him as he progressively discovers that there's more and more out there that he can't control.

Robin Yes, if he gets the responses he needs from the mother, he can slowly recognise his edges, his boundary, and then he can go on later, as his awareness of the world expands, to get other boundaries right too.

John But it occurs to me that when the mother is playing with the child, making that kind of deep emotional contact you were talking about, she's doing *more* than just mirroring the baby, she's always adding something new. News of another tiny difference.

Robin That's right, I think that in that lovely spontaneous activity we call 'play', we're improvising, inventing, always adding something new. So when an ordinary mother plays with her baby, makes faces back, talks, mirrors his behaviour, what she does will be very supportive and affirming, because it *follows* what the baby does. Nothing unexpected, nothing new is happening, and the baby is gradually learning about himself as if he's looking in a mirror. But a healthy mother will also *play* with the baby. She'll change things slightly, her responses won't *just* be copies of what the baby is doing. They will add little bits of herself as a different, separate person. The baby will be getting information that there are other people out there, because she's not following his expectations completely, he's not in control, but he will be getting it in a context of great support and enjoyment, and at a rate he can manage.

John The baby's getting the stability, the sameness, the support, but also little bits of strangeness, differentness, separateness.

Robin Yes. So if the 'tuning in' has taken place and the mother's sensitive response has earned the baby's full trust, then very, very slowly the baby and mother will start drawing apart on the baby's mental map, from almost overlapping completely

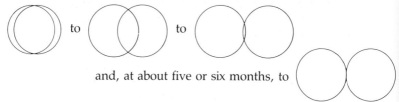

and, at about five or six months, to

the first realisation that mother is *a separate, different person*!

John And this process occurs more or less naturally if the support's there?

Robin Provided the baby's getting the information that Mother's different.

John Well how could it *not* be getting *that*?

Robin Well . . . if she can't separate from the baby.

John I don't understand.

Or stay fuzzy . . . . . .

Robin In order to tune in to the baby, the mother's got to let go of her adult way of thinking, and allow herself to drift back into her own babyhood memories and ways of feeling. Now some mothers can tune in all right, but *can't* get back out again.

John They can't reclaim their adult boundaries when they need to? But why can't they?

Robin Because *their* boundaries are fuzzy. Because *their* mothers' boundaries were fuzzy.

John Because their grandmothers' boundaries were fuzzy?

Robin And so on. As usual, it's not anybody's 'fault', it's the old cycle.

John So if the mother's boundaries are fuzzy, she can't separate from the baby when she needs to . . .

Robin So the baby will be able to control her too much and for too long. Which means the baby isn't getting the information that he needs, the news that Mother's different. So he can't become clear about his edges, and will have difficulty. distinguishing himself from his mother. They'll stay fused, mixed up to some extent.

John The baby's boundaries stay fuzzy, like the mother's. So what's the effect of this on the baby, or rather on the person the baby becomes when he grows up? What problems do fuzzy boundaries bring?

Robin Well, according to the degree to which the boundaries are unclear, you get a whole range of problems. At one extreme, the 'fuzziest' end of the range, many psychiatrists believe that this lack of clear boundaries is a basic factor in at least some of the severe mental disorders called schizophrenia, though there's now no doubt that in most cases inherited factors play a very large part too. At the other end of the range, you've got families who get through life all right, but who remain extremely involved with each other all their lives.

John They don't achieve normal adult independence.

Robin No, they can't get apart emotionally – or can only achieve separation by living far apart – sometimes, indeed, even with every different member of the family in a different country!

John And in the middle of the range?

Robin There are a lot of cases called 'borderline' where there may be no actual breakdown or need for admission to hospital, but where the person appears very odd and eccentric to others.

John How do the *most* severe cases seem to other people?

Robin They'll seem 'insane'. You see, because of these fuzzy boundaries, the person can be very confused about what's him and what's other people, what's inside himself and what's outside himself. So he may suffer from hallucinations – the inability to distinguish dreams or daydreams from the real world of the senses. He may feel that he's affecting others through his thoughts and feelings or that others are influencing him by methods that are quite impossible. So his behaviour seems *very* strange to ordinary folk – meaningless, in fact, unless his confusion and lack of boundaries is recognised.

John Meaningless because his behaviour has no relation to ordinary folks' maps of the world.

Robin More than just meaningless. A lot of it is contradictory too because people like this are caught in a lot of 'double-binds'.

John Now wait a moment. You get a double-bind when a child is getting a 'double message' from the parents, right? When the parents are giving the child two contradictory ideas about how to behave.

Robin Broadly, except of course that it's not deliberate and it's not even as if one part of the family is *doing anything* to another part, even accidentally. The system is such that they're all in it together, all reacting the way they are because of the way everyone's reacting to them. In fact, everyone in a family like this is having a pretty difficult time and suffering a great deal.

John There are two things I don't see. One, is the 'suffering' more than just confusion arising from shaky boundaries? Two, why are people sending – and receiving – contradictory messages?

Robin OK. Well, remember that Mother has very hazy boundaries. And one of the first principles we established was that she'll probably have married someone with pretty equally fuzzy boundaries too.

John Ah. You mean both parents are, *in a way*, stuck at the same level as the baby *himself*?

Robin Exactly. Of course they may have built up a shaky façade to conceal it, which enables them to cope after a fashion and which may deceive others, but underneath this the foundations are insecurely built and they are functioning emotionally, in many ways, at this baby-level. And remember what the baby-level is. The baby *is* everything *as far as he knows* – 'all powerful'. And you remember that every step he takes towards establishing his own limits and boundaries will be painful because he'll have to lose this original God-like feeling of omnipotence.

John So to some extent the *parents* haven't got over these baby-like feelings of omnipotence.

Robin That's right! Their boundaries are fuzzy because they weren't able to differentiate themselves from their mothers, their families, so they've still got these feelings! So they all inevitably end up in a competition with each other to avoid giving up these omnipotent feelings. Automatically, unintentionally.

John So how does a family like this behave?

Robin Imagine a box and a number of balloons in that box which can be blown up somehow from outside. The balloons represent the family members or, rather, their unrealistic maps of themselves, and the box is the world. Well, if each balloon – family member – believes it's omnipotent, it's like every balloon trying to fill the whole box. And it can't do that without squeezing all the other balloons out of existence. So all the balloons – all the family members – are tending to do just that – to wipe the others out. So there's an endless struggle, punctuated sometimes by periods of very uneasy truce.

John So that's why it's so painful. But why is the struggle endless? Why doesn't somebody *win*?

Robin They're all stuck at this stage so they're all aware that they *can't* stand on their own. Each one *needs* the others desperately. So they're in this impossible dilemma of wanting love from the others, yet finding themselves constantly in danger of getting into a terrible struggle with them.

John If one of them got too big, he'd realise he would be in danger of wiping out the ones he's dependent on.

Robin And if he got too small, he'd lose that vital feeling of omnipotence. So wherever they are, they're uncomfortable . It's a terribly unhappy and painful situation for them all. Actually you can catch the tiniest echo of this conflict in everyday life when people are *relating* at a baby-level. Lovers, for example, indulging in baby talk, or adults talking to very small children. 'I could eat you up,' we say. That's expressing love and need, but in a way it's also big-balloonery, filling up their space and wiping them out. Normal people say this playfully, in fun, and it adds a little excitement, a tiny thrill of delicious fear to the endearment. But the really disturbed families feel uncomfortably close to *being* like this, even doing it. They feel as if the emotional hunger of the others could swallow them up, devour them, if they don't watch out.

John What can a therapist do to help 'fuzzy-boundary' families?

Robin At the milder, 'less fuzzy' end of the range, a lot. You can help them all to develop clearer boundaries by seeing them together and behaving in a very clear and definite way in your dealings with them. The clarity gets passed on through your example. But you have to be not only firm, but also very supportive at the same time.

John Because as their boundaries clarify, they have to cope with their baby-like 'egos' being shrunk.

Robin You have to support them through that. But it's quite astonishing what an effect it can have if the therapist establishes very clear boundaries for himself in this way – saying what he will and won't do, and avoiding being manipulated into changing those decisions, while being very friendly and encouraging through it all.

John And how about the families at the more severe end of the range?

Robin Here it's very difficult to bring about any *basic* change. What you generally have to do is just support the family in times of stress because these families do manage to cope a lot of the time without anyone breaking down, and can still carry on *even* under stress provided they're given some support. The most vulnerable member, that's the one with the fuzziest boundaries who ends up breaking down and becoming the 'patient', may be helped by certain medicines which damp down the overload of impressions getting through the weak boundaries. And if that doesn't work, getting that person to a protected situation away from the family pressure – like a hospital or special community – may be needed for a while till they've settled down and the boundaries have got a bit firmer again.

John But if they go back to the family, they may crack up again?

Robin If the family stresses increase again, and support isn't available, they may. But recently, it's been found that even reducing the amount of time some of these vulnerable indi-viduals spend in contact with other family members – by arranging for them to spend periods apart during the day – greatly reduces the number of breakdowns. And meetings with the families to encourage them to give each other a bit more emotional 'space' – for example, less intense involvement, less unconstructive criticism – has had very encouraging results too.

John So let me try to recapitulate . . . provided there's enough emotional support, the child can allow himself to take in inform-ation about the world . . . so he can start drawing his boundaries. But if the *mother's* boundaries are very shaky – she's not a separate enough person – then the baby won't be able to do this and may *stay* at this rather primitive, undifferentiated, fuzzy-boundary stage as it gets older.

Robin *Unless* some other person later provides the experience of clear boundaries he missed, in a way that's supportive and not too stressful.

John But if the person stays at this baby-like level, in the *worst* cases he or she may even be diagnosed as a schizophrenic later on.

Robin Yes. Due either to an inherited vulnerability, or family 'fuzziness', or both. Remember this is a very broad outline, and my personal bird's-eye view of a subject where knowledge is still extremely confused and full of conflicting opinions. Still, there's more agreement than most people realise about some basic principles, and I'm trying to put them together in a way that makes sense of my own personal and professional experience and which seems to work in practice.

John Now, if Mum's boundaries *are* OK, the baby will presumably be able to go on to define himself more and more, getting a better map and going on to find his boundaries with father, his brothers and sisters, and then in the wider world outside the family.

Robin That's the way I see it. But I should say . . . there *is* one more hurdle to negotiate before the boundaries get sorted out.

John How naive to imagine it might be otherwise. So what's this hurdle called?

Robin The 'paranoid' way of dealing with stress.

We're all paranoid . . . . . .

John Have we finished with 'fuzzy boundaries', then? Is this a new phase?

Robin Not really. This 'paranoid' way of functioning isn't possible until there *are* some boundaries, but it's only possible *because* they're still a bit fuzzy. You see, there's a certain advantage for the baby in having fuzzy boundaries. He can make use of that fuzziness, that uncertainty about where his edges are, to protect himself when stress and pain get too great for him to cope. It's like a safety-valve, an overflow pipe. The baby can offload painful feelings when they're too upsetting. This is important because it explains some of the differences between children and adults, as well as behaviour that's called technically 'paranoid'.

John 'Paranoid' in the sense of not wanting to go to rugby matches because the forwards keep huddling together to talk about you?

Robin It's the same principle, yes. In the extreme case, it's clinical paranoia, what people often call a 'persecution complex'. And in everyday life it's at the root of a whole lot of problems where *blaming others* is a big contributing factor.

John Why is this important to the baby at this stage?

Robin It's thought that, at this early stage of life when even the 'wiring' of the brain is far from complete, the emotions a baby feels are very extreme because they are not yet connected together by memory, they're not integrated, they're not balancing each other up.

John You can certainly see they're very extreme. You can't help hearing it either. There are few sounds that set the teeth on edge like a baby screaming.

Robin Yes. Life is pure bliss after the feed, and pure rage and anguish when the next one is late. Now, it seems that when that rage and pain is too great to bear, the baby at this stage has the option of moving the boundary in such a way that those feelings are experienced as though they are *outside* rather than *inside*. They've become 'not me' instead of 'me'.

John Hang on. That came out a bit glib. You're saying that if I'm a baby, I can *move* my boundaries – on my mental map – so that those nasty feelings become '*not* me' instead of staying as part of 'me'?

Robin Exactly. Think of the boundary as like those moveable plastic cones they use to mark the edges of the open lanes during motorway repairs, rather than like the fixed crash-barrier. So what's 'motorway' and what's 'not motorway' can be altered – or, in the case of baby, the line between what's experienced as 'me' and 'not me'.

John So the baby can, in a way, 'pretend' that a part of himself – some of his own feelings – aren't really in him at all.

Robin That's right. If he can't bear them, he can disown them.

John And then he feels better?

Robin Yes and no. I have to explain what happens *next*. The baby had these nasty feelings, and now he's pretending that they're not inside him. But, of course, they *haven't* just *dis-appeared*. He senses that they're still around. But if they're not *inside* him . . .

John They must be coming from *outside* him?

Robin That's it.

John Is this what's called 'projection'?

Robin Yes, that's the technical term. I'll recap. It happens when the baby has nasty frightening feelings, which he pretends are not inside him. He 'pretends' this by putting a dent in his boundary to leave the painful feelings outside himself

The painful feelings don't go away, of course, so it now seems to the baby as if they're coming from outside.

John He's 'projected' them on to the outside world?

Robin That's right. So the world itself will now seem more angry and cruel than it really is. So when you ask if the baby feels better . . . yes, he does because he doesn't feel so bad *himself*, but no, because the world *around* has become a more dangerous place. And, of course, at this stage the world is still more or less Mother. So instead of baby feeling like tearing Mother to pieces and gobbling her up when he's hungry and furious, he'll 'project' these feelings on to the mother herself. Here's a slow-motion replay . . .

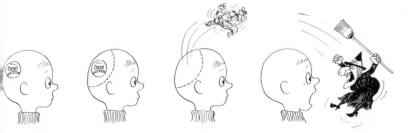

Robin So Mother herself now seems to the baby like a terrifying witch who might gobble *him* up.

John He's no longer in a terrible rage, he's simply scared to death.

Robin Out of the frying pan into the fire, really.

John I suppose this explains why children's fairy stories are so astonishingly nasty and populated with hordes of awful women, wicked stepmothers, witches, ugly sisters, and so on. There don't seem to be any *normal* mothers about. Fathers are vague, ineffectual creatures, who hang around at the back. And the only good women are the fairy godmothers, who are absolutely perfect and who always arrive, like the Fifth Cavalry, at exactly the right moment to make everything all right – with the next 'feed' presumably.

Robin Don't forget there's plenty of scope for projecting bad feelings about Dad into ogres and giants, and there are kings, princes, magicians who put things right too.

And then a horrible ogre came along — you know the type: weak chin, thinning hair...

John So these stories have been so fascinating to small children for so long just because they correspond to all the fantasies and projections they've just been experiencing.

Robin Yes, because everything is polarised into extremes of love and hate, just like what the baby seems to experience and young children are still very close to. Getting the boundary in the right place between 'me' and 'not me', and being able to balance out some of the hate, when it comes, by remembering past feelings of love, are tasks that continue into early childhood and indeed are never completely finished. Throughout our lives, though to a lessening extent, extreme feelings will lead us to use this method as a safety-valve.

John Do fairy stories help children to cope with this?

Robin Yes. Such tales actually *encourage* them to project any unmanageable feelings into the witches and ogres, so if it's the parents or other loving grown-ups who are reading the stories to them, the children are getting reassurance that the grown-ups can cope with such feelings.

John If they see their parents aren't frightened of these feelings, they'll feel they don't have to be so scared of them either?

Robin Right. And the safer the feelings feel, the less they'll need to be projected. So the children can begin to 'own' them, to contain them. Which means that the emotions are being brought together, so they'll balance each other up more and therefore become less extreme. Then they'll produce less fear and it becomes less and less necessary to deny painful feelings and redraw the boundary to put them outside. The tendency towards 'paranoia' diminishes.

John This is interesting. So the people who believe children should be protected against the violence in these traditional fairy stories could be giving children the wrong message – that there *is* something in the stories that scares the *parents*.

Robin Yes. When I meet a family where the parents want to shield children from such tales, I expect to find a very frightened child. The stories *help* a child cope with his own baby-like vio-lence, *provided* the parents supply the reassurance and love, and are not frightened of the child's violent, hateful feelings themselves.

John So to sum up, at this stage in a baby's development, the baby's not able to connect and balance up his emotions, so some feelings are very frightening. The baby projects these, which makes him feel better. But the world around him becomes more frightening instead.

Robin That's it. And of course, if the baby gets enough support and nurture during this phase, that'll ease the pain and rage and frustration he feels. Then he doesn't have to go on pretending those emotions are outside himself, and they become *manageable* enough for him to own them again. So he can start getting his boundaries right.

John And carry on happily mapping the world. OK. Now what happens if he *doesn't* get enough support and nurture?

Robin Then to that extent he will tend to stay stuck at this phase.

John You mean he will *go on* projecting 'bad' feelings. Incidentally . . . are these 'bad' emotions usually anger and violence?

Robin With a baby, they probably are the most difficult ones.

But as a person who's stuck at this stage gets older, it can be any feeling at all that is too painful or alarming for him to own – sexual feelings, envy, jealousy, sadness . . .

John But whatever it may be, it gets projected on to the world outside, which therefore becomes a very hostile, threatening sort of place. Now what's the link between this and someone who's 'paranoid' – who has a 'persecution complex'?

Robin Well a person like that – who's really clinically paranoid – is an extreme case of someone who's not grown out of this stage. But perhaps I ought to say here that I reckon we're *all* a bit paranoid from time to time.

John . . . Well, if I disagree with that, it'd look as though I was taking it personally and that'd prove I *was* paranoid. So . . . I'll agree.

Robin All I'm saying is that almost everyone shows a bit of paranoia from time to time. In other words, very, very few people ever grow *completely* out of this stage. For example, haven't you ever tried blaming someone else for something, when it's partly your fault?

John But that's thoroughly healthy. And normal.

Robin *And* paranoid.

John All right, what do you mean by 'paranoid'?

Robin Well, whenever you're in a situation where there's some disagreement or confrontation, no matter how mild, and you adopt the position that you are blame*less* – 'good' – and try to pretend that the other person is *totally* to blame – 'bad' – well that's paranoid behaviour. And it's significant that you use the word 'healthy' because behaving in a paranoid way does make you feel 'better'.

John Better in a *moral* sense?

Robin Better in every sense. If you feel you're in the right, then everything's simple. The other person's to blame and, yes, you do feel morally better as well as not having to deal with uncomfortable feelings, like guilt. That's why the baby did it, remember? To feel better.

John But to anyone watching you, you'd seem *worse*, because you can't see anyone else's point of view, admit your mistakes, or compromise.

Robin Right.

John For example, I've noticed that when I'm driving I can get very irritated with other drivers who fail to indicate in time where they're turning; but if *I* fail to indicate and someone hoots, I'm inclined to catch myself feeling that I was perfectly justified not to signal because it was bloody obvious, even to the worst cretin, what I was going to do. That's paranoid?

Robin Yes. It doesn't mean you're a clinical paranoid psychotic, of course, because you don't take it very seriously and five minutes later you stop feeling like that and accept the reality without any trouble. But it *is* paranoid *behaviour*.

John And if I crack my shin against a coffee table and feel a flash of anger . . . that's a way of avoiding admitting I've made a mistake, by blaming the table?

Robin That's another example. If you want more, just think of Basil Fawlty, blaming everyone else, indeed finding it hard to credit how stupid and inconsiderate they *all* are, while preserving an image of himself as morally perfect.

John And I suppose if you want to see an exhibition of organized paranoia you go to a football match. If their player kicks ours, it was deliberate, but if our player kicks theirs, he was going for the ball. Our team is hard but fair, theirs is villainous, and the referee's bent.

Robin It's all part of the fun, isn't it?

John But why do we do it? It's something to do with the simplicity isn't it? Like putting the 'baddies' into black hats in Westerns to tell us we don't have to worry when they get shot.

Robin Yes, splitting everything up into neat compartments of 'good' and 'bad' does several things for us, all of which make us feel better. First, it helps us to feel part of a 'good' group – that's comforting. Second, we can relax our usual standards of 'correct' behaviour for a bit – avoid those difficult 'grey' areas of moral decision we normally have to wrestle with. And third, we can let off steam, that is, get rid of our own 'bad' feelings on to the 'baddies'.

John You mean get rid of some of the frustrations that have been building up over the week while we behaved 'correctly'? And dump them on the 'baddies', who *deserve* them – so we don't have to feel 'bad' about doing that.

Robin That's it. I think that's why most people enjoy some kind of competitive game. In fact, one of the most striking differences that was noticed in one study of mental health was that the really healthy people enjoyed competitive sports. The less healthy, badly adjusted ones, didn't. But, of course, healthy people *know* it's *play* and they know what they're doing. They can deliberately work themselves up into a very competitive frame of mind and then switch it off and return to normal when the game's over. It's just a bit of fun. They've had a good time. They don't take it too seriously.

John But what about the ones who do? The soccer hooligans, the people who write hate-mail to snooker players?

Robin Well, they're somewhere between the healthy normal people and the clinically paranoid ones. They really *need* to keep the bad feelings in other people, the same way that paranoid people and families have to believe the outside world is bad and persecuting in order to keep themselves on an even keel.

John They need to do this because if they realised the 'badness' was really their own, they might crack up?

Robin Yes. The more stuck people are at this kind of level, the more they'll need to make the outside world bad to keep themselves feeling good. The more they need to do that, the less they'll be in touch with reality and the nearer they'll be to 'clinical' paranoia, or 'persecution mania'.

John So if they're really stuck at this level, it's because as babies or children they didn't grow out of it as 'normal' people do. That must be because their parents didn't provide enough love and nurture – presumably because *they* found 'bad' feelings very frightening themselves. In other words, the parents were stuck at this level too.

Robin I think that's right. Children can't really develop much beyond their parents' level, without a lot of input from outside the family, anyway.

John So someone who's close to clinical paranoia will tend to come from a pretty paranoid family. How does a family like that work?

Robin Well, as you'd guess, a family where everyone is stuck at this baby stage of adjustable boundaries will be trying all the time to get rid of their 'nasty feelings'.

John By projecting them on to each other.

Robin Yes. But nobody wants them, so the family ends up playing 'pass the parcel' with all the bad feelings.

John Each getting them in turn, and having to load them on to someone else.

Robin Instead of realising that they're their own and trying to deal with them. And as no one can handle them, the child as he grows up soon gets the message that they're not 'safe', so he joins in the game too.

John And does the 'parcel' just go on being passed around indefinitely?

Robin It can happen like that. But if the painful feelings among the family members increase past a certain point – as they might do if there'd been an upsetting experience like a death or some other bad loss – they may find it impossible to keep handing them all round and may pick on one family member and blame him or her for all the discomfort. We call this 'scapegoating'.

John The scapegoat has to carry all the family's bad feelings?

Robin Yes. One way of looking at it is that they redraw the *family* boundary so that the scapegoat is now outside it. Everyone else in the family is now 'good', while the scapegoat contains all the badness, and 'causes all the trouble' that the family suffers. And of course, since the scapegoat is now such a 'bad' person, it gives everyone else the chance to express all their bad feelings – with the excuse that it's all the scapegoat's fault that they're having to behave so badly towards him or her.

John Isn't the scapegoat going to crack up under this sort of pressure?

Robin Not necessarily. But if the stress in the family is high, and more and more painful feelings get loaded on to the scapegoat, he or she may well finish up in hospital.

John But if that happens . . . it's hard to treat the scapegoat unless the whole family can be persuaded to take back the bad feelings that he's carrying.

Robin That's right! That's the point! But, unfortunately, many professionals who don't know what's happening – and even *today* many don't – accept the family's demand that the scapegoat be excluded from the family and 'cured'. In other words, they *agree* with the family that the scapegoat is a 'patient' and should be removed to a mental hospital.

John In other words, they treat the scapegoat as if he was really to blame. They take the family's side, in fact. So the scapegoat's gone – what happens to the family next?

Robin Well, they may feel slightly better for a bit. And then, of course, the old patterns reassert themselves – they all start feeling the bad feelings again – and worst of all, the scapegoat isn't around to be blamed!

John So what happens then?

Robin At this point, they may try to get the scapegoat back.

John So that they can go on shoving their bad feelings on to him?

Robin Yes.

John This is mind-boggling . . . *or* I suppose they might try and shove them into *another* family member.

Robin After a period of time that often happens. I've seen it frequently in families where a 'problem child' was dealt with by sending him off to boarding school, when that child was really acting as a sponge soaking up the problems of the whole family.

Someone else becomes the family sponge.

John Now if you can only treat such a family successfully by getting them to understand what they're doing to the scapegoat, and to take the bad feelings back from him, presumably you need the whole family in therapy.

Robin And that's often a real difficulty. Getting them all together. The parents will often come but they'll resist bringing the other children – they usually just want to bring the scapegoat.

John Why?

Robin Well, as we've seen, the whole point of this paranoid way of operating is to keep the 'bad' feelings away from the 'good' feelings. So that the one can't spoil the other. So they want to keep the 'good', happy child, or children, away from the one they now see as full of badness . . .

John So that the 'rotten apple' doesn't affect the others.

Robin That's how they see it. Deep down, I think they sense that it's going somehow to blow the story. But they would be shocked if you suggested that, and I'm sure they aren't conscious of it. What's more, it involves everyone. You see, the scapegoat is always to some extent a volunteer.

John . . . You're joking!

Robin No, it's something most family therapists would agree about. Certainly the scapegoat *is* pushed into the part by the others; but he or she always knows that they're helping the family in some way by 'taking the rap'. When you're very small, it usually feels preferable to have parents who at least stay together to look after you and who are not too miserable and depressed and desperate to do that . . . *rather than* parents who are going to tear each other to pieces and perhaps commit suicide or abandon you.

John But the child can't really be aware of all that.

Robin Well let's just say he begins to notice things are more stable when he accepts that he's the 'baddie'.

John So the child 'accepts' the role to *help* the family . . . by becoming the family dustbin. Which, I suppose, in a *perverse* way, does mean at least that he gets a lot of attention.

Robin That's right. And of course the child also senses he has a very important role for the family.

John This is extraordinary. You mean the scapegoat feels 'needed'?

Robin That's right. The family does need him so long as he accepts the dustbin role, so in a crazy way that gives him security.

John So if you are going to treat a family like this, you need to get them all together, and to avoid taking the family's side.

Robin *Or* the scapegoat's. You mustn't take anyone's side because then you'd be joining in the 'blaming', joining in the paranoid behaviour. That's why I believe the ideas of R. D. Laing and Cooper have done a lot of harm. It's natural, from an emotional point of view, to side with the scapegoat, but the therapist's got to avoid it because it doesn't work. Supporting only the scapegoat makes the rest of the family less secure, more paranoid, even less able to 'own' their bad feelings, and therefore more likely to dump them even harder on the scapegoat when they all get home. You've got to treat the family as a system, without blaming *anyone*. Indeed, for reasons which will now be obvious, you need to make them *all* feel supported, to reduce their use of blaming as a safety-valve.

John OK. So to sum up, before about six months, the baby is going through a paranoid phase, which means that he gets rid of 'bad' feelings by projecting them into the outside world. Which doesn't work very well because it only makes the world around him seem nastier than it is. However, the baby will correct his boundaries and get a proper grasp on reality provided he gets the support he needs – because this allows the feelings to become less nasty and therefore more bearable and 'ownable'. So the baby will pass out of the paranoid phase – *unless* his family is very stuck there. In which case they may all play 'pass the parcel' with *all* their individual bad feelings until sometimes these get dumped on one family member – scapegoat – who accepts them to help everyone else.

However, very few of us ever get totally free of these paranoid tendencies so that, even in the most normal families, an individual who's under particular stress may become mildly paranoid for a time, saying things like 'it's not my fault at all, you're entirely to blame'. The crucial difference is that this person will soon get his boundaries right again and realise it was only a temporary aberration, while the 'clinical' paranoid may never emerge from his paranoid world or be able to see the real world correctly at all.

Recognising Mummy . . . . . .

John So, given the right love and nurture, the baby's coming out of this paranoid phase at about what age? Six months?

Robin Somewhere round about there. It's a gradual process, of course, there's no sudden change.

John What's the next lesson he has to learn?

Robin Well, what's characteristic of the paranoid phase is that the baby's perceptions and emotions are not connected up together, and so not unified, balanced.

John The feelings are kept separate.

Robin Not just the feelings. For example, before about five months the mother is probably still unconnected breasts, voice, eyes, arms, face, and so on.

John But the baby recognises her before then.

Robin Oh yes. I'm trying to give you an outline of a lot of different kinds of information, but most people would agree that definite social responses are developing between mother and baby after one month or so, the baby's beginning to recognise the mother's voice, for example; by about three months, the baby's reaction to the mother is stronger than to other people; and at about five months the mother's clearly recognised.

John And after that?

Robin During the second six months of life, the baby begins to develop the ability to stick the various bits – face, breasts, hands – together, to make a person!

John And if he's beginning to perceive his mother as a whole, presumably he's started to do the same with *himself*?

Robin Yes, he's getting a greater sense of his own continuity. So he's not quite so much at the mercy of his extreme emotions. It's still awful to be hungry and left to cry, but less terrifying if the baby can remember, however faintly at first, how happy he was last time he was fed, and can feel that it's likely to happen again soon.

John The feelings are beginning to connect up and balance each other out, which brings the possibility of more self-control.

Robin That's right. Now let's go back to the baby's awareness of the mother. Just as he's putting the physical bits together, he's beginning to realise that the mother who comes and feeds him and gives him so much happiness . . . is the *same person* as the one who sometimes isn't there, or who deliberately leaves him to cry, causing him a lot of pain.

John You mean that before this he's had *two* separate mothers in his mind? A good, fairy-godmother one, and a wicked witch-like one?

Robin That's how it seems. Now, after six months these two totally opposite figures are beginning to get fused into one in the baby's mind.

John And his totally opposite, extreme *feelings* about them must be getting put together too. Which must be pretty confusing to say the least.

Robin And painful. It's very difficult to discover that you hate someone you love.

John Especially at this time when you're so completely *reliant* on her.

Robin But there's a very positive side to all this too. It's the beginning of a new kind of love – the beginning of *concern*, the kind of loving worry you have about someone that you're close to, that they're *all right*.

John As opposed to 'cupboard love', you mean – where you're only interested in them because of what you can get from them.

Robin Yes. The baby's taking a *first step* towards being able to feel a more grown-up, *equal* kind of love where people look after each other because they care about the other person. People who never get to this stage treat others like breasts or bottles to be sucked dry. Drug addicts and severe alcoholics operate rather like this. They're stuck at the same level as the pre-six months baby, or schizophrenics who can only treat others as objects; that is, disconnected things, voices, lips, bodies, minds, breasts, genitals. Obviously you can't feel the same kind of concern for a mother's breast as you can for a real, live, whole mother.

John So the baby's now getting a better map of the world, and seeing both his mother and himself as wholes. This brings the possibility of real concern for another human being. The price of this is that the baby has to put together in himself a lot of conflicting emotions that he kept apart in the paranoid phase. Which must make him anxious, particularly when he discovers he feels hate for the very same thing he loves and is completely dependent upon – his mother.

Robin And he's made even more anxious by another aspect of what's happening. You see, as the baby starts perceiving his mother and himself as 'wholes', he starts realising his separation from Mum. Up to now they've been overlapping.

John You mean, as he draws a line around himself and Mum on his mental map, the penny starts to drop that there's a line *between* them.

Robin Yes. Drawing a line defines both what's inside *and* outside. It's even expressed in our language – as you become 'all one' you become 'alone'. So his insecurity increases as the baby becomes more aware of his separateness – while the boundaries were overlapping, he must have felt less insecure. Now that he's realising that his mother is separate, the baby must sense the *possibility of losing her* – losing his lifeline. And that's really what this next phase is all about, going from

to

John Realising you're separate from your life-support system – and that you can therefore lose it – must be pretty hair-raising. How long does this separating process take?

Robin It goes on throughout childhood, and in a sense throughout our lives, particularly at the point when we face up to death. But so far as the young child is concerned, the toughest part of the separation process will go on from this age of six months up to about the age of three. This is when the child is most anxious about the possibility of losing his mother and most needs reassurance that she isn't going to disappear.

John Does the anxiety arising from the baby realising he's separate come on suddenly or gradually?

Robin Some time shortly after the six months' mark the penny begins to drop quite rapidly that the mother is separate. And there's a high point of anxiety at that time which then gradually decreases. So during this six months-to-three years period the child is extremely vulnerable to any prolonged separation from his mother. And because of this, and because he now recognises his mother, 'attachment behaviour' is very strong.

John What happens if there is a long separation during this period?

Robin Some British experts, John Bowlby and James and Joyce Robertson, studied children who had been separated from their families, and they described three stages that the child would go through as the separation got longer. The first stage they called 'protest' – distress, angry crying, searching, trying to find the mother and get her back. The child who is reunited at this stage will, interestingly enough, usually be quite difficult for a time. It's as though he is punishing the mother for going away. When he's got these feelings off his chest, he returns to normality. He's got his confidence back, though he can still remain sensitive to any further separation for quite a long time.

John That punishing the mother is interesting, isn't it? I've noticed it the other way round. When a child's gone missing and the mother finds him, she often rewards his return with a terrible walloping, to punish him for the fears that he has caused her.

Robin That's right. It's easy to forget that attachment behaviour goes both ways, and that the separation anxiety works in both directions too.

John So what did Bowlby and the Robertsons find if the separation continued for *longer*?

Robin Well, then the child may go on to the stage known as 'despair'. He's very quiet, withdrawn, miserable and apathetic. He stops playing – seems to lose interest in everything. Now before this was all properly understood, hospital staffs used to think the child had stopped making a fuss and was settling down. But in fact the child now fears that the mother is never coming back. And when he gets home he'll take much longer to get over the experience. He'll cling to his mother more. He will seem to have lost confidence and spirit, and may be depressed for some time. Before he starts to get better, he'll usually then have to go through the protest phase on the way, and go through a period of being very difficult. It may seem strange, but this is a *good* sign.

John It's as though he's got to get his confidence back a bit before he can start to have the courage to express his anger.

Robin Now, the third stage – 'detachment' – is the most serious. After the stage of 'despair', if the mother still remains absent, the child *seems* to recover. He perks up, appears to have got over his unhappiness, and begins to play again and to respond to others. In the old days again, the medical staff in the hospital used to think he was back to normal. Now we know that, in fact, he only seems to have recovered, and at the cost of killing his love for his mother.

John He needs to kill his love off to be able to face the loss. Losing Mum isn't so bad if you don't love her.

Robin That's right. If the child and the mother are now reunited after the 'detachment' phase, it can be very distressing for the whole family. The child can seem quite changed and now appears superficial, emotionally distant. This is because the love for the mother is dead, or rather, in the deep freeze, as it were. This is the most difficult stage to undo.

John But supposing that a good, reliable mother-substitute has been provided?

Robin The child may still go into the first or second stages, protest and despair, temporarily but this worst third stage will usually be avoided.

John It sounds very bad indeed.

Robin It was a great problem. Luckily, now that we understand the process, hospitals are making it easier for parents to visit more or live in the hospital with younger children so that the two later stages are reached much less often.

John Why isn't the child vulnerable before six months?

Robin Well, remember the child isn't fully aware of his mother as a whole person until he's reached about five or six months. This seems very startling to some mothers but the fact is that a substitute mother can be brought in during this period without so much harm, because the child isn't yet completely aware of the difference.

John That explains something I've never understood before, why all the wet-nursing that went on in England over the centuries didn't result in terrible deprivation for the child. Now, at the end of this period, you say the child is not so badly affected by a long separation. Why's that?

Robin After the age of two and a half or three, the child is more able to keep the memory of his mother alive, indeed to carry his whole family around in his mind. Even if they can't be there with the child, he can understand they are still alive and that he will be reunited with them.

John OK. Now let's go back to what you were saying earlier. I asked what happened if the mother's emotional support wasn't there for the child and you explained about Bowlby's and the Robertsons' work. But you also said something else. You implied, at any rate, that the mother might be there, *but* nevertheless she might not be able to give the baby the right kind of . . . what?

Robin Call it what you like – nurture, support, parental love . . .

John Seriously, all mothers want to love their babies, don't they?

Robin I'm sure that's right.

John So why is it that . . . how shall I put this . . . one mother's love isn't as . . . as efficient as another's?

Robin It's very interesting that you hesitated then. It's because we're getting into a very ticklish area, a very emotive one. On the one hand, people seem to react quite spontaneously when they sense a mother is not treating a child well. One of the worst insults in the human vocabulary is to call a woman a bad mother. On the other hand, few people except the mother understand the tremendous demands that the child is placing on her and she's often having to cope without enough support. Nevertheless there *are* some women who are not able to give the child as much love, in the sense of emotional contact, as he needs. But – and I cannot emphasise this too strongly – it would be a terrible mistake to blame the mother for this.

John Well you said earlier that the reason she can't empathise with the baby is because her own *babyhood experiences were painful*. Which means *her mother* couldn't tune in to *her*.

Robin And *her* mother didn't give enough to *her*, all the way back generation after generation. It's called a cycle of deprivation. You remember Harlow and his experiments with baby monkeys.

John They preferred the furry frame to the wire frame, and so on.

Robin Yes. Well Harlow showed this cycle of deprivation very clearly. The baby monkeys that were brought up apart from their mothers were very incapable mothers themselves when they grew up. They usually either ignored their babies and didn't bother to feed them, and often tried to push them away when they tried to cuddle; or in the worst cases they actually attacked them so that they were in danger of their lives and had to be removed.

John Did the ones who had been given furry frames turn out to be a bit better at mothering than the ones who'd had the wire frames or been completely isolated?

Robin The results suggested that they were, and if the motherless mother had at least had playmates, her ability to care for her baby was much greater.

John OK, but hang on a moment, I'm getting a bit super-saturated. So let me just try to recap for a moment. We talked about change. Too much change in too little time can floor us. We talked about what we need to cope with change – shielding from stress so we can rest, reassurance, and emotional support.

Now after that we noted how much stress the parents of a new child suffer, and then we looked at the astonishing rate of change the baby himself experiences – which is why he needs so much shielding and love. Right. Now, that shielding and love usually comes from the mother, and nature's evolved an instinctive behaviour mechanism called attachment behaviour. This keeps the child and mother close together. It's not just for physical survival, it's so that the child can get the love from his mother to enable him to grow, to become, tiny bit by tiny bit, more confident, more independent. What was next?

Robin Well next we saw that the human child doesn't get completely 'attached' to a particular person until he's about five or six months old – when he can identify and recognise his mother pretty reliably.

John Whereas with animals this attachment behaviour can operate much earlier?

Robin Yes. Do you remember Konrad Lorenz and his geese? He found they became imprinted, attached to, the first moving thing they saw.

John Yes. The first thing one brood of goslings saw after the inside of their eggs was Lorenz himself, so they adopted him as their Mum.

Robin And if you remember another's little eyes first fell on a large yellow balloon. So he followed that – until it popped, I suppose.

John It must be frightfully alarming seeing your mother explode. Somewhere in Germany must exist an unusually detached goose. Anyway, from six months up to about two or three years of age, the normal child is very, very strongly attached to his mother and if, during this time, the mother is separated from the child and he is not given *tremendous* support to compensate, he's likely to go through a very difficult time. And if the separation is *really* prolonged – as with a hospitalisation – he will go through the three stages Bowlby describes of protest, then despair, then detachment. Now, you also pointed out that even if the mother is with the child throughout there can be a problem if the mother is unable to achieve full communication with the child; that is, if she can't establish empathy by reaching back to her babyhood and childhood feelings because those memories are painful. The child will sense this and feel that he is somehow not fully loved despite everything he is given. *But* it's foolish to start 'blaming' the mother because she probably had a difficult childhood herself. And you can't blame the grandmother because the great-grandmother, etc., etc., etc.

Robin Yes, leave blaming to the politicians.

John All right. Now next, I want to know more about what you call 'deprivation'.

Looking after the baby inside . . . . . .

Robin Well, what do *you* experience when you start feeling deprived?

John When I come under particular stress?

Robin Yes.

John Well, the first thing I notice is that certain muscles tighten up, especially round my shoulders and neck. In fact my shoulders start moving up towards my ears! The jaw muscles tighten, and also those round my temples and forehead.

Robin And psychologically?

John I get resentful. It feels as though I'm giving a lot out and not getting anything back. I feel tetchy, although I hide this a bit. But somehow the underlying resentment comes through. It's as though I'm complaining non-verbally. And then I start feeling slightly paranoid – that the world is somehow getting at me, that people are making unreasonable demands. I *know* that's absurd, but my mind doesn't seem to be able to tell my emotions to pack it in. Actually I start feeling as Basil Fawlty must every day of his life. And I dislike myself in this mood.

Robin Do you feel like screaming?

John . . . Not these days, but five years ago I would have said 'Yes'. You know . . . it suddenly occurs to me that this feeling is a bit like having an angry baby inside you. Is that a peculiar thing to say?

Robin No. I think this kind of experience is common enough, though people don't often describe it so clearly. But I'm most intrigued you use the phrase 'a baby inside you'. One way of looking at this is that we have *all* got a baby inside us. When things are going normally, it's quite dormant. But under stress it starts squawking. And if we don't look after it ourselves, give it a lot of nurture, *and* perhaps get others to help nurture us too

. . . we can finish up in hospital. We collapse. The lack of emotional nurture can have a physical effect as severe as that.

John You said 'all of us'. You believe *everyone* has a baby inside them?

Robin Certainly I do. When I first read Bowlby I thought that he had a bit of a bee in his bonnet about the importance of maternal care. But the more experience I got, the more I came to believe he was right.

John So some people have a big baby inside them and some a tiny one.

Robin Let's say that some internal babies are more distressed than others.

John And genuinely tough guys? Do they really have a baby at all?

Robin Well, I've interviewed all sorts and I've never met anyone who didn't.

John So even if the internal baby is very, very quiet, nevertheless, given enough stress it'll start squawking.

Robin Yes. Actually it's very revealing to examine what we mean by 'tough guys'. If we mean the hard, 'macho' variety, they're trying to pretend they don't have any sort of a baby inside. So they'll never nurture it. That's why these types have nothing to 'give' other people, and indeed tend to be bad-

tempered. They'll stand up to stress so far and then
suddenly crack. The person who's really tough acknowledges
the baby inside and knows how to look after it. These were the
people who stood up to everything the Gestapo could do to
them, and were still able to support and nurture colleagues at
the same time.

John In a way, interrogation techniques are almost designed to
bring out the baby inside, aren't they? By applying maximum
stress while cutting off any possibility of emotional support.

Robin Prisoners are deliberately allowed to lose track of the
time, are even hooded and subjected to meaningless noise so
that they can't even connect themselves with the outside world –
cutting off even that source of support.

John The phrase 'looking after yourself' is very revealing, isn't
it? A tough guy is someone who can 'look after himself'.
Mothers look after you. So what makes somebody tough and
independent is his ability to mother *himself*.

Robin That's right. To give himself or herself what he or she
needs. People who can do this regularly as a matter of course
are the ones who seem very strong and independent.

John They keep their internal baby satisfied. So let's come back
to the mother and her baby. Or rather bab*ies*: the real one and
the one inside her. Presumably she has to look after *both*?

Robin Exactly. For example, one thing that may surprise you is
that 'good' mothers, the ones who have had more nurture – the
ones with happier childhoods – will probably stop breast feeding
at an earlier age and put the baby on the bottle.

John Why?

Robin So they can share the baby around. The husband can do
some of it. Someone else can look after the baby while they go
out for a bit!

John You're not saying that the healthy mothers who've had
more nurture give *less* to the baby?

Robin Not overall, no. The point is they know when to stop. In
other words, they know when they need to do something for
themselves. Sometimes they even go on breast feeding for a year
or more.

John Why?

Robin They enjoy it. They're getting a lot out of it. So it's the
same thing. They can give to themselves, look after themselves.

So that when they're with the baby they can *enjoy* giving him their *full* attention. If you can love yourself, it kind of brushes off on other people, doesn't it?

John So the Buddhists say. I had a friend who felt he needed to be able to give more to others, so he went to a weekend organised by Buddhists called 'Loving Kindness'. They spent the entire time showing him how to be more loving and kinder to himself. For them, that had to be the starting point. So . . . the 'good' mother can enjoy giving the baby her full attention because she's also taking care of the baby inside her.

Robin That's right. But I'm not comfortable with that phrase, the 'good' mother. Winnicott, the great paediatrician and psychoanalyst, preferred 'good enough' mother. Actually, if any mother was perfect – if she *always* arrived at the moment the baby needed her and always gave him exactly what he wanted – it'd give the baby problems, as we've seen.

John Permanently fuzzy boundaries.

Robin So we're not talking about perfect, 24-carat, Olympic-gold-medal mothering here. We're talking about mothers who give the baby a *lot* of attention *some* of the time – 'good enough' mothering.

John Now tell me about the mothers who *can't* do that – the ones who are more 'deprived'.

Robin The ones who haven't had the love themselves? Well, they'll find it very difficult to give the baby to anyone else to look after. They'd feel that was *wrong*. So they're with the baby nearly all the time. But it's very difficult for them, even for very short periods, to give the baby their full attention. They'll tend always to have their minds on other things; so it's hard for them to tune in to the baby's wavelength because they're avoiding tuning in to that wavelength in themselves. And, of course, they'll be feeling terrible. Their own baby, the one inside them, will be screaming for attention because they're spending so long with the child, but they won't have any idea how to give themselves what they need.

John And of course they feel 'inadequate'.

Robin Oh yes! They sense they're failing in some way, although they're doing *everything they can think of* – more, in fact, to all appearances – than the 'good enough' mothers whose babies are thriving. Of course they believe that everyone else around them is doing perfectly and that they're the only ones who can't cope.

John But if they *did* look inside themselves . . .?

Robin But that's the whole problem – they *don't*.

John So what do they think is going wrong?

Robin Well, all they can generally recognise is that they have very difficult babies. And their babies *are* difficult . . . they keep them awake, they're often very colicky, they scream a lot.

John Like the baby inside them.

Robin Absolutely. The baby inside them is screaming because it's getting completely ignored. What they're doing to themselves is just like shutting the door on a real baby to stop him screaming, instead of picking him up and comforting him. So the baby screaming outside in the cot is the mirror image of the baby 'screaming inside'. The baby's miserable and tense because the mother's miserable and tense.

John This is fascinating because it's taking us right back to the first big lesson at the start of this book; that it is not 'difficult' emotions that cause the problem, it's *denying* that you have these 'difficult' emotions. And you deny them because your family all find them uncomfortable, which forces you to put them behind the screen. Here the emotion is what . . . deprivation, unhappiness . . . in other words, a squalling baby is firmly hidden away behind the screen. So the way to deal with the problem, to make the person feel less deprived, is to get the baby out where they can see it, recognise it, and give it some care.

Robin Well, do you remember what normally stops that from happening?

John The feelings of family disapproval. If the family disapproved of the emotion, which is why it got shoved behind the screen in the first place, when you try and bring it out – even years later – you'll feel the same disapproving feelings.

Robin And because you were young and dependent when all this happened, these are very, very strong feelings. So it's not easy to go through the process.

John No, I can remember that personally. Being a good public-school chap I used to see myself as jolly independent and quite tough and, above all, *supremely* normal. I certainly didn't need any affection – namby-pamby nonsense – and I developed a pretty healthy contempt for anyone who looked as though he needed any mothering. It wasn't till I got into your group, at the age of thirty-five, that I began to realise how much I needed warmth and affection, and also how difficult it was for me to *show* that I needed it.

Robin What did you feel if you tried to ask for it?

John Ashamed. And inadequate. After all, I had this image of myself as . . . 'manly', so my first reaction was that people would treat me with contempt if I told them I needed affection. Also, I discovered I didn't feel 'entitled' to ask for it. Then I made the amazing discovery that, if I actually showed a woman I wanted affection, she liked me for it! Instead of, as I think I'd always unconsciously assumed, kicking me out of the door for being so pathetic! But it still took me a long time before I could really trust it.

Robin Well it had been a long period of 'conditioning' so it's not surprising that it should take quite a time to turn your attitudes round on that point. But those are the sorts of feelings – shame, inadequacy, thinking that you're not entitled to ask – that make it difficult for mothers to accept the baby behind the screen, once they've stuck it there. They don't have to worry about being 'manly', but they are equally worried about feeling 'like a baby' again. And that makes it hard to come to terms with these needs, even though everyone has them.

John But wait a moment, Robin. Supposing they're right. I don't mean right in pretending that they don't have needs. But supposing they're right in thinking that there *won't* be any care available. If there isn't affection around, it might be better, *safer*,

t) keep your distance and not take risks stirring up painful
feelings when you won't get the support you need to handle
them.

Robin Well, in my experience of trying to help people who
think like that, there's always plenty of support available.

John But surely that isn't true for some people.

Robin Let me try to convince you.

Sources of support . . . . . .

John You believe that there's nearly always care and affection
available if people *ask* for it.

Robin If they stop shutting themselves off from it, yes. It's their
attitude that stops them *receiving* affection. Just as their 'baby' is
shut away behind that tightly-held-down screen, they'll also be
sending out signals – by the expression on their faces and the
movements and posture of their bodies – which tell other people
to keep their distance.

John It's as though they're sending out messages that they
haven't got a baby behind the screen. Just to make sure nobody
behaves as if they had.

Robin But of course they don't realise they're doing that. To
others they will look slightly forbidding and fierce so that we'd
almost feel foolish offering them encouragement or warmth.

John I've just remembered a girl who came into our group, who
spent the first three sessions putting everyone's back up. You
could see she actually took pleasure in annoying people. And
when people returned her aggression she liked it even more.
And then, in about the third session, you suddenly ignored all
the angry signals and spoke to her for perhaps just a minute
very warmly, with a lot of support and affection. And to our
total astonishment she dissolved into tears and cried for about
ten minutes. And she came in next week looking almost radiant.

Robin That's right. The confrontations she liked to produce
were simply a way of keeping her needy feelings at bay.

John It's a good example of how group therapy works, too.
People often tend to think it's a frightfully dry process of
intellectual analysis. Actually there's very little of that.

Robin Yes, what the therapist is trying to do is to wait for the moment when someone is ready to deal with a difficult feeling and then gradually try to introduce it to him, help him to face it. And, as you say, very little of this is to do with verbal analysis. A great deal of the benefit even of 'analytic' therapy is to do with modelling. To the extent that the analyst is behaving in a natural, open way and is comfortable with his or her feelings, it frees other people to do the same – even without them understanding how it's working.

John Back to the needy mothers. Now you say there will be affection available if they're giving off the right signals. But the needy mothers come from deprived families, so their parents, brothers and sisters will have a similar problem. And the mother's likely to have married someone who's stuck at the same stage too. And presumably some of their friends will be similar.

Robin There will still be plenty of others, neighbours and so on, who can give support. And even if they're *all* stuck, don't forget one important source. As the family grows up, it's interesting to see how the children often give the parents the love they need.

John The *children*!?

Robin Certainly!

John Surely that's not always good for the children, is it?

Robin Why not? As long as it's open, freely given. Children are naturally very generous and they enjoy giving to their parents if only the parents will accept it. Also, if the parents haven't been too possessive and jealous, the children will have got love from the other sources – relatives, neighbours, friends, the school, and so on – and in some ways may be more grown up than the parents! In other words, they'll have something to give. And they'll enjoy giving it. Moreover, it's by playing at swopping over the parent/child roles sometimes that children practise for being parents themselves later, and learn how to care for others.

John So you really believe there are enough sources of support around for everyone, *if* they're sending off the right signals.

Robin Yes. For example, take the father of the newly born baby. He's feeling left out, right? He's supposed to be giving the mother a lot of support while getting little back from her, and not really getting much from the intimacy with the baby either. He needs to plug in to other sources – his parental family, his work mates, his friends – and lean on them a bit while he is holding the lifeline for his wife and child. If he asks for a bit of help, he'll usually get it. People are programmed that way.

John All right. So if the early years haven't gone right for someone, he or she can still get a lot of the good experience to make up for that provided that he or she realises that they still need it, and start sending out the right signals. But we have to be prepared to deal with some pretty difficult emotions – feeling rather ashamed, and suspicious that if anyone sees that we're really like this they'll reject us for being so inadequate.

Robin I don't want to over-emphasise these unpleasant feelings. Some people may be quite aware that they need some love and attention for themselves now and again and just need to realise that they require *20 per cent more* than they're taking. That realisation will be pretty easy for them. Then there will be others with rather more of a baby hidden behind the screen. But they may not find it too difficult either. For instance, in the mothers' groups Prue runs, she says the deprived mothers often simply see that the mothers who are doing well also have problems with their children and needs of their own, but also that they don't hesitate to admit the problems and satisfy the needs. This frees the more anxious ones to be more relaxed and natural too. They no longer have to pretend that everything is perfect, and once they can be open and ask for help, people automatically seem to move to help them.

John Well, this is all rather encouraging. But I want now to ask you about the really bad cases of deprivation. I'm thinking of the things that make us all wince a bit, like 'battered babies'. What can you say about them?

Severe deprivation . . . . . .

Robin If we study families where there's a battered baby, we find a cycle of deprivation again. Parents who batter their babies have usually been terribly neglected when they were young; or threatened with terrible punishments; or even actually battered by their own parents. In fact it's quite instructive to look at some of the other conclusions that Harlow reached in his research on the deprived monkeys. As I've mentioned, when the motherless ones grew up and had babies of their own, they were more often able to care for them if they were allowed to play with other little monkeys as they grew up, or even, it seemed, if they'd just been given a furry cloth-mother to cuddle as babies.

John That was enough to help them connect.

Robin And more surprising than that, some of the most deprived monkeys who had rejected and injured their *first* babies – maybe in one or two instances even killed them – when these monkeys had second and third babies they *were* often able to care for them – at least after a fashion.

John What had made *them* change?

Robin Well, Harlow thinks that the mothers were changed by the first babies.

John The ones they treated so badly?

Robin Yes. Because the babies themselves always made such tremendous efforts to cuddle and love their mothers, no matter how much they were punished and rejected. So the mothers got some love from their first babies even though they didn't want it. And that seemed enough to begin to change them.

John So what can be done about the most difficult *human* cases?

Robin The surprising thing is that the most deprived parents are ultimately very responsive. But they're terribly difficult to get through to, to reach, to *start with*.

John So how do you get started with people who have a particularly needy baby behind their screens? How can you help them to start becoming aware of it?

Robin You have to find a tactful way of expressing things that enables them to accept support without having to face too suddenly the fact that they need it so desperately. Being friendly, and complimenting them on the job they're *trying* to do *as parents* is one way.

John What – even parents of *battered babies*!?

Robin Yes. Even with them. Even there you can say, 'I can see how hard you both try to bring up your child the right way.' Which in fact is true. The *intention* is always good, though violence and punishment is the only way they understand. So instead of *criticising* them, which would only make things worse, you offer to help them find a *better* way, and you can also *show* them a better way by how you treat them yourself. In other less serious cases you can be more direct. In one of the first cases I treated as a family, the problem *appeared* to be the daughter. But she was just the scapegoat. And it soon became clear that she was carrying the can for the problems of the whole family. The story was that she had upset the parents from the age of two up to the age of fourteen – which was when she was sent to me – and the mother had actually spent many spells in mental hospitals and made several suicide attempts. After four sessions of family therapy, the mother began to be able to acknowledge her deep craving for love and affection. As this happened, the daughter stopped her misbehaviour and became the one who gave the mother the love she'd never had. The mother didn't need to go to hospital again.

John All this could happen once you'd helped her to face her unsatisfied needs.

Robin Yes, when she'd become aware of the crying baby behind the screen, with our encouragement she was able to let the rest of the family look after it.

John But that needed a shrink.

Robin Yes, but that was a *very* serious problem, present over twelve years and involving several suicide attempts by the mother. But for the vast majority of the people one ordinarily meets, it's enough to say that anyone can help anyone else, provided, that is, that they all acknowledge their needs for affection and support. If we could get every family in the land to think about that for ten minutes, I believe there'd be a lot of much happier families around in three weeks!

John You know, there's one last question I want to ask. We've talked about emotional support, affection, care, love, attention, we've called it everything except mystery ingredient X. Doctor, what is this thing called 'love'?

Wider attachments . . . . . .

Robin What do you think 'love' is?

John Neatly turned . . . well, in the sense of emotional support, it's certainly partly to do with the physical act of touching. Handling, stroking, embracing, everything they used to call 'gentling'. If you're stressed, all these things make you feel better, more relaxed, give you a sense of inner calmness. They seem to help you to get things in perspective. But it's something much more than just that. If I'm feeling a bit worried about something and I simply sit and talk with someone that I like and trust, it's as though the act of being with them in itself calms me and makes me feel better. Even when there's no physical contact, and even when the person I'm talking to can't really give me any advice or rational reassurance. Just being with someone who's got this inner calmness seems to count. I remember Koestler talking about Indians flocking to a village to listen to one of the great Indian religious figures. He was surprised at first that they didn't seem to listen much. They just looked up occasionally and then went on playing with the babies that they'd brought along. He suddenly realised that they were simply getting something from the guru's presence, and not from the content of what he was saying.

My shrink died, but I still go to him.

Is he as supportive as ever?

Oh, much more so.

Robin But don't you see that fits in with what we concluded about the effect of physical comfort? Remember when you asked earlier what I thought 'love' was, and what the little monkey was getting from the 'cloth-mother'? We agreed it had something to do with having a spell of comfort, quietness, calmness, to enable us to settle down and get steady and organised again after a bit of upsetting change. To get a chance to 'get ourselves in order', to 'pull ourselves together', to 'get back in one piece' after being 'in pieces', 'all over the place'. How much of that we need will depend on the size of the stress. If you think about it, when we're under pressure we may need a kind of gear change upwards to engage with a bigger system. When the baby's under pressure, he needs to plug in to the mother for stability and support. The mother may need to plug in to the father, the father in to his family, his work place, and so on. In other words, when the stress is too big for the individual, he may need to engage a group that can handle the change. The bigger the change, the bigger this group may need to be.

John Our 'attachments' are going wider and wider.

Robin That's right. A cut on the knee may need a plaster and cuddle from Mum; something worse may need the doctor to come round; if the injury's too bad for the doctor to handle, he may have to send the child to hospital.

John And I suppose if you plug in to the biggest system of all . . . well then we're talking about some religious feeling, something to do with God.

Robin Well, at least, let's say the person plugs into a feeling that the universe is ordered and there's meaning and purpose in everything that happens. Despite the bad thing that may be happening at that moment, nevertheless the person can feel that the universe is basically 'all right'.

John Parallel with that, I'm constantly surprised at the extraordinarily beneficial effect that meditation has.

Robin I think it's for the same reason. Anyone who feels that they're in some way plugged in to a meaningful, cosmic system is given a greater psychological balance and stability as a result – whether or not they believe it contains a God-like figure at the control panel. And lots of people have this beneficial sense of being plugged in to something bigger, even if they're not religious in the going-to-church-regularly sense.

John I've always found the energy of those great Victorian figures daunting. I suppose it was something to do with the deep faith many of them experienced. They seemed to be able to adjust to disasters and be up and off again disappointingly easily.

Robin I think I've mentioned before about the research on healthy families that they did at Timberlawn, in Dallas. One of their most intriguing findings is that the healthiest families seem to subscribe to some transcendent value system, something beyond themselves. I'm sure the fact that they were plugged in in this way, to the greatest of all possible systems, helped to give them such remarkable psychological stability and resilience. I've always been struck by the way so many patients, if they do really well in therapy, develop an interest in the meaning and purpose of life.

John This is rather neat, isn't it? We start by talking about all the stress caused by changes; we go on to discuss the importance of attachment – of the baby being able sometimes to connect himself 100 per cent with the mother so that he can handle his own huge changes; and we finish up discovering that the healthiest families – whose chief characteristic is their ability to cope with change – share the characteristic of having an attachment to some transcendent belief.

Robin Must be time we changed the subject.

Afterthought: Paranoia and Politics

John You know, ever since you've explained about paranoia and how the projection mechanism actually works, I seem to see more and more examples of it all around me.

Robin More and more people plotting against you behind your back, that sort of thing?

John Thank you for being so understanding, Doctor. But not that, in fact. Not yet, anyway. But you said that any time we find ourselves thinking that we have behaved impeccably over some matter and that other people are entirely to blame for problems that may have arisen, then that's paranoid – *not* in the sense that we're permanently clinically paranoid, but in the sense that that *particular* piece of thinking is paranoid.

Robin Yes, if we split our feelings up into 'good' and 'bad', or love and hate, and then project the nasty ones on to someone else, or some other group, that's a paranoid way of functioning.

John But it doesn't do us any harm if we let that happen now and again, say at a football match?

Robin No, it just allows us to let off steam, to relax, and to feel part of our group.

John And normal people can simply let these feelings go afterwards?

Robin Yes, they just switch them off at the end of the game. They've had a bit of fun, that's all.

John But the truly paranoid will have to keep on doing this.

Robin Yes, they *need* to keep the bad feelings in other people permanently.

John So if we look at politics, where justifying yourself and blaming others is a fine art, we see rather a lot of paranoid behaviour, don't we?

Robin Well, I think ordinary, healthy people engage in political arguments the same way they play or watch football. They may get angry when they argue with people of different views, but afterwards they can drop the hostilities and see them as human beings again. In other words, I think most people know deep down that politics is a kind of game, the working-out of conflict between groups of people according to certain agreed rules.

John So if we look at mainstream British politics, it's perfectly healthy that the parties should get worked up and angry with each other during a debate or an election, because they can let those feelings go later and talk to each other on a friendly basis.

Robin Yes. After all, politics is the art of the possible, isn't it? No one's going to have exactly the same views, so you need to respect each other's differences and try to reach a reasonable compromise if you can.

John But the real extremists have difficulty with this, don't they? They don't seem to be able to see their political opponents as people who happen to hold different opinions. They really seem to view them as bad people.

Robin Well, you see, people like this need to use their opponents as dustbins, somewhere they can dump all the bits of themselves that they can't accept. Just like the scapegoat in a sick family. So they need to hate their opponents to keep themselves sane.

John You mean, while they're hating, they can keep their screens down and avoid seeing their own faults.

Robin That's right. An intense preoccupation with politics is usually a way of putting painful personal conflicts outside ourselves, disowning them.

John So what would happen if they started to listen more to their opponents' views?

Robin That might be positively dangerous for them because then they would have to start to face up to their own faults or weaknesses. Their screens might flip up, and then they'd see in themselves the dreadful things they're attributing to the other party. So if there's any danger of this, they quickly arrange to make an inflammatory speech accusing *others* of wanting to see rivers of blood or fascist dictatorships in the country and thereby stave off the breakdown for a bit longer; or at least reduce it to sufficiently manageable proportions to pass for normal in the House of Commons.

John You mean they couldn't cope with the faults they might see in themselves?

Robin That's right. They're protecting their precarious sanity by blaming others.

John Perhaps that's why extremists are so politically active. They *need* to be! If they went off and had a nice time, they might go mad. The political struggle keeps them sane.

Robin In fact, it is very hard to treat someone with really militant political views, except just to relieve the symptoms by drugs. It's like paranoia – in fact it *is* paranoia – adjusted to seem to fit neatly into the political scene, so that people won't see it for what it really is. But when someone in psychotherapy realises this about themselves, it's a tremendous step forward. A foreign patient in one of my psychotherapy groups, who was a militant left-wing activist in her country of origin, and who resisted any attempt to examine that part of her life, came back recently from holiday looking absolutely marvellous – really alive, full of confidence. Everyone noticed it and told her so. She said that what had happened was that she'd realised at home that her attachment to Communism had been a way of dealing with her painful feelings about her mother, and with this realisation she'd suddenly become free of both.

John How much did that affect her political views?

Robin It didn't change her political orientation, but now she can talk about her views without feeling threatened by disagreement. She's able to listen, where before she was closed off and absolutely rigid. It's interesting too that when I asked her whether she'd be more, or less, effective now in her political aims, she said at once, 'More effective.' Which I am sure is right, because she's more realistic and practical now that she is less dominated by her own psychological needs. She would be able to form alliances now, and compromise to get strategy agreed.

John What's so funny about really extreme political sects is their inability to get on with each other. They're always splitting up and forming separate groups, which themselves split up after a time. We had a lot of fun with this in Monty Python's *Life of Brian*. I checked the political scene recently and came up with the following lists of the parties of the extreme left and the extreme right. In the red corner, the Communist Party of Great Britain (Marxist-Leninist), the New Communist Party, the Vanguard Group, the Socialist Workers' Party (Trotskyist), the Socialist Party of Great Britain (Marxist), the International Marxist Group, Revolution Youth, the Workers' Revolutionary Party (Trotskyist), the Revolutionary Communist Party, the Spartacist League (Trotskyist), the Communist Workers' Organisation, Big Flame (originally Maoist), the Chartists, the Revolutionary Marxist Tendency, the Workers' Party, the Institute for Workers' Control, the Anti-Nazi League, the International Communists League, the Revolutionary Workers' Party, the Socialist Workers' Revolutionary Party, the Workers' Power Group (Trotskyist), Workers' Fight, Workers' League, the Revolutionary Communist Party of Britain (Marxist-Leninist, strongly pro-Albanian), the Communist Party of England, the

Association of Communist Workers, the Socialist Union
Internationalist, the Communist Workers' Movement, the Young
Communists League of Great Britain, Solidarity for Social
Revolution, the Revolutionary Communist League of Britain
(Maoist), People's Democracy (Marxist-Leninist), World
Revolution, Alternative Socialism, Young Socialists, the Militant
Tendency, the Workers' Socialist League, the Revolutionary
Marxist Current (Trotskyist), the League for Socialist Action,
Marxist Worker (Trotskyist), the Revolutionary Communist
Tendency (Trotskyist), the Revolutionary Socialist League
(Trotskyist), International Socialists, and the Independent Labour
Party. And in the blue corner, complete with swastikas and
various symbols from Nordic mythology, we have the National
Front, the British Movement, the British National Party, the
National Reorganisation Party, Column 88, the League of St
George, the Northern League, the Odinist Committee of
London, Viking Youth, SS Woton 18, the Eleventh Hour
Brigade, the Adolf Hitler Commando Group, the Iron Guard,
the Knights of the Iron Cross, the Dirlwanger Brigade, the
British League of Rights, Self-Help Organisation, Choice
Organisation, the Immigration Control Association and the
Racial Preservation Society.

Robin Haven't you missed some out?

John Probably. Because they're all splitting up so fast, it's
practically impossible to get the latest score. It's rather like
watching cellular activity under a microscope. But I still don't
really understand why they split off from each other as often as
they do, nor why they seem to attack each other more than they
attack their 'real enemies' on the other side of the political
spectrum. What on earth is it all about?

Robin Ah. I think this is a rather different principle from the
one we've been talking about so far. The paranoid person is
trying to keep the good separate from the bad by putting all the
bad outside; that is, drawing the boundary more closely, more
narrowly, to exclude the feelings he can't stand. But at least the
person who's operating in a paranoid fashion has got boundaries
of *some* sort, and can bear to admit there are other people in the
world. So a person who operates to some extent at this level
could cope reasonably well if he joined a political party which
stands for the kinds of attitudes and feelings he likes in himself,
provided there's another party, very different from the one he's
joined, standing for a lot of the things he can't bear to see in his
own personality. Then he can support his own side, and hate
the other lot, and he'll feel really good. This kind of life will suit
him down to the ground, and keep him from cracking up. Of

course, he won't be able to 'bury the hatchet' when the heat of the debate is over, like the more normal members of his party do, because he can't afford to stop being hostile to the other side. But at least he can get on reasonably well with his own crowd, as long as the enemy is there to hate.

John So he could fit in to one of the *big* political parties?

Robin Yes. But if the need to use this paranoid defence is really intense, and he's even in danger of slipping back severely into the fuzzy-family stage if he doesn't work overtime at it, he'll start doing the same thing with his *own* side too. And his feeling of God-like omnipotence – having to be the big balloon filling the box – will be threatened by the existence of *anyone* else, unless that other person's views seem so identical to his own that he doesn't really perceive him as 'different'. So, because people are bound to be at least a *bit* different from each other, and that difference will emerge sooner or later, there'll be a constant splitting of the party into fragments as each person strives to hang on to the feeling of purity and perfection. So they either boot each other out or leave to start a new party that *really* stands for the pure, unsullied truth.

John Ah, that's right, isn't it? Real extremists are very proud of the purity of their beliefs.

Robin Yes. Of course, there's nothing wrong with trying to improve yourself, as long as you're realistic. But the moment you try to convince others, and even try to convince yourself, that you're *purer than you actually are*, that means you've got to start screening off the bits of you that don't match your claim.

John And once they go behind the screen, they get projected on to other people or groups.

Robin Now if you're the person doing that, of course it does make *you* feel purer, more perfect – for a while.

John Just as during the Inquisition they thought they were getting high marks from God and doing Christ a good turn by burning people alive.

Robin It's likely that most of them seriously believed they were only doing it for the victims' own good. Consciously, the Inquisitors could feel that they had saved them from a fate worse than death, and also saved the world from a terrible evil these victims were imagined to contain. But the hidden agenda would be the Inquisitors' need to screen off the same evil in themselves; to deny it, to project it into their victims and to get rid of it by destroying them.

John And that would actually make them feel better for a time.

Robin Yes. Till the chickens come home to roost again.

John No doubt that's why they'd torture a confession out of their victims if they could. Proof in writing that the Inquisitor is really a nice chap, just doing his job. That would make him feel better for even longer.

Robin Probably. It would confirm them in their belief in what they were doing, dispelling any traces of doubt. It would reassure them that the bad things were *really* outside, out there in the victims, and not inside in themselves. A confession would be very comforting.

John Presumably the same applies to the witch-hunting in Britain in the seventeenth century. Because the Puritans felt that sexual feelings were so wicked, they all screened them off, and projected them on to other people – the poor old 'witches'.

Robin That's right. Then if they did have improper sexual thoughts themselves, they could blame the witches for putting these into their minds.

John So they burnt them. And they went on doing so until things relaxed a bit and naughty thoughts became permissible. Then we got lots of dirty Restoration comedies and didn't need to burn witches any more.

Robin It all goes to show how dangerous it can be if we try to be too *good*. Someone else ends up having to be the 'baddie'.

John But why does it make us feel so good to fall into this paranoid way of thinking and behaving? I can see you feel better because you've got rid of all the 'bad' feelings. But there's something else going on, isn't there? Once you've got them safely projected into other people, you can be really foul to them because your behaviour is fully justified by how 'bad' they are. And that means you can actually let out all your nasty, cruel, envious, negative feelings by behaving badly towards them. So you get it both ways, don't you?

Robin True. And notice also that there's another of these psychological vicious circles built into that process, which helps to explain why human beings can be so fiendishly cruel to each other. No matter how much the persecutor justifies his treatment of the victim, the fact that he's torturing him or burning him alive puts him in danger of seeing the *enjoyment* he's getting out of it – seeing his *own* 'badness', in other words. So the projection has to be stepped up, making the victim seem even more bad, therefore justifying more cruelty, which again increases the danger of the persecutor seeing himself – what he's really like – and so on. So, far from feeling any mercy, the persecutor will be driven to be steadily more awful, more angry and cruel, the more the victim is seen to suffer. Also, this vicious circle of cruelty, guilt, projection of the guilt on to the victim, and then greater cruelty still, is reinforced through the persecutors all reassuring each other that they're doing the right thing. For if one of them begins to have doubts whether the cruelty is right and necessary, that person will threaten everyone else's peace of mind. So they'll first try to reassure and support him in the good work; but if he continues to waver, they'll turn on him and put him on the fire as well. And this principle operates in more ordinary life too. In politics, for example, everyone can get an extraordinarily comforting feeling of mutual support from their group by focussing on an enemy. The need to fight your enemy gives you a common purpose, which by making you aware of your dependence on the others and their dependence on you, brings a feeling of greater cohesion.

John You see this at Party Conferences, don't you? They're all sitting there looking rather grim, and then a speaker gets up who's got real fire in his belly, and he says: 'The other lot really are the most awful bunch of rotters, the *most* left-wing – or right-wing – bunch there's ever been in this great country of ours, and it would be a disaster if they got into power – or continued in power – so *we* must get into power – or hold on to power – but that's going to be a tremendous struggle, a terrific fight, and we can't relax and enjoy ourselves and have a good time, we must struggle and fight and fight and struggle and then struggle a little bit more at the end of all that.' And then he sits down, and there's a lovely warm glow throughout the hall, as if they've all had tea and crumpets, and everyone looks relaxed and happy and cheerful. They're simply radiant with contentment and goodwill. Although if he'd said to them, 'We must all have an absolutely tremendous time and have lots of fun and be nice to each other,' they'd probably have lynched him. So why is it that these hilarious exhortations to fight, fight and fight again, always relax everyone and make them so much more agreeable?

Robin The same principle. It splits off the angry, rejecting feelings from the warm, affectionate ones and directs the 'bad' ones entirely at the opposing party. That leaves the 'good' ones undiluted and therefore more positive. Of course, the cosy glow this produces can't last, because it isn't realistic, and over a period of time you can't help seeing that people on your own side have faults too. But it does give a temporary respite from having to face the reality that *everyone* is both good and bad, including yourself. That's a more complicated, grown-up kind of attitude which can be a bit sobering, almost depressing. So we all get on better when there's an enemy to hate, which is why people who lived through the last war remember an extra warmth and friendliness then, and wonder where it has gone in peace time.

John I've heard that there was less clinical depression then.

Robin There is some evidence to support that. And this paranoid way of operating often seems to be called into play on a big scale when depressing events are affecting society as a whole. For example, do you remember the industrial dispute at Grunwick in 1977?

John It ran for weeks. Huge numbers of pickets, shoving and fighting at the gates, pictures on every edition of the television news, everybody who was anybody turning up to demonstrate. It really captured the public's imagination, didn't it?

Robin But the degree of public interest never seemed justified by the size or importance of the dispute. I couldn't see why such a huge cross-section of the public were getting so involved emotionally, until I found myself wanting to go along and throw a few bricks too. Then I noticed that I'd suddenly felt more cheerful and lively while having that thought, though I'd been rather flat and morose just before. And that made me realise that the Grunwick dispute had become the focus of attention just at a time when events were forcing us to face up to the dreadful state of the British economy – the fact that, from then on, we were all going to get poorer. I remember I'd often felt depressed about that, but getting worked up about Grunwick and imagining joining in the fight there always gave me a lift, a shot of adrenalin.

John And eventually all the interest and excitement died away although nothing had changed. So it works like this. Everyone's standard of living is going down because the world is changing in a way we can't stop – that's depressing for us all. But if everyone divides up into two big teams, one team saying we'd all be well-off if it wasn't for the greedy, selfish bosses, the other lot saying we'd still be well-off if it wasn't for hide-bound union leaders and lazy workers, it becomes like a Cup Final where everyone can get aggressive and excited, and forget the depressing and complicated real economic problems.

Robin That's it. Of course, the *real* problem doesn't get solved, because we have to face reality to do that, despite the gloom it causes. And we also have to cooperate in order to succeed.

John So, in the short term, paranoid behaviour really does cheer us up. But there can be a cost . . .

Robin Yes. And in small doses it does no harm. Provided we know we're doing it, and can drop it and return to ordinary behaviour – as most people do after taking part in a competitive sport or a political debate – it stimulates us without any ill-effects on others. It's just one example of the way normal people can revert to more childish ways of thinking and behaving when they don't need to be serious and careful, and can let themselves free-wheel, relax and play around a bit. But they can drop it immediately and return to a more adult way of thinking if some important event requires accurate, balanced judgement.

John And, as you said, the real extremists can't do this – they have to stay in the paranoid mode of functioning. So what happens if they get control of governments?

Robin It depends how extreme the lunacy is. If the leader is stuck back at the fuzzy-family stage in many respects, but is also clever and plausible, you get the kind of situation that arose in recent times in Nazi Germany. All the paranoid ways of operating will be carried to extremes and used systematically to scapegoat some minority group, so that any angry, frustrated feelings in the population are deflected away from the regime and on to these scapegoats. But in addition, the leader will be very unclear about his own boundaries. He'll still have the idea of himself as omnipotent, with no limits of any kind – that he's God – so he'll have to control everything, everybody, every aspect of life, in an attempt to avoid any contradiction of his fantasy. To take the simplest example, every time Hitler held his arm up, he wanted everyone else to do the same.

John And presumably that works the other way round too. The more everyone behaves as the dictator wants, the more confused he'll become about the boundaries he does have.

Robin I think that's one reason why too much power corrupts. The holder is bound increasingly to lose contact with reality because he won't be getting the frustration he needs to define his boundaries. And the worse he gets, the more he will be threatened by any kind of individuality or difference that he hasn't created himself. Because these differences show his limits, show he isn't everything, he isn't God. So dictators love uniforms and uniformity, and they particularly hate, and have to destroy, anything that's different, separate, anything that has a strong identity of its own. The Jews have a particularly strong, separate and unmistakable identity, so they're a natural target for anyone who thinks he's God.

John People of different colour are another obvious target – the dictator can't avoid seeing, or forbid, that difference.

Robin Right. So the dictator has to get rid of all these people who differ from his idea of himself. At the same time, he can attribute to them all the things *inside* himself that he doesn't like, the parts of himself that make him feel weak, bad, less than God-like.

John Next, I suppose, the existence of other, different, independent nations presents the same problem.

Robin Yes. So the dictator obviously has to conquer them and either make them the same – absorb them – or wipe them out if they're too different to absorb. Terrible though it is, it all follows quite logically, automatically. And once someone has set himself on this path, he's driven on to *more* projection and destruction, *the more he succeeds*. The dictator and his clique obviously haven't really got rid of any of the bad feelings in themselves at all, they simply projected them on to another group, who became public

enemies number one. So they liquidated them and, after a
pause, they're off again, projecting them on to the next group,
and so on.

John Memories of dear Oliver Cromwell. He started off with the
support of Parliament, the Army and the Scottish Puritans. They
helped his side get rid of the Royalists. Then he dealt with the
Scots. Then he purged the Army. Then he purged Parliament.
Then he got rid of Parliament altogether. By the time he died,
he'd got rid of practically everything that had supported the
Protectorate in the first place. No wonder there was a
Restoration of the monarchy within two years. The Nazis
worked on the same sort of principle. Hitler eliminated the
Communists, the Socialists, the Trade Unions, Catholics,
Protestants, Jews, Gypsies, and so on. He also purged his own
Brownshirts, and was eventually polishing off the High
Command of his Army, Air Force and was even having a go at
the SS when events rather overtook him. And Stalin – he
eventually wiped out virtually every single major figure who'd
helped to bring about the Revolution, accusing each one in turn
of counter-revolutionary behaviour. If you're a leader like this,
once you've got rid of your enemies, you have to start on your
own side.

Robin You have to find more and more dissidents, traitors, and
so on, within the movement. If he ever ran out of them, the
dictator would reach a point where even he might not be able to
believe any more that all the bad feelings were coming from
outside himself.

John His screen would actually start flipping up.

Robin And then the logical conclusion would be that he would
have to wipe himself out as well.

John It's funny you mention that, because I've always had a
suspicion that the Ayatollah would finish up as the only man
left in Iran, sitting there sternly chopping his own limbs off . . .
It's just struck me that the mass suicide of the Jim Jones cult
happened after they'd moved to the promised land in Guyana.

Robin That's a particularly good example. They'd finally got
completely away from the bad, persecuting outsiders and they
no longer had anyone else to project their bad feelings on to. It
would then become more and more difficult to avoid facing the
truth – they would have to take the bad feelings back into
themselves and they just couldn't cope with that. You see how
death and destruction on a large scale is the ultimate logical
result of these paranoid ways of avoiding the truth about

ourselves, avoiding criticism. But, of course, it's criticism, negative as well as positive feedback, that keeps us sane. You remember the mental map analogy we keep coming back to. Well, we have to keep redrawing the boundaries on our mental maps, and we can only do that if we're getting accurate information back from others. So if you start out a bit batty, and then wipe out anyone or any group that makes any criticism, your mental map gets less and less representative of the real world – so you get madder and madder and madder. And it's typical of any group that operates in this way that they maintain a tight control of communication, to stop any corrective information coming in from outside the system. So families of the kind I've been describing usually have a rule that members shouldn't talk too openly with people outside the family.

John There's a marvellous speech in *The Godfather*, when the Godfather reprimands one of his sons after a meeting with another Mafia family. He says, 'Dino, has your brain gone soft? Never tell anyone outside the family what you are thinking again.'

Robin Well, there was quite a bit of death and destruction in that family by the end of the story, if I remember rightly. There weren't many left *inside* the family to tell either. And these are the same principles that crazy families, and also the more extreme cults and political groups, apply to their members, to restrict the passage of information across the family or group boundary. No information must be allowed that contradicts the 'family' map, for fear that the whole system might break down and have to change.

John And totalitarian states similarly control the news and censor history, and discourage their citizens from listening to foreign broadcasts.

Robin It makes you appreciate the freedoms we have in this country, doesn't it? We take them for granted most of the time, but they really make the difference between sanity and madness.

John The really shattering fact is that, according to Amnesty, in over 110 countries of the world people can be locked up for the peaceful expression of their views. Still, I suppose there's one thing you can say for paranoia ... it makes you feel better.

Robin Temporarily at least. That's why there's such a lot of it about. And no doubt it's why we've both just enjoyed indulging in a spot of it ourselves by blaming the paranoids.

John Ah, so *that's* why I'm suddenly feeling so cheerful.

3 The Astonishing Stuffed Rabbit

Becoming separate......

John We've just dealt with the baby's first attempts to construct his map of the world, and how he needs the right combination of emotional support and information about his difference from Mum to do that. What's the next group of ideas?

Robin All the next lot of ideas are connected with the baby becoming more aware that he's not *a part of*, but basically *apart from* Mum: why teddy bears are vital; why we feel open and relaxed on some days, and 'up-tight' on others; the difference between depression and sadness, and how *useful* sadness is; why Basil Fawlty is irritable; why all depression is 'chemical'; and why mothers need to allow their babies a little distress now and again.

John What's the starting point?

Robin It all begins when the baby realises, somewhere around seven months, that he's a separate person from his mother. He becomes increasingly aware of this yawning gulf between them which he now has to deal with.

John You said his general level of anxiety leaps up at about this point – rather as if that particular penny drops quite rapidly.

Robin Right. Noticing that space opening up between himself and Mum is an alarming experience, a bit like that awkward moment when you've got one foot in the boat and the other still on the river bank. Of course, attachment behaviour – his need to stay close to Mum and his anxiety about being separated from her – is also developing. Which is why 'Peep-bo' is such a splendid game about now.

John Mother's there, and then suddenly she isn't! A little frisson of anxiety . . . and there she is again. The anxiety's relieved, gurgles of delight.

Robin And laughter. Which usually signals a release of tension.

John But as the baby gets older, his level of anxiety falls. . .?

Robin Because he's learning to do for himself what he previously had to rely on Mother to do.

John You mean his anxiety about separation is, crudely speaking, proportional to his dependence on his mother?

Robin Well, let's just say that the more he can mother himself, the less reason there is for anxiety.

John When you say 'can mother himself', are you thinking of practical mothering or emotional mothering?

Robin Both. He has to learn to do up his own buttons and feed himself . . . and also to give himself pleasure and support.

John You mean, tell himself that everything will be all right, or that he *can* do such and such if he really tries? I suddenly think of tennis players talking to themselves at crucial moments – 'Come on, Jim, you can do it.'

Robin Yes, a child will learn to reassure himself like that later on.

John But, until he can, any separation from his mother will make him anxious?

Robin It may *tend* to, but fortunately the baby has an equally natural desire to explore, to venture out into the world away from Mother. So at about nine months the baby starts crawling off to explore and finds it very enjoyable – provided only that he's had the love and emotional support that will give him the confidence to 'go solo' for a bit.

John But Mother still needs to stay pretty close in case he gets scared.

Robin Or so that he can crawl back and discover her again! And it's obviously important that the mother should encourage these adventures, give the baby the basic message: 'You can go when you want to, and come back when you need me.'

John But wait a moment. It's all fine if Mother's close by, because if baby gets anxious about the separation, she can come and reassure him. But the baby has to learn to become more independent. We're agreed that's desirable?

Robin Right.

John So he needs to be able to do without her sometimes. But that makes him anxious, so she has to come to reassure him.

But then he's *not* learning how to be independent. In other words, if the baby needs the mother to be *there* to help him do *without* her . . . well, we've got a Catch-22, haven't we? So what can the mother do to help the baby while she's not there?

Robin She can give him a transitional object.

John Well that's put a layman in his place.

Robin It's what we doctors call a teddy bear.

Permission to grow up. . . . . .

John Why is a teddy bear called a 'transitional object'?

Robin Because it helps a baby to make the transition between the point where he can't cope for long without some emotional support from his mother, to a position where he can start to get that emotional support from other people.

John How can it help the baby bridge that gap?

Robin Because it allows the baby to *transfer some of the powerful feelings* that have bound him so tightly to his mother *on to the object* instead. Which is any cuddly toy that's specially important for a child – something he carries everywhere and hugs as he goes to sleep.

John Like Linus's security blanket in *Peanuts*?

Robin Yes.

John Mine was a stuffed rabbit called Reggie. So the baby actually transfers some of his emotions on to the 'transitional object'.

Robin You can almost see this happening before your eyes when the mother gives the baby the stuffed rabbit or whatever. As she leaves, you can sense the way the baby moves part of his attachment behaviour on to the rabbit.

John So *that's* why these cuddly toys take on such an importance in the child's life. I never quite saw what that was about. And that begins about when?

Robin It happens at different times for different children – for most it begins during the second or even the third year. So now the baby has a kind of portable 'support-system' to help him manage the separation from his mother that's now under way.

John It's a kind of *substitute* for the mother?

Robin Yes, that's a very important *part* of what the transitional object helps to achieve. Often the first thing the baby uses is just a bit of sheet or blanket which goes into his mouth with the thumb, so it's associated with comfort and feeding. It *represents* the mother.

John And when he carries the blanket, or teddy, or stuffed rabbit, it's a reminder of the mother's availability, a 'memory-mother'.

Robin That's a good name for it because the child's *memory is still shaky* at this stage. Even after he can connect the different bits of the mother together to make a complete person, the picture of her is easily broken up again by a strong painful emotion. If she is away too long, he'll get in a rage, and the anger will destroy the image of her, like a jigsaw will be shaken up into pieces again if you bang the table too hard, *especially* if the jigsaw isn't finished. Then the child can't conjure up the picture of the absent mother to comfort himself. The stuffed rabbit, however, helps him to recall her image and that will help him not to get so upset. The child will be able to remember support that his mother gives him without her actually being there.

John You said that's only a *part* of it. What other uses does it have?

Robin Well, secondly, the baby will discover a lot about himself by playing on his own with the stuffed rabbit. If you watch a child playing with a 'transitional object', you'll see that he uses the object to stand for himself, while he plays the mother's part. When he does this, the baby is in a sense becoming the *mother, looking after* the stuffed rabbit.

John 'You're a good little rabbit' . . . or 'Don't do that, your Mummy doesn't like it.'

Robin Yes, when he can talk, he'll say things like that. So, he's finding out about his feelings, by projecting them into the toy. One minute the child plays at being the mother, caring for the toy, the next minute he makes the toy the mother and clings to it for support.

John So by alternating between the mother's role and the child's role, he's learning more about how it feels to be a mother . . . and as he understands his mother more, the other side of that coin must be that he understands *himself* better too. He's continuing to clarify his boundaries in a way, slowly sorting out what's going on between himself and Mum.

Robin That's it.

John It occurs to me that the fact that the rabbit is inanimate helps. The rabbit's not changing or reacting or having emotions itself, so that must help to clarify things.

Robin Go on.

John Well, take an emotion I have some confusions about – competitiveness. Sometimes I can be with someone and I'll suddenly realise that there's a lot of rivalry about, but it's very hard for me to know to what extent I'm providing that feeling and to what extent it's coming from the other person. The 'on-going interaction' – the continuous ebb and flow of the feeling – makes it hard for me to work out the boundary between my rivalry and theirs, even if I can sort it out later. So, by analogy, the fact that the rabbit's not a *variable* must help the baby's learning process.

Robin Yes, I think that's right. Incidentally, that's one reason – in fact I think it's the *main* reason – why the psychoanalytic technique works as it does. A patient with unclear boundaries will be able to clarify his own edges and disentangle which feelings really belong to him and which are imaginary, projected, because the analyst is 'keeping still', not reacting except for an occasional neutral comment.

John And presumably by 'playing with the mother's role', the baby's discovering how to be a mother and therefore how to mother, to look after, himself. Which is vital for the separating process.

Robin I believe so.

John So that's the second benefit from the transitional object. Is there anything else that this talented rabbit is achieving for the child?

Robin There is. And it's just as important as the other two, the security and the learning through play. In fact, it's almost more important. The rabbit is carrying a kind of message from the mother to the child. 'Permission to grow up.'

John You're sounding oracular.

Robin Well, remember all this is about the baby growing up – growing away from the stage where the mother is *all*-important, towards a later phase where the child can begin to transfer some of his attachment to others – father, brothers and sisters, and so on. Now, *if* the mother is happy for this to take place by giving the child the rabbit, and by her subsequent attitude to the rabbit, she's sending this vital message to the child.

John The message being, 'I am happy for you to grow away from me.' I think I see. By showing that *she's happy* for the baby to play with the rabbit when she's *not there*, she's telling the baby that it's fine to *enjoy himself* when she's not there; but at the same time there's a bit of her there, in the rabbit, to comfort the baby in her absence. It's a kind of solution to the Catch-22, isn't it?

Robin And I think the rabbit's carrying a further message which reads: 'And you can grow away from me at whatever pace you like – you don't have to go faster than you can comfortably manage. And, eventually, I can bear you to leave.'

John What, leave completely?

Robin Yes. It's saying, 'I want you to grow up and in the end not need me at all.'

John I'm sorry, I can see the rabbit's carrying the rest of the message but that last bit seems a bit fanciful.

Robin It seems to me it's just another way of putting the message we've already agreed about, carried to its logical conclusion.

John Well, you're the pundit. Now let me see if I've got this. Somewhere around six months the baby needs to start separating from his mother a little – that is, to move from being totally emotionally dependent on her to a position where he can get support from other people too. He finds that a transitional object helps him to do this, for several reasons. First, the baby can transfer some of his feelings for his mother on to the stuffed rabbit. So when he becomes anxious he can use the rabbit to remind himself of the comfort the mother gives him. Second, by playing with the rabbit, the baby can try out both mother and baby roles, which helps him to learn about being a mother, in other words how to mother himself . . . as well as to clarify his own edges by understanding his own mother better. And third, the fact that the mother approves of the baby playing with the rabbit carries the message that it's good for the baby to become more independent. In other words, this rabbit is a memory-mother, an edge-clarifier, a teacher of self-mothering and an independence-approver. No wonder they're the price they are.

Robin So as the baby begins to lose a little of his closeness with his mother, he feels supported and is learning to give himself support too. And that makes him feel relaxed. He'll gradually develop a confident and 'open' attitude towards all the changes he'll encounter as he grows up and away.

John It's the same with adults, isn't it? If we can remind ourselves of the sources of support that are available to us, it helps us deal with stress and stay more open to new possibilities. I suppose that's why people carry photos of their families with them, or rings and other objects of sentimental value, that

connect us with loved ones . . . and even crucifixes?

Robin They all help us to keep that internal feeling of confidence that we can handle the changes life throws at us, and keep moving on.

John Thinking about the baby's transition at this stage has given me another slant on why changes are stressful. It's because you can't move on to something new unless you let go of something old first. The baby can't start to enjoy Dad unless he's got a little freer from Mum. And he can't start to enjoy school until he can give up some of the delights of staying at home.

Robin That's right. You can't even have a really new idea till you've let go of an old one.

John . . . Maybe that's why thinking is hard work. Anyway, if you've got to let go before you can move on, you've got *two* possible sources of anxiety. First, the letting go – which means some sort of loss – which usually brings feelings of discomfort; and second, the fact that you're getting something *new*, which at best you don't know how much you can rely on, and at worst *may* be quite alarming. It's unfamiliarity that scares us rather than actual danger.

Robin True. And the anxiety is greatest when you're in between, not hanging on to the old any more, but without a secure grasp on the new. So this all explains why it's so vital for the baby at this stage to develop confidence that he can let go, trusting that what he's going to get instead will be all right – if not better. If he gets this confidence, he'll be able to handle life in an open and relaxed kind of way and keep growing.

John And if he doesn't, he can get stuck? Closed off, scared to try anything new, up-tight?

Robin That's right. If we've been given this confidence, we can face the world in an open, relaxed way. When we have to let go of something, we can do so because we have the confidence that we can handle the scary feelings that the loss will bring. But by allowing ourselves to go through that discomfort, we get free of the need for what we're leaving behind. Then, when we're confronted by something new, instead of being scared and having to close ourselves off from it, we can be open to the discovery that the new things are not dangers at all, but on the contrary are helpful and supportive to us.

John And if we *haven't* got through this stage properly, we don't want to let go of anything because we haven't the confidence that we can handle the feelings associated with losing it.

Robin So then, when we're in an unfamiliar situation we tend to tense up, to be on edge, on our guard. And while this is a perfectly natural way of protecting ourselves against real dangers, it's not an appropriate way to respond to something that's merely 'new'.

John It's like being at battle-stations, isn't it? You're on full alert and the frontiers are closed.

Hermione must be in an unusually relaxed, trusting mood.

Yes — no lance today.

Robin Exactly. So the child who isn't allowed support when he needs it – a transitional object to help him cope with separation, or a run back to his mother when he gets a scare – will have to use this 'battle-stations' way of protecting himself against too much change and stress. He's likely to become tense, holding on to himself tightly, rather mistrustful . . . as you said, 'up-tight'.

John So that he'll never give himself the chance to find that new things are not dangerous.

Robin Or of course that they'll provide him with new kinds of support that will gradually take the place of his mother's care, as he opens up to his father, brothers and sisters, friends, schoolmates, clubs and teams and groups, and eventually, of course, a lover.

John So the 'open and relaxed' attitude, and the 'closed-off and up-tight' one are two different ways of experiencing life.

Robin The first way will lead to growing and changing, and the second to staying 'stuck'.

John But surely most people experience *both* moods. I mean sometimes I feel relaxed so, even if there's a difficult situation to face, I can go into it with a very pleasant, almost detached curiosity about what's going to happen – and then because I'm more open to people, arguments get resolved rather easily. But if I'm stressed and in the 'battle-stations' mode, I'm more inflexible, so things don't get sorted out, there isn't the same happy compromising. The point is, I operate both ways, depending on mood.

Robin Fair enough. Even the most open person will put up the shutters if they've had a lot of stress without time to recharge their batteries, and even the most rigid will open up if given sufficient warmth. But people will tend to operate more in *one* way than the other most of the time.

The right track . . . . . .

John So you're saying that there are two tracks that we can take through life. One is the 'open, relaxed' track. The other's the 'closed, up-tight' one. And which track we find ourselves on is largely determined by how we and our mothers manage this separating phase between about six months and three years old?

Robin I believe that's right, though putting it that way makes the mother seem too responsible. You see, if she's stuck on the 'closed, up-tight' track, that's because her family was. She can't help it. And she won't easily be able to 'switch the points' to get her baby on the 'open, relaxed' track.

John To do that, she'd need considerable support from *outside*. Which isn't likely to come from her husband as she'll probably have chosen someone on the same track as herself.

Robin That's right. But this idea of the two tracks is so important with respect to the way people grow up as adults that I want to look at the mother/child relationship as it happens on each track. Let's take the 'healthy' track first. Here the mother – the normal mother – is what we call the 'good-enough' mother. You remember what characterises her?

John She can take care of herself. She's aware of her own needs and feels happy about satisfying them. So she hands the baby over to others when she needs a break, and can ask people for love and support when she needs it.

Robin That's right. So the result of all this is that she has *enough* love or emotional support or relaxation or confidence or whatever you want to call it. Now this has two results. First, as she's got enough for herself she can give to the baby, so the baby gets the emotional support he needs. And second, as she's got enough, she's not *dependent on the baby* for love and support. So she'll be able to let him go when he's ready.

John So she'll allow him his smelly bit of blanket, give him a stuffed rabbit. And that'll help him separate, not only because he connects it with love from his mother, but also because she *approves* of him having it. It shows that she wants him to be free of her when he's ready.

Robin So he's more secure, he's therefore more courageous, and able to enjoy taking a few risks. He won't need to get up-tight to close himself off from new experiences. So everything becomes more fun. Life is more enjoyable. The baby makes friends more quickly and has more support available when he needs it, even when Mum and the family aren't around to help. So he'll need his mother less, and later he'll need his family less. And that, incidentally, means he'll be able to *enjoy* them more.

John Why?

Robin Because when they're with him, he won't always be anxious that they might disappear. So worries like that won't spoil his enjoyment. He'll be much more able to cope with change and loss and stress of all kinds, and his life will not only be richer but will *go on* getting more rich and varied.

John So that's the healthy track. Whereas a mother on the other track can't be selfish in this healthy sort of way? She can't take what she needs.

Robin No. So she won't have enough. And if she hasn't got enough, then how can she possibly give? So the child will be short of emotional support to start with. And the second half of it is that as she hasn't got enough herself, she'll be dependent on the child for *his* love and support of *her*. She'll cling to him as he will be clinging to her. And so, even if she does give him a teddy or a rabbit, her *attitude* to it all is going to be *quite different*. She'll be possessive of the child and won't be happy about the stuffed rabbit getting all the attention and becoming almost as important as herself. It will seem too much like a rival!

John So the rabbit won't carry the message, 'I support you in growing away' and the baby won't be given the confidence to try to do so. In fact he's getting the opposite message.

Robin That's right. Now that's one way things can work on the 'unhealthy' track. But it happens another way if the mother's learned to *deny* her own needs for nurture.

John If she's put them behind the screen.

Robin Yes. Then she'll feel unhappy about *any* kind of clinging, whether its hers or the child's. She'll try to deny both their needs and will tend to push the child away if he does try to cling. So naturally she'll be embarrassed by the child clinging to the stuffed rabbit, especially as he gets older, so she'll discourage the child from playing with it too.

John So either way the child gets a negative message about the rabbit if the mother's on the unhealthy track.

Robin Yes, and as the child needs the mother's approval of the rabbit – that is, the *freedom to go* which the rabbit *stands for* – before it can help the child to grow away from her . . . well, the child simply can't do that. He'll remain stuck, very tied to her apron strings, a clinger.

John He's 'stuck' because he can't make the transition between Mother and the other sources of support in the world outside.

Robin So you find that children on this 'unhealthy' track hang around their mothers or any other source of security they can find.

John And yet they're not getting enough from their mothers. So even being with her isn't quite satisfactory.

CAN'T GO BACK TO
GET WHAT HE NEEDS...

Come and play!

...AND
FRIGHTENED
TO GO ON

Robin No. These children always seem to be wanting something, hoping for something. Yet they never seem to get much. So they're not very confident or open to new experience.

John The poor child doesn't know what to do, does he? I sense that the main emotion he feels is not sadness but more a feeling of being perplexed. And a little bit up-tight. Yes. He's frozen without knowing why.

Robin Of course, his puzzlement is even more complicated by the attitude of the outside world. Because pretty soon the other kids stop shouting, 'Come out and play' and start shouting different things, *especially* if the child's a boy.

So his puzzlement and distress is increased because he's now getting orders to leave his mother, without having any idea how to do it. And he's getting criticised and made fun of for being stuck where he is.

John If he and his Mum were left to themselves they might at least be able to cling together and get some mutual support, as I think girls traditionally can do with less criticism. They're just called 'home-bodies' or 'quiet'. The boy's a 'cissy'.

Robin Which complicates things for the boy because his unsatisfied desire to cling is now going to get shoved behind the screen because of all the outside disapproval.

John So *now* he even has to deny that he's stuck! So what can you do for a person who's stuck? How can you move them across to the other track – the more relaxed, confident way of functioning that will let them grow?

Robin It's not easy. Once a family gets on to either the healthy track or the unhealthy track, it's hard for them to switch across. That's fine if you're on the 'relaxed' track, of course, but a family on the 'up-tight' track is probably not going to be able to cross over without outside help.

John The family members can't help each other much because they're all functioning in the same way?

Robin Yes. That's why the parents chose each other in the first place. And of course all the children will grow up with the same unconscious attitudes. So the whole family's locked into the tense, fearful way of approaching life. That's how the family works – it's the family *system*.

John They *all* have difficulty being healthily selfish – taking what they need?

Robin Yes. And if one parent can't give himself or herself enough 'attention' or 'love', then everyone else has to hang around trying to do it for them.

John So families on the unhealthy track will all be clinging together.

Robin That's right. They're all 'stuck'. And these families are the ones which are more likely to produce people who suffer from the second big group of emotional illnesses – depressive illnesses.

John What was the first big group then?

Robin Illnesses connected with fuzzy-boundary problems – in the extreme cases, autism and schizophrenia.

John All right. Now I'm getting a bit lost. Let me try and sort it out. We saw how the baby can only grow up, become more independent, if he can grow away from his mother. If his mother's normal, 'good-enough', she'll approve of this. She'll give him a transitional object to aid his going solo; and her positive attitude to the transitional object will make the baby feel supported as he tries to learn to go it alone. This gives him the confidence to let go of previous attachments and move on to new things. And that means the baby will be on the 'healthy track'.

Robin So far so good.

John Now if the mother can't give herself what she needs . . . well, *first*, the baby's a bit short of support to start with; and *second*, the mother will need the baby's love, so deep down she *won't* like him becoming more independent. So even if she does give him a rabbit, it won't have the right message with it. So both ways the baby is failing to get the confidence he needs to let go and move on. So he's bound to finish up 'stuck', clinging, unable to become more independent of Mother. He's on the unhealthy track and more likely to grow into an adult who suffers from a depressive illness.

Robin Wordsworth could not have put it better.

John The poet in me sometimes craves expression. But prithee, why do you say 'depressive illnesses'? Why not just 'depression'?

Sadness – and worse . . . . . .

Robin Straightforward depression is only one kind of 'depressive illness'. There are many others, called 'depressive equivalents', which means that the depression has been covered over and is being expressed in disguised ways.

John Like psychosomatic illnesses?

Robin Yes, for example where there's pain – genuine pain – but there's no physical cause for it. But in many other ways too, like eating problems, alcoholism, many phobias, worrying unnecessarily about one's health . . . there are so many . . .

John But they can all be disguised depression.

Robin Yes. When you look into them, you find they've been brought on by the kinds of events or upbringing that you'd expect to cause depression. And incidentally they can't be treated properly unless the hidden depression is recognised as such, and relieved.

John So what is depression, Doctor?

Robin Well I need to start by pointing out a fundamental difference – the difference between depression and sadness.

John I see. People usually use them interchangeably.

Robin Do you?

John A lot of the time. Partly because saying, 'I'm depressed today' sounds less dramatic than, 'I'm sad today.' But I think 'depression' to me means feeling rather dead inside, whereas sadness is something to do with feeling the emotion more fully.

Robin Well let's examine it, because I think the difference is crucial, and we lose a lot of understanding by confusing them. Now you pointed out earlier that a person can't 'move on' without leaving something behind. In other words, without suffering a loss. So how do we react to loss? If a lover leaves us, or someone close to us dies, or we lose a job?

John I think there's always a quick flash of pain. But then we often cover that up with anger, feelings of resentment towards people who are 'responsible', to numb the pain, I suspect.

Robin But after a time these feelings die down and we get 'the blues'. We feel sad.

John We feel the real pain.

Robin Which will last for a certain natural time. But then, if we're reasonably healthy, we let ourselves go through that and we get better. We start cheering up and getting over it. We can begin to leave whatever we've lost behind, and to turn our attention to something else.

John And the reason is that we've allowed ourselves to be miserable?

Robin *Exactly*. Because we've mourned whatever we've lost, we can let go of it and move on.

John But if you don't mourn it fully, you can't let go of it.

Robin That's right. The feeling of loss will hang around indefinitely, and you *won't* feel really free to move on.

John You said once in talking about healthy families that what you found so surprising when you first discovered the research about them was the ease, the naturalness, with which healthy people remarried if they lost a spouse.

Robin That's right. They mourned *very* fully and deeply. And *because* they could allow themselves to go *so thoroughly* through the process they were able to recover from the loss much more rapidly than most of us. Then they could go on and rebuild their lives again.

John So mourning – really *feeling* the pain of the loss – is not just natural, it actually accomplishes something.

Robin Yes. We have to allow the old connections to come apart before we can reorganise ourselves to fit the new situation. Like dismantling a house before rebuilding it. And *that's* what I mean by 'sadness'.

John Yes, I think the idea that sadness was actually *useful* was probably the most important, and for me the most surprising, single thing that I learnt when I was in your group. Up to then I'd always felt that being sad was a waste of time. As well as very self-indulgent. I'd feel, 'What are *you* feeling sad for when there are millions starving in India?' Or, 'Why can't I stop feeling sad and go out and enjoy myself?' It always seemed so *pointless*. But in your group I learned not only that being sad was 'all right', but also that it *accomplished something*. Which of course helps one to go through it more fully and get rid of it quicker.

Robin And of course people are often immensely relieved to learn that feeling sadness is a completely *healthy* reaction.

John But why should we feel that it isn't? Is it because people who have repressed sadness, put it behind the screen and denied it, would have to disapprove of it?

Robin Hold your horses, we're coming on to that. For the moment just remember that what we've been saying about big losses is obviously true for small losses, except that the anger and sadness is much less and therefore overcome much more quickly.

John So if West Ham lose it takes me an hour to recover,

Fulham takes about three minutes and Arsenal 0.0006 of a second.

Robin Very graphic. Now let's apply this idea to the mother and child. This stage of development is all about the child learning to separate. Every time he separates just a tiny bit more, he'll have to cope with a small loss. He'll have to get sad for a little bit. And this is healthy and natural. It's these little moments of sadness and anxiety that are helping the child to separate.

John If he doesn't go through these painful moments, he can't let go of his Mum a bit at a time.

Robin Right. So the mother has to be able to bear to watch a certain amount of anxiety and sadness in the child, when it's part of a change towards being more independent. Of course, she'll judge it. If the child's very upset, then of course she must go in to relieve the distress. But if she senses it's just a 'growing pain', then she'll not dash in, she'll be able to hold back and watch to see if the child can handle it.

John So she shouldn't rush in to relieve every little discomfort.

Robin Not when the child has reached this stage when he's learning to be a little more independent of her. Now, going back to our two tracks . . . the healthy, 'good-enough' mother senses this, so she can let her child struggle a bit with the distress, 'go through it' a little while she stands by just in case he can't cope.

John It's quite a delicate bit of judgement, isn't it?

Robin She only has to get it more or less right, over a period of time. There's no tearing hurry about it. She'll make mistakes, but she'll gradually correct them. In the long run, most mothers can sense the difference between real distress and wingeing, 'trying it on', especially as the child gets older. And if she manages to get this right, more or less, the child will become more resourceful and confident by slow degrees – she's helping him slowly to lose his utter dependence on her.

John So what you're saying is that if the mother *can't* bear to do this, if she dashes right in to relieve the child's distress *every* single time he shows any, even as he grows older, there's no way that he can learn to let go of her, step by step. She stops the child from mourning the little bit of closeness he's just lost.

Robin That's it! She never lets it happen. So if the Mum isn't taking what *she* needs, she'll be a bit anxious and depressed herself, and this may make her over-sensitive to the child's pain. So, on the unhealthy track, the mother tends to rush in too quickly to relieve the child just when he's having a little *normal*, healthy sadness caused by taking a small step away from her. So the child can't now make the jump. He'll keep going back to where he was. She's stopped the process.

John In a sense the child is not getting a chance to learn how to *cope* with sadness – how to allow himself to feel the sadness and go right through it, without being panicked by it.

Robin Now we're getting on to depression.

John *Olé.*

Robin Because if this happens a few times – if the Mum always dashes in at the first sign of distress – the child learns, *not* how to let himself feel sadness and go through it, but the opposite. He learns how to *stop* feeling that discomfort by sending out distress-signals that Mum can't resist.

John So he's learning how to *avoid* coping with sadness, so that he won't be able to handle loss. So the child can't grow up.

Robin Correct. The healthy sadness which would allow him to separate a little at a time, automatically, instead brings the mother in on a rescue bid. And the child learns – as automatically as a dog learns to sit up if it gets a dog biscuit each time it does so – to fit in with this behaviour. He forms the habit of making a miserable face whenever anything is a tiny little bit difficult, *long before* there's any real suffering. So he's always getting the mother to remove the stress he really needs to learn to cope with. And as long as the mother responds to the 'stop it for me, Mum' face by rescuing the child from his difficulty, the pattern will get more and more deeply ingrained, more and more of a habit, and therefore more and more difficult to change.

John It's a kind of malingering?

Robin No. Not at all. That would mean the child knew what he was doing.

John No, I meant *unconscious* malingering.

Robin He's quite unaware of what he's doing. And the pattern is learned so early that as the child gets older he thinks it's quite natural to feel as he does. He thinks, 'I can't help it', and that's true – he can't imagine that there's any other way of doing it *at all*. Because he's never been taught any other way. So I think 'malingering' is quite the wrong word.

John Let's put it like this. He's sending out 'Help, I feel terrible' messages without really feeling very terrible.

Robin That's it. He's giving off all sorts of miserable, complaining sadness-signals, but he's never given the chance to go on and let himself actually *feel* that sadness.

John But he's feeling *something* he's not enjoying much.

Robin True, but it's a quite different experience from the sadness he's avoiding.

John . . . You mean what the child is experiencing is *depression*.

Robin *Olé.*

John Or rather, what *you* call depression, O Fount of All Wisdom.

Robin Well, let's compare the experiences themselves. If you try to recall what it feels like when we're sad, it's a rich, deep emotion. And it makes us feel very alive, even though it hurts. We don't feel cut off from the world – on the contrary, we're strongly in touch with what's going on round us.

John And you feel, in a way, 'full' – you're in your body and aware of it, as well as of what's going on around you. Also you don't seem to be struggling against anything. When I feel like this I seem to accept what's happening, so I stay open and I'm aware there's a lot of support around. And although it's painful, it's somehow tolerable because you do feel so alive.

Robin I think this is why most of us feel so alive and full after watching a tragic play or film that really grips us. On the other hand, if you try to cut yourself off from this feeling, you're left with deadness, emptiness, a lack of life and a lack of real emotional connection with other people.

John Well that's how I felt a lot of the time a few years ago. Life seemed almost pointless. I felt very cut off from everything – including my body. I carried a lot of muscular tension which must explain that. And because I felt closed off from what was going on around me, I felt rather isolated. The feeling, as you say, was of a kind of deadness. And emptiness too. Also, I seemed to be fighting the feeling instead of accepting it. So just getting through life was a struggle. And the sense of humour was an early casualty. In fact when I began to be able to laugh at it all, it began to clear. Of course the other thing you notice is a feeling of weight pressing down on you. I suppose that's where the word comes from.

Robin Yes, the posture of someone who's depressed gives that impression.

John What surprises me now, talking about it, was that I *didn't* realise that I wasn't *sad*. In fact I remember watching a TV programme about depression with Spike Milligan and Olivier Todd, and someone pointed out that they weren't actually feeling sad when they were depressed, and I had to go away and think about it. But why should I not have seen the difference before? Is it just the way we use the words interchangeably?

Robin I think so. It would be much clearer if everyone used the word 'depression' in the limited sense that psychiatrists do. It helps us not to confuse the two experiences.

John But do you think people would agree with the way we're describing these feelings?

Robin Most people, yes. I've heard the same descriptions over the years, and the 'feeling dead' or 'feeling alive' always seems to be the key difference. Don't forget that the whole purpose of depression is to *avoid* feeling sadness. And you *can't* choose to stop feeling one emotion without cutting all the others off too. So if you cut off sadness, you cut off all your other emotions. And when your emotions go dead, *you* go dead. So it's hardly surprising one doesn't feel like doing anything when one's in this mood.

John And there's another difference I'm aware of, too. If I'm feeling sad I can say to someone, 'I'm sad but I'm fine.' And I can be with them and enjoy them without feeling that I need anything from them, except perhaps simple contact. But when I was depressed, I think *deep down* I was expecting someone else to change it for me, and in an absurd way feeling resentful that they weren't!

Robin Think of Basil Fawlty. He's depressed all the time, isn't he? Though he could never admit it. He spends his life sending out signals to everyone else that it's their fault for making his life so difficult.

John And we don't blame others in that way when we're *sad*. Does that mean that *complaining* is a sign of *depression*?

Robin Yes, most communications by depressives, even if they're disguised, have that 'nobody loves me', 'this shouldn't be happening to me', 'somebody should be putting it right' quality.

John Well, if you've been trained to put on the 'sad face', to make mother put things right for you, and she *doesn't* . . . presumably a part of you feels like blaming her for failing you. So that's why you'd be giving off a general air of complaint that *somebody* isn't putting your life right for you.

Robin And of course if you're sitting around, waiting for someone else to put your life right for you, you're going to be stuck.

John So this is another way of explaining why people on the unhealthy track can't move on. But what can move them on? What can get them across to the 'healthy' track?

Robin You've got to find a way of helping them realise they're sending out signals to *other* people to change things for them, and instead get *them* to change things themselves.

John How can they do that?

Robin Only by getting in touch with their sad feelings. And they'll need help to do that because that's exactly what they've been trained not to do.

Switching tracks . . . . . .

John Looking at all this in terms of the 'unhealthy track' mother and her child . . . you could say that the child's sad face and distressed behaviour has *stopped* being a *sign* that he's coping

with some necessary change . . . and *become* a *signal* to others to remove the stress.

Robin That's quite a neat way of putting it, yes. But if you talk about 'signals', that might give the impression that the whole thing happens much more consciously than it does. The mother doesn't observe the reaction, note it, and make a decision to act on it. Any more than the child makes a decision to send the signal. It's all much more automatic than that.

John Neither of them has the slightest idea why they're doing it.

Robin Or even *what* they're doing. It's like a washing machine just doing what it's programmed to do. And of course it's not just the mother. It's the father and the children too, the *whole* family who are operating in this way. Because as usual it's a family pattern that has been passed on over generations to both the parents. So everyone in the family will be stuck in this way even if they pretend they're not.

John How do they 'pretend'?

Robin Well, Mother may seem to be too indulgent and Father may look to outsiders as if he's critical of this. He may sometimes tell her to 'stop spoiling the child'. *But* when you look more closely at the family while they talk to you *together*, you soon find that he's simply jealous and wants to be 'spoiled' like that too. So he can't really help. So whichever way it is, whether the father is also obviously needy or denying his needs, the child learns to escape from stress by switching on his helpless, inadequate, suffering face.

John So if this is all happening so automatically, the *whole process* is 'behind the screen'?

Robin Yes, it's behind everyone's screen in that kind of family, not just the person who's complaining of symptoms at a particular time. So it needs someone from *outside the family system* to help them see what's going on and accept the sadness behind the screen so they can get free of the pattern.

John Friends perhaps?

Robin Possibly, if the tendency's mild. But if it's severe, deeply ingrained, that's not very likely. You see, the person who's learned this pattern of behaviour from his mother will tend to choose friends like himself – who won't confront him about his behaviour.

John Just as they'll marry someone who will have learned in *their* family to obey the signals automatically.

Robin So it's a bit unlikely that someone who can do what's necessary is going to arrive by chance.

John Well, what is necessary?

Robin You've got to do several things simultaneously with someone like this. You have to put them into a situation where the sad face *doesn't get the pay-off*; and at the same time where the reason for the 'sad-face' signal is *understood* and not condemned; and where *emotional support is offered* to help them begin to feel the sadness.

John Hang on. I need to take them one at a time. The sad face mustn't get the pay-off. What's the pay-off?

Robin Quite simply someone dashing in and saying, 'You don't have to face up to difficult experiences that upset you.'

John In other words, putting it crudely, the therapist has to say, 'You need to face up to painful things in life, even though they make you sad.'

Robin *Very* crudely, yes.

John And next, the reason for the sad face has to be understood, not condemned?

Robin That means it's got to be conveyed to the person that it's *'all right'* for him to have the sad feelings, it doesn't make him a 'baby'.

John That helps to get the feelings out from behind the screen, so he can deal with them.

Robin Right. So he can feel them. That's all he has to do.

John But as he's never done that, the prospect must be very frightening to him. So that's why he needs emotional support.

Robin Yes, and giving that is as important as the other two things.

John Of course the person on the healthy track has been getting rid of the various sadnesses that have come from all his many small losses by feeling them at the time. To take a silly example, if it takes 1,000 sadness units to separate from Mum, the healthy-track child has been able to do them one at a time. So each loss is small and manageable. But the person on the unhealthy track has got all those units piled up there behind the barrier.

Robin And, in fact, any later losses he's suffered may add to that total, making him even more apprehensive about getting in touch with such feelings. Of course, once he starts to feel the sadness, he is not going to feel it all at once, it can be let out a bit at a time. But he certainly senses how much there is stored up there and is often scared he may be overwhelmed by the feelings if he stops avoiding them. Which is why, as I say, giving steady support to the person is just as important as not giving him the pay-off, the automatic family response he's used to.

John It was a revelation to me when I began to get an understanding of this in your group. I think before that, when I'd been with someone who was depressed, I'd felt there were only two possible responses to it. One was to get sucked into it, to be pulled into the 'Oh poor diddums' routine, feeling no doubt that one was being wonderfully loving and supportive by just agreeing with everything the other person said – giving them the pay-off as you put it. On the other hand, if I was in a different mood, possibly if I was depressed myself, I'd adopt the brisk British 'pour yourself a Scotch and pull yourself together' approach. I don't think it had ever occurred to me that you could quite simply sit with someone and say, 'Yes, this is very difficult for you and you have some unpleasant feelings to cope with. So I'll just sit here and be with you while that's going on.' I remember now that after one of my relationships broke up, the girl told me that when she was depressed I could never 'just be with her'. I didn't understand at the time but I hope I do now.

Robin This depressive pattern was certainly strong in my family and I took a long time to see what was really required to help people change this pattern. Of course, it's easier to give people this experience in a calm, supportive, neutral way if it's just a professional relationship, because your own feelings aren't so involved. With people you're close to it's obviously harder to keep that balance of support and firmness.

John Your own needs get in the way!

Severe depression......

John What about really severe depression? I've often heard it's supposed to be chemical in origin rather than psychological, and that consequently it can be helped only by drugs.

Robin Well, we're all *made* of chemicals. Everything that happens in us involves chemical changes, doesn't it? If you see a pretty girl, or observe a bus bearing down on you as you're crossing the road, or if you get angry with someone, there'll be chemical changes in your blood. So, of course, it's possible to interfere with some of these reactions at the chemical level. So some kinds of depression can be relieved that way. In fact drugs are particularly helpful as a *temporary measure to undo a vicious circle* of chemical changes that occurs in severe depression when these interfere with the patient's ability to cooperate and think clearly to the point where psychotherapy is useless and life may even be in danger. But, of course, taking chemicals doesn't change the personality, it doesn't alter these underlying automatic patterns we've been talking about. So these patterns go on causing the body to produce the same chemicals which the drugs are intended to counteract. But if you can change the *automatic pattern of reaction*, the person may not get depressed again in the same way or need drugs at all.

John Even with the worst depressions?

Robin It's hard to say because so many cases which were previously treatable only by drugs are now responding to the new family methods of therapy all over the world. And more effective methods are being discovered all the time, so we can't really say for certain that even cases we can't reach now won't be curable by these means a year hence. But certainly at present, and maybe for a long time to come, drugs, professional support and hospitalisation – with electro-convulsive therapy for cases where everything else fails – are often the only practical remedies for the most severe depressive conditions.

John What do you think is the reason why some depressives are worse than others and consequently harder to help?

Robin There are different views about it. But the one that makes most sense to me, and works in practice, is that people with depressions of different severity are stuck at different points in this period from six months onwards, when separation is the task to be coped with. Someone who's got only a short distance through this process is likely to be more severely handicapped and harder to treat.

John So if the child gets stuck when he's only just begun to get his boundaries sorted out, only just begun to glimpse his mother sometimes as a separate, whole person, he'll be more . . . vulnerable?

Robin Yes, if his boundaries are still slightly fuzzy and easily dissolved, someone at this level can lose touch with reality again more easily under stress. The loss of something vitally important to that person – it may be a loved one, an ambition, or some idea about himself that made him feel good – produces more pain, distress, and anger than he can cope with. He hasn't reached the point where he can hold on to good memories of people he loves and of happy times in order to counteract the pain and keep his balance. So the present pain seems even worse and, sometimes, the only way he can cope with it is to go back down the developmental ladder and use the safety-valve device of the earlier stage where the painful feelings are projected on to the outside world and into others. Or he may even go right back to the stage where he thinks he can control the world.

John He can regress all the way back to paranoia and even schizophrenia?

Robin Yes, in some ways he can slip right back to these earlier stages and develop that kind of 'insanity', with delusions or hallucinations and all the rest of it.

John But if he's got a bit *further* in this separation phase . . .

Robin Well, then he can hold his memories of good experiences together in his mind despite the distress caused by a serious loss, and that'll help him to hold on to his 'depressive' position and *not* retreat. Also, as he's more advanced, there's more of a grown-up personality both to cope with the problems *and* for the therapist to work with if the person comes in for treatment.

John Is there any evidence that the really severe depressive illnesses are genetically transmitted?

Robin Yes. I think most people would agree these days that at least some *vulnerability* is probably passed down by heredity, and there seem to be differences in that inherited influence in different types of depression. This vulnerability could make particular families or family members more sensitive to certain stresses, and more likely to develop the different kinds of automatic patterns we've talked about.

John And where does manic-depression fit in all this – where the mood swings go right up as well as down?

Robin A lot of doctors think that's just an inherited disease, but there's quite a lot of evidence of environmental factors too. At the moment we just don't really know how they're connected.

John But where does it come on the spectrum?

Robin I would put the manic-depressive personality down towards the earlier end, next to paranoia, in terms of the clarity of boundaries and the degree of separation achieved. And I see mania in the same way as most analysts, as an even less adult way of operating than ordinary depression; in fact as a defence against it.

John That would put mania *in between* depression and paranoia.

Robin That's right. In fact, it makes use of *some* of the features of the stage which can lead to schizophrenia or paranoia – fuzzier boundaries, loss of touch with reality, keeping the good and bad feelings apart and projecting unpleasant ones outside. But it's done in a much more sophisticated way because in some ways the manic-depressive has progressed past that stage.

John It sounds almost like an emergency retreat back towards paranoia, but going only half-way.

Robin Yes. It tends to be triggered by loss, as a defence measure against severe depression.

John But mania is almost the opposite of depression, isn't it? If a person's manic, they're wildly over-optimistic, as opposed to being depressed and over-pessimistic.

Robin That's right. In a manic mood, a person's behaviour is closer to our own experience of being excited or triumphant, 'up in the air'. They've lost contact with the ground, as it were, so they become tremendously expansive and feel very big and powerful, and start all kinds of over-ambitious projects.

John And spend a lot of money that they don't have but are *certain* they're going to earn shortly.

Robin That's right. They feel unrealistically in control of things. And so they're quite hard for others to control!

John It's a bit like going back to being a big balloon, isn't it?

Robin Yes, but there is a difference here between mania and schizophrenia. Unless, of course, they do reverse right back into schizophrenia. An ordinary manic-depressive in the manic phase is much more rational and understandable than the schizophrenic.

John They're more in contact with reality at some level?

Robin Yes. It's as if the schizophrenic has *never* been brought down to size so he *still* thinks he *is* a big balloon. The manic, on the other hand, has discovered earlier that he isn't able to control everything – he's had to face this and learn that lesson – but he's desperately trying to *pretend* he's a big balloon. And *as he knows* deep down this isn't the case, eventually the balloon goes pop . . . and he shrinks down to being depressed again.

John The manic phases can last for months, can't they?

Robin They can, yes. Sometimes there's a rhythm to the swings but more often it's hard to see any pattern at all. However, people who've studied this have found that a stress, usually a loss of something important, triggers the swing, either up *or* down.

John All right. Finally, what about the cases up at the milder end of the range? Presumably such folk suffer much milder depression, but fairly continuously.

Robin Yes, they have better-developed personalities and don't seem very abnormal. They've just had parents who've protected them a bit too much against ordinary stresses so they've developed a strong habit of feeling hurt and wounded if things get difficult. And, of course, as families they'll tend to cling together more than healthy-track families.

John So that's the depression spectrum, is it? Down the severe end, the person may even reverse to paranoia or schizophrenia under severe stress and will in any case find it very hard to function in ordinary life. Then, less severe than that because they're more in contact with reality, is the manic-depressive who has bouts of feeling wildly elated and over-optimistic alternating with bouts of depression. And towards the milder end of the spectrum, you have people who can function in life but who just aren't having much fun.

Robin That's roughly it.

John So what about treatment? What can you do about the more severe cases?

Robin Well, the more severe the case, the more likely it is that you'll need drugs to help some members to get out of their really acute episodes, and also that you'll need the whole family present to achieve an effective cure.

John And the milder cases?

Robin Well the prognosis for psychological treatment of these is very good indeed. *If* they come for treatment! Remember, people like this can be *very* successful in life. The fact that they've got to be loved and approved of makes them very hard workers, people who sacrifice themselves for the company, the organisation, and so on.

John And for their families.

Robin Yes, that's part of the problem! As you remember, they can't take for themselves. So being rather stuck, not only to their family but to other groups with whom they come in contact, makes them loyal and reliable and sometimes painfully conscientious. *Pain*staking. So they may go far and get big rewards.

John And ulcers. I remember that all the people in the group I attended were near the top of their professions, including *all* the wives. It was just that they never seemed to be able to enjoy themselves, partly because they were so dependent on their spouses. In families like this, there's a lot of clinging, isn't there?

Robin Even if it's disguised, yes.

John But since no one's able to take in a healthy way for himself or herself . . . well, that must mean, as you've said a million times, that they haven't much to give. So what *are* they getting from each other by clinging together?

Robin What they're getting is the best compromise they can manage. Given that everyone has the same difficulties in relationships, is stuck at the same level, they fit together better than they would fit in a normal situation. It isn't as good as it might be but they're giving each other as much as they can. The system works after a fashion, as long as there's no severe loss like a death, or some other kind of separation or major change. It's more precariously balanced than a normal family, more easily thrown into a crisis where the system breaks down. That's why the big, extended family of the past was so good and why the present nuclear family 'hot-house' can cause such problems.

Nobody's perfect . . . . . .

John Many of the symptoms of depression you've been describing are things I recognise in myself. Although I don't
nowadays get anything like the prolonged and quite deep
depressions that I used to get seven or eight years ago, I can still
see echoes of these symptoms in my behaviour when I'm in
certain moods. For example, if someone says something hurtful,
then, rather than relaxing and feeling the momentary loss of
self-esteem, I often catch myself tightening up in order to avoid
doing that. Or if I'm under heavy work pressure, I'm not good
at taking periods off to 'give to myself'. I tend to stay at the
grindstone, which again involves tightening up and losing
awareness of my body and the world around. And then I
sometimes start developing the attitude that I dislike most in
myself, a resentment of the Supreme Being for deliberately
playing a cosmic practical joke on me by making things go
wrong. And I know a lot of my friends have similar 'depressive'
reactions to stress. The point of this interminable preamble is to
ask . . . what about you?

Robin Well, when I began working as a child psychiatrist, I
used to joke to colleagues that if I was any good at the job it
was mainly because between everyone in my family we seemed
to have had a *bit* of just about everything going – so I knew it all
at first-hand! Partly that was the usual medical student's disease
of imagining he's suffering from whatever illnesses he has just
been reading about, but there was obviously a lot of truth in it
too. At first I thought I was unusual in this respect, but later,
when I joined a therapy group as part of my training, I found
on closer inspection that the other trainees seemed to have as
many problems in their families as I had in mine. After
understanding a bit more about myself, I realised with hindsight
that I had come into the profession to help myself as much as to
help others, and that maybe I was also, without anyone realising
it, sent on a mission by my family to rescue them too. Luckily,
this is the one job where you can turn such difficulties to
advantage.

John What about politics?

Robin Maybe. But in mine, if you acknowledge that you need

help, you can *also* get some for yourself, and maybe sort things out to some extent.

The other day, I turned up an old tape-recording of the first big family therapy conference held in Britain. It was back in 1973, and for the first time, encouraged by visiting American family therapists from the Ackerman Institute in New York, we all got involved in role-playing. That is, play-acting scenes from our own families, as well as our patient families, in order to understand them better. It's interesting to see the seeds of this book there in what I said at the final session:

> One of the most valuable things I've got from this conference is to become connected up with my own family. This is something I knew I needed and didn't know how to achieve. But I've realised that the families I've seen presented here *are* all *my* family – that we've been watching the same family all the time.
>
> Each time, we see an uncertain *mother*, who hasn't had a secure base from which she can venture out. So she still has an ambivalent attachment to *her* mother and is looking for *nurture* from her husband and children but is defending herself against realising this by giving it to others instead, regardless of their needs for autonomy. And she's depressed, naturally, because she hasn't got past that stage.
>
> And each time these families seem to have a *father* who had a bad relationship with *his* father and couldn't escape from the need for *his* mother, and who is angry, impotent, opting-out and excluded.

The couple aren't having a good sexual relationship because they haven't got to that stage yet in their development, and they are still looking for parents to look after them instead. Until they get that parenting, which they obviously can't get enough of from each other, they can't go to bed and fully enjoy each other. And the children are all following the same pattern. Because of this, the parents feel very impotent; and because of that, they're trying to be *omnipotent* and trying too hard to bring up the children properly.

Seeing this same pattern being presented in the role-plays not just of patient families but of families of colleagues, I wonder if I'm like the man who goes outside in the garden, sees the moon, and thinks the moon is shining just for *him*. Maybe everyone here is seeing that same moon, the same family, their *own* family. Maybe there's only one family, the *human* family, and there are just different ways in which we get stuck or pushed off course.

John So I suppose it's not unreasonable to assume that a lot of people reading this will identify with some of the behaviour, or at least identify their own families or friends.

Robin Yes, I think a great many of them will, even if the behaviour they recognise is a very mild version of what I've described.

John And if they don't recognise anything?

Robin Well, then they're *completely* clear of this phase in a way that, I believe, only a smallish proportion of people ever achieve.

John But, of course, there are always the ones who think they're clear of it and who aren't.

Robin Well, they'll be able to recognise themselves if they *want to*.

John How?

Robin They'll find they get strangely cross reading this for reasons they won't quite be able to put a finger on.

John Very glib, Doctor, very glib. But you must get people like this in therapy sometimes – people who just get angry and defensive when you suggest *they* might have needs they're not satisfying.

Robin In fact, it's even more difficult with those who skillfully provoke *you* if you get near their feelings of sadness, instead of getting angry themselves. I remember one chap who used to wind me up successfully every time he came – a borderline, paranoid personality, who'd had lots of therapy but whom I'd agreed to see occasionally because his previous therapist had died. He would come along every few months, lay out a lot of books on the table – *Winnie the Pooh*, Freud's *Interpretation of Dreams*, *Alice in Wonderland*, Melanie Klein's *Envy and Gratitude*, or whatever – and he'd talk about what he'd understood while I would try to figure out the message I was supposed to get. I usually felt irritated, and that I had been unhelpful, but he kept coming back and he seemed to change slowly for the better. One day, along with the books, he brought an enormous paper bag from which he carefully extracted a giant white stuffed rabbit two or three feet high which he placed on the table with the books. However, this rabbit kept falling on its back, so I got more and more books off the shelves to support it till finally it sat upright, though he kept telling me not to bother. In the interview that followed he *really* got me going. I felt so irritated I decided we were wasting each other's time, though I didn't say so. To my surprise he looked very pleased as he left, gathering up his books and putting this great rabbit back in the bag. 'Thank you so much,' he said, 'for what you did for the *rabbit!*'

John You mean he couldn't ask for himself, but when you supported his rabbit he felt you'd supported *him*.

Robin I think so. It was the nearest he could come to asking for help. And he had cued me in some way so that, even though I hadn't been aware of it, I had intuitively responded to his need in the only way he could cope with. And I also realised afterwards that he had probably cued me to get angry too, to make him feel safely distanced from any concern he was evoking.

John ... I've been thinking about what the transitional object does for the child – providing support, while at the same time carrying the message that Mother's not going to come rushing in unnecessarily – and comparing this with your behaviour when you're treating depressives, and I've come to the conclusion that professionally speaking *you* are nothing more than a stuffed rabbit.

Robin But you've no idea how difficult it is to be a *good* one.

John Perhaps it'd be easier if you got stuffed.

4 Who's in Charge Here?

Shall I be an angel, Mummy?......

John What's the next group of ideas you want to take?

Robin Rather an interesting batch. Attitudes to authority, why people conform or rebel, how strict parents need to be, what jobs the father's vital for, why some people are good team members and others, with big 'egos', won't fit in, why children misbehave or get ill to keep their parents together, obsessions, toddlers' tantrums, why it's good for parents to fight sometimes, and the Garden of Eden.

John Oh, is that all? And these all come next presumably because they're to do with the next stage of development of the baby.

Robin The baby's becoming a toddler, that's the point.

John The baby was more or less helpless . . .

Robin More or less. But the brain's been growing and the nerve cells have been connecting up with each other and with the muscles. Now, *somewhere* between one and two, the toddler starts to walk on his own and to produce his first real words.

John And what about his 'natural functions', as we call them in Weston-super-Mare?

Robin Well the 'wiring' connecting the bladder and bowels to the brain has been getting completed. So that these functions can now be switched on and off when the toddler wants, instead of just happening automatically. And at about one and a half the toddler shows clear signs of being able to think for himself.

John Poor parents! Before he could only express dissent by howling or refusing his food.

Robin Or getting ill. But now his options are endless. He can come when he's called, or run away! He can say 'Yes' *and* 'No'.

He can throw things and knock them over although Mummy doesn't like it. And when he's put on the pot, he can do his duty or perform at a less convenient moment. And as he gets more active the parents begin to show him what they like and what they don't like.

John They're beginning to make demands on him, because he's beginning to be able to *choose* what he's going to do.

Robin Exactly. He's getting some real independence and freedom so he's having to start to face the choice between 'Good' and 'Evil'!

John Evil is now available in many exciting new varieties. So this is why we get the tantrums now, at this stage.

Robin Yes. Of course he's just testing his strength finding out all the new things he can do. And if he encounters an obstacle, he'll push and struggle to overcome it. And sometimes the parents will be that obstacle!

John In a way he's just experimenting.

Robin Yes. Sometimes the parents think they're doing something wrong, that they're failing the child in some way. They're not. Tantrums are normal.

John Why are they so violent?

Robin Well, look at it positively. The force of the tantrums is a kind of measure of the strength of character the child can possess eventually, *if* he's helped to harness that energy. The

violence is due to the fierceness of the self-will that's being blocked. Think of it as the energy that powers the space rocket away from earth. And the tantrums as those early rockets blowing up on the launch pad or exploding after take-off, before they'd discovered how to control all that energy and make the rocket go where they wanted.

John It had never struck me that a tantrum starts with energy and not with anger. It explains why anger can be such a good source of energy, doesn't it? If I'm struggling with some writing problem and get stuck and then get angry with myself . . . I can use that anger as extra energy to keep battering away at the problem, often for longer than I could have done if I hadn't felt so frustrated in the first place.

Robin That's what the child has to learn – to control the tantrums so he can ride all this wonderful new energy, as a good rider manages a horse, letting it run but controlling its direction. The tantrums stop when the child learns to handle this energy and make it *work for him.*

John It's just a matter of time before he learns how to do this?

Robin Yes. Provided the parents realise that it's perfectly normal, they'll be able to be calm and firm with him and he'll learn to control it naturally.

John So the toddler's got all these new physical skills and he's becoming able to think for himself . . . so what's he got to learn at this stage?

Robin How to fit in with others; first with his family, and eventually with the rest of society.

John Because if he doesn't . . . he'll lose the affection, support and help from other people which he'll certainly need.

Robin And in any case his life will be much more rewarding and interesting if he's able to get on well with others.

John So he's got to learn to choose to be 'good'.

Robin No.

John No?!

Robin Well, you see, it's no use his *just* being 'good'. If he's going to develop into a healthy, independent, self-reliant sort of person with a mind of his own, he's got at this stage to begin doing things for himself, creatively, things that are quite original for him. Things that his parents won't be able to predict. And sometimes *won't like.*

John So he's got to be confident enough to explore *and at the same time* . . . learn how to fit in with others?

Robin That's it. He's got to learn not to be too 'naughty' and not to be too 'good'. He's got to find the path between.

John Hang on a moment. I can see he's got to learn not to be too 'bad', because if he's completely selfish, his lack of consideration will make him lonely and unloved. But what's the danger of being 'too good'.

Robin If he's not encouraged to explore a bit, to think for himself, if he's forced to give in too much, he'll become very much of a conformist. He'll certainly be no trouble to anybody – but he'll be dull, boring, uninteresting. He'll get pushed around and so won't be able to get what he wants or needs. There won't seem to be anything of himself there, he'll have no clear sense of his own identity.

John A chartered accountant, in other words. It's funny, isn't it, but when I was teaching I noticed that the one or two children who never did anything wrong didn't really inspire much affection.

Robin No, this is the problem. They're *not* very well liked or loved. So they tend to lack support in later life, like the very selfish ones. So, as you can see, the parents have quite a difficult task at this stage, steering the child on a course between these two extremes.

John Allowing the toddler the freedom and encouragement to explore and become confident and independent, but also enough control and firmness for him to be able to develop self-control.

Robin That delicate balance between conformity and independence, which we've all got to struggle with for the rest of our lives.

John Once we get kicked out into the hard world. After lying happily in our cot being the apple of mother's eye, getting twenty-four-hour room service.

Robin And speaking of apples . . .

John Do, please.

Robin Well, some people think this is what the myth of the Garden of Eden is all about. Babyhood is our 'Garden of Eden', with everything provided, and *nothing* demanded in return. The 'fall' is when we begin to have choice, the option to do what *we* want or what our *parents* want. After this we've 'eaten of the tree of the knowledge of good and evil'. Before that, we're 'innocent' – good and evil have no meaning at all.

John So we have to be evil – as well as good – before we can be fully ourselves.

Robin We have to be *able* to do both – to have the *choice* between good and evil. Which *must* bring with it the possibility of going against the system, *even* at the risk of being destroyed by it!! Yet we often forget this and *hope* that we can be free and true to ourselves without risking being unpopular and unsafe.

John . . . Yes, we do. Or *I* do. So, you're suggesting a child can't develop a clear sense of his own identity if he can't be naughty.

Robin And we're all individuals, all born different, so the toddler is like a test pilot flying a new plane. He has to test himself out, experiment, push things to the limit, and that'll mean going too far sometimes.

John But what about the fig leaves? Adam and Eve discovering sexuality?

Robin The real flowering of sexuality in children doesn't actually come until later. This toddler stage is the time when children first become *aware* not of sex itself, but of physical sexual *differences*. And very curious about them, too. So I think this toddler phase is concerned not just with discovering the possibility of being 'good' or 'bad', but also with accepting that you are *either* male *or* female . . . but not *both*.

John So the myth isn't about sex, it's about sexual identity.

Robin Right. Adam and Eve become aware of their difference from each other, and *this* makes them realise their separateness, their aloneness. So naturally they also then feel cast out from the Garden.

John Away from that blissful union with the Lord Mum Almighty. So 'The Fall' is about the knowledge of good and evil – that is, about discovering there are rules which you can keep or break . . . *and* it's about leaving Mother. But you said earlier that separation was to do with the period from *about* 6 months to *about* 3 . . . whereas this toddler phase is about the period from . . . what? . . . 12 months to the age of 4?

Robin Yes, more or less. I'd put the start around 15 months.

John Well the point I'm making is that they're overlapping.

Robin Obviously. A lot of these events – lessons we have to learn – are overlapping each other. Like a meal being cooked: the joint has to be started before the potatoes, and the potatoes have to go on before the peas, and the soup has to be ready before any of them; but most of the time several things are happening together.

John So the toddler is undergoing a very complex series of changes. He's having to learn to separate from Mum, he's learning to explore the new, exciting but slightly frightening world outside, he's beginning to accept his sexual identity and at the same time he's having to learn to fit in with the rules of the family. So he's redrawing his map frantically every ten minutes, isn't he?

Robin And he's now adding to the map all the lines that get drawn for him by his parents. The lines that indicate the family rules. So he's now learning for the first time to make a map of how society works.

Firmness. . . . . .

John I saw a Python sketch in my local supermarket about three weeks ago. Mum was there with two expertly naughty children and every time they did something they shouldn't have – which was about every eight seconds – she'd shout and threaten them with unimaginable deprivations and tortures, whereupon they'd go straight off and do something else naughty. And she'd increase the threatened punishment by five thousand lashes and two more goes in the Iron Maiden. So then they'd do something *really* naughty to let her know who was boss. In the end she had to give them a lot of sweets so they wouldn't burn the place down.

Robin I can imagine it. When there are a lot of rows in a family it's because the parents aren't providing the kind of clear guidelines the child needs. Usually, anyway.

John OK. Now I want to get more into this 'drawing lines' business. I mean if the toddler's going to learn to fit in, he can only learn where the lines are if they're drawn clearly, can't he? And presumably enforced. Which brings us up against that difficult word 'discipline'.

Robin From the Latin word for 'to teach'.

John Right. A disciple was not someone whom Jesus systematically punished. But if you mention it nowadays, people immediately conjure up a mental image of a lot of smacking and unkindness and kids having a rotten time.

Robin The point is . . . a lot of smacking usually only occurs if the lines *aren't* clear. If a father *can* take complete control when it's necessary that'll mean that he hardly ever needs to do it.

John Well that was my experience with my daughter. I'm afraid I didn't get really involved in her growing up as early as I should. But when she was about four, she was getting very, very difficult and I finally lost my temper and I smacked her hard for the first time. And to my absolute amazement I could sense that our relationship *immediately* got better. I had to smack her again sometimes, but the intervals between the smackings were getting longer and longer. So that after she was six, I hardly ever had to do it. And the really nice thing is – because I think one always feels a bit of guilt even when you sense that it's right – that she never seemed to bear any ill-will about it. It seemed to bring us closer in some paradoxical way.

Robin Well, that's a universal experience. I found the same with our children, and families in treatment always discover it too if they're willing to follow advice and take a firmer line. The children always forgive you – indeed, they love you more because acting in this way can show how involved you are, how much you do *care*.

John That'll go down a treat at the GLC. I can hear the derisive snorting from here. But this 'drawing lines' kind of caring can be just as loving as the maternal nurturing kind, though it's so different.

Robin That's right. In fact, in some ways, it's almost more profound because it involves the parent risking temporary dislike, even hate, since the parent is doing something to frustrate the child. Even if it's for the child's own good. So in some ways, it's the harder kind of love to give a child, because you don't immediately get something nice back. You get temporary rejection. The gratitude comes later on!

John Talking to my daughter during the holidays, I was reminded how kids really despise teachers who can't keep order. They resent them too. They quite like the strict ones . . . and the easy-going ones are fine provided they *can* keep control. The other teachers they can't stand are the inconsistent ones, who are strict one minute and lenient the next.

Robin Children need consistency. The poor little devils don't know *how* to behave unless they know the limits of what's tolerated and what isn't.

John Why do they dislike the uncertainty so much? Because it makes them *anxious*? Why *do* they want clear lines?

Robin They feel secure if they know how far they can go. Children like achieving, learning, being stretched a bit, and they also feel safer if they know just how much they can relax and fool around too. So they're much happier if there's enough structure to help them control themselves.

John I'm getting a mental image about how the child feels. I see the child sitting on a chair in the middle of a dark, unfamiliar room. And the child's got to have the courage to leave that chair and explore the room. But it's murky, he's not quite sure where the walls are. But he needs to be able to go off and explore and come up against them and establish where they are, good and firm and clear. Then he can explore the room full of curiosity and without fear. But if the walls *aren't* there he'll get scared. He'll not be sure how far he can go. Perhaps if he goes too far he'll fall over the edge! Or perhaps he won't be able to get back to base, the chair, when he wants to. By giving him the walls to bang up against, the parents give him the confidence to explore.

Robin That's good but you missed one bit out. When he finds the wall, he's got to be *able* to bang on it!

John That's the anger or frustration he feels, at that moment.

Robin So the wall's got to be firm. And he bangs on it, and nothing terrible happens, the ceiling doesn't come down and then he knows . . . 'Well, there's the wall then.' You see, to feel really safe with yourself you need to have had the opportunity to go to the limit of your feelings, so you know how to cope with your most extreme emotions. Once you've gone to that limit and you know where it is, and you know you survived and other people you loved survived, you can feel at ease with yourself and trust your anger from then on. You know you can handle it. Obviously, to have the opportunity of an experience like that *someone has to look after you*; and look after *themselves* despite the fact that you feel savage or murderous or whatever. They have to hold the situation, contain it, accept the full force of the feelings but prevent any real harm. Now, if the parents provide clear limits, as well as continuing their emotional support, the child can try out his strength to the full and learn to feel safe with it, gradually learn to control it.

John Then you're not frightened of your anger. Fascinating. So . . . that's why kids need clear, consistent guidelines.

Robin Yes, and sometimes a child does something naughty to try to force the parents to lay down a guideline.

John I suddenly think of the phrase . . . 'the child was asking for it'. Not a smack necessarily, but a clear limit.

Robin So they 'know where they are' and can stop feeling anxious. If the parents don't give guidelines, then the only thing the kids can do is to keep testing the limits! The longer the parents remain indecisive because they want to please everyone and are worried that a firm line will make them unpopular with the children, the more impossible the children will have to be to try to force a definite response. And, of course, the worse the explosion will be in the end.

John You mean if the parents do eventually draw the line.

Robin Yes. And the later the parents leave it, the bigger the explosion will be and the longer the dust will take to settle. One sees a lot of parents who've put off the confrontation till the child is eight or ten or even until teenage arrives. In such cases I warn them, when I advise them to make a stand, that it will be like landing on the Normandy beaches again and that they can expect a week of absolute hell. Then they usually cope. But it's obviously better to draw clear lines when the child 'asks for it' at the toddler stage, and help him to learn how to fit in slowly, stage by stage, as he becomes able to develop more self-control.

John I get the red mist sometimes when I hear very progressive parents and teachers refusing to take responsibility for giving kids the guidelines they need simply because somebody might think them unloving or fascist. It seems to me the most contemptible lack of responsibility.

Robin And of course Freud gets most of the blame for it. Though in fact he was remarkably sensible and down to earth about the matter. But people interpret him as they want, as with the Bible.

John But hang on. Suppose the parents were *very* strict? What effect would that have?

Robin Well, in my experience, as long as there's plenty of *love as well*, a strict upbringing by itself doesn't seem to cause many problems. It may produce a person who's narrower and who tends to conform more – who might have rather conservative views and accept hierarchy and authority more easily than you or I do, but that would help them to fit in particularly well in organisations and professions where conformity is needed, like the army, the police, the civil service, the law and so on.

John You forgot accountancy. So they'd toe the line, and they wouldn't see anything wrong with that.

Robin In fact, interestingly enough, I've noticed that people are almost always *grateful* to strict parents. Even as children, they seem to sense that it costs the parents something.

John Provided it's done for the *children's* good.

Robin Yes. If the parents are being strict in order to hang on to the child to satisfy their own needs, or for some reason like that, then it's a different story. And just as children are grateful to strict, loving parents, they never forgive over-indulgent ones.

John They sense in some way that it's not ultimately good for them?

Robin Yes, they seem to realise that over-indulgence is caused either by laziness, or by a childish need of the parents to be

constantly loved and approved of. And even if the children don't see that at the time, they usually recognise it in later life.

John So you're suggesting that, provided there's love, even old-fashioned 'Victorian' strictness is not likely to cause psychological damage.

Robin Provided we keep saying, 'so long as it's done with love and for the child's good' I think I'd go along with that.

John It sounds as though, when in doubt, it's better if the parents err on the strict side.

Robin I'd say that, yes. But fortunately, there's a kind of built-in mechanism to help the parents get this right. It's a simple rule really. 'If the kids are driving you crazy, it's because they want you to read the riot act.' So if in doubt, *read* it early on before they've become impossible. But interestingly, there's another reason why erring on the strict side is the right mistake to make, and it's that the effects of too-harsh discipline tend to fade with time, and so the person who's suffered it tends to get more normal. But on the other hand, someone who's had too little help in controlling himself, or herself, when young, will find it much more difficult to move in the other direction, towards *gaining* self-discipline.

John But surely you hear some children, indeed some adults, complaining that their parents *were* too strict.

Robin Ah yes. But when I've looked *more closely* at the family backgrounds of people who blamed their difficulties on 'over-strict' parents, the parents have usually turned out to be too weak, too easily manipulated.

John So where does the 'too strict' idea come from?

Robin Because the parents are *worried* about being too strict for fear the children won't love them if they are. So the children pick that feeling up, and take it at face value. After all, if the parents are so busy blaming themselves, it's not unreasonable for the children to give them the benefit of the doubt and blame them too!

John They have only their parents' standards to go by.

Robin And once they discover the parents *are* frightened of being accused of strictness, they learn to play upon this guilt to get their own way.

John I see. OK. Let me see if I've got the gist of all this. Children need clear boundaries. Drawing these for them accomplishes several things. First, it teaches them how to fit in; second, it means they don't experience the anxiety of 'not knowing where they are'; and third, it gives them the chance, particularly at the toddler stage, of experiencing extreme emotions under 'controlled conditions', so they can become acquainted with them and learn to control them.

Robin That'll do for the time being.

John Now there's something I haven't understood. The child mustn't be 'too good', right? Well, if real strictness – provided its loving – doesn't produce the 'can't say boo to a goose' type . . . what *does*?

Robin Well the cowed, timid types have usually received very powerful pressure to conform to their parents' expectations. *But* this pressure has not been exerted through firmness, but by means of *guilt*. Such parents don't say, 'Don't do that or I'll be cross,' or 'You'll lose that treat,' or 'It's off to bed with you'. They say, 'Don't do that, it makes me so unhappy'.

John 'It'll give Father a heart attack, it'll upset your Mum, the universe will disintegrate.'

Robin 'You'll be sorry when I've gone.'

John 'If you loved me you wouldn't do that.'

Robin *Or* . . . it can be done by instilling a fear in the child that if he doesn't behave, his parents will actually *abandon* him.

John Both of which are putting a terrible responsibility on the child, aren't they?

Robin They're putting the child into a strait-jacket, or worse, making the child put himself into a strait-jacket.

John By making him responsible for the parents' happiness and even their lives! And the family's stability, which to the child is almost his own life.

Robin So of course such a child becomes unable to explore his emotions because of the damage he fears he might do.

John He's never been able to bang on the walls because he's been told that if he does, the whole house will come tumbling down.

Robin And so, naturally, he's terrified to stand up for himself.

Father comes in from the cold......

John Right at the start you said the toddler stage was when the father has some vital jobs. Presumably that's because he now has to supply the support and encouragement the child needs if he or she is to start exploring the world outside Mother.

Robin Not only that. There's something else too. He's now got to begin to reclaim his wife.

John Come again?

Robin Since the birth, the usual arrangement is that Dad's been holding the lifeline for Mum while baby needed so much of her time and attention. Now Dad should begin to haul her back, to reclaim her as it were, from the baby. So that the two of them can put their own relationship as a married couple first again.

John Because as she lets the baby separate, she'll be feeling a loss – the loss of an incredibly close relationship – so if Father's on hand to make up that loss with a renewal of her bond with him, that'll ease her letting the baby go.

Robin So if Dad doesn't step forward at this point to reclaim his place as husband and lover, rather than just as a father, he's not helping the mother, *or* the baby, to cope with *their* next move of stepping *back* from each other.

John So Father's first role is to help the separation by reclaiming Mum. And then, as the next source of love and support after Mum, he's uniquely qualified to help the baby to explore.

Robin Yes, he's offering baby something a bit different. Usually a less cosy relationship, but perhaps a more robust, vigorous and stimulating one. So he's not only supporting the child during his first adventures away from Mum; he can even make leaving her for a bit seem rather attractive.

John So he's acting as a bridge between the mother and the outside world, helping the toddler to build up confidence for his explorations, so he can start to make the map he needs of how society works.

Robin That's right. And by reclaiming Mum, by getting in between the mother and the child, the father's already helping to draw that map. Up to now, baby's been in this position

and now he finds himself in this position.

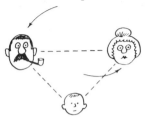

John The baby's being forced to share. Having been such a selfish little beggar up to now that's a pretty huge step, isn't it, to come to terms with the idea that there are *other* people 'out there' who have their needs too. So in a way Dad becomes a rival. Do people get a bit uncomfortable about that idea?

Robin Only because children have been 'in vogue' in recent years, while Dads have been definitely 'out'!

John In what way?

Robin Well, for the last couple of decades or so, some of the 'fatherly' virtues have been a bit out of fashion, and there's been a tremendous concentration on 'motherly' virtues. At the beginning this change was a thoroughly good thing. But most people felt the pendulum swung too far one way, especially when it was at its extreme in the 'sixties, and now I believe that's being corrected, that we're going back towards the middle with both father *and* mother being seen as important in different ways. But to go back to your point about rivalry. Please understand that although it's only natural for the father to be a bit *jealous* of the baby, he must also be able to love him and offer him care. It's his *loving presence* which helps the child to face the problem of sharing and coping with groups bigger than two. And, of course, for that to work he must be *there*.

John So each new baby in the family will have the exclusive relationship with Mum to start with, and then, as Dad reclaims Mum, each in turn will find that he has to relinquish that special relationship and become part of the team.

Robin And if all goes well, they'll end up in this sort of formation:

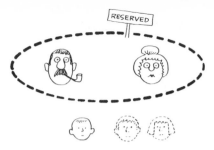

The two parents should be Number One for each other, in a special compartment of their own, separated from their children.

John And if the parents aren't in a separate compartment, the children won't be able to separate?

Robin It'll certainly be that much more difficult. Parents who claim their own space apart from the children are helping the children to separate and grow up. They're setting a good example.

John So Dad needs to reclaim Mum for *everyone's* sake. Right. Now this 'exploring the beyond-Mum world' business. Father's encouraging the toddler to do this. Is this the same as 'drawing lines' or is it parallel, so to speak?

Robin By 'drawing the line' when that's necessary – setting limits – he's helping the child to draw the lines on his internal map of the world.

John But now we come to the $64,000 question. Why should the father – the *man* – be any better at drawing lines than the mother? It may have been the traditional view, but what about Meir and Indira Gandhi and Thatcher?

Robin I don't really think this has much to do with any inherent psychological difference between males and females. Except that the physical difference that the woman will have given birth and is more likely to have been the main support in the earlier stages *will* affect things *at this toddler stage*. Because the child will still need to run back to Mother often, for comfort and an injection of self-confidence when the demands of the world get too tough.

John It's a jungle out there.

Robin So the toddler needs a loving mother who provides the opposite – softness, warmth, cuddles – safety!

John So?

Robin Well, when the child's still very young, even up to the toddler stage, I think it's very confusing and disturbing for him if Mother has to try to play *both* roles too much – being very soft and supportive one minute, and tough and demanding the next. You remember he's having quite enough trouble already trying to put the jigsaw together to make her into one whole person.

John So, for the time being, it's best if she presents one more or less consistent image to the child. Easiest for the child to *understand*?

Robin That's one reason why, *at this stage at least*, Dad needs to be the one who expects the child to learn to fit in with the rest of the family. All this takes place bit by bit, of course, as the baby gets more able to control himself. But it's Dad who'll be asking more of the child.

John I think there's another possible reason. Many women I know have a worry, deep down inside, that they're not quite 'a good enough Mum'. That makes it much harder for them to be firm with the child because that voice inside is saying, 'Hang on, are you being loving *enough*? Wouldn't a really good mother be more understanding?'

Robin I admit that does seem to be a very common feeling in mothers, however unjustified, and if the father takes a firmer attitude that will help her – particularly at this toddler stage. Naturally, as the child gets older and more secure, and gets a clearer picture of his parents, he won't be so confused by the same parent being supportive at times and firm at others. And then *both* parents can *share* giving the support, on the one hand, and drawing the lines, on the other hand. And, in fact, that's what happens in families, quite naturally, as the children grow up.

John So you've given me two reasons why the father is specially important at this stage. What other jobs has he got now?

Robin Well, another is that so far mother and baby have usually been quite a mutual admiration society. And though this uncritical, unconditional love will help the baby to build his confidence and his trust, they may both have been enjoying each other so much that the mother may have some difficulty in being sufficiently realistic about the baby's actual virtues and faults.

John So the baby may not be getting the accurate feedback from her that he needs to draw his map?

Robin A map which has got to include the baby himself.

John What? . . . Oh I see! *He's got to be on his own map.* Of course! He needs to get his *own* size right in relation to everything else if he's not going to have unrealistic ideas about his own importance . . . which would make him too selfish?

Robin Not only that. If he doesn't get his own size on the map right, know where his limits are, how far he can go without running up against others, he's not going to have a good guide as to how he can most efficiently use the rest of the world to get what he wants. This is what 'drawing lines' is all about.

John Yes, I see that. So if our maps of the world are to help us, we've got to include *ourselves* on that map, and get our size right.

Robin So that's why they may both need the father, who's a bit more detached, to help them both to be a bit more objective about the toddler's capabilities.

John . . . Any more jobs for father?

Robin Yes, I think there's at least one more. As we've said before, at first the baby feels as if he's everything. Then, as he finds his edges, he shrinks, losing that feeling of omnipotence gradually. But he compensates for that come-down, because he's *so* close to Mother, and *she* must seem at this stage as powerful as God. So he must lose *that* illusion next. So after a time, if he sees that Mother isn't running the world, that she has to share power with Father, that's another step on the way.

John And later he'll have to discover Dad isn't God either.

Robin Of course. And if Dad is doing his fathering job properly, he'll make it clear that *he's* part of something bigger too and has to fit in like everyone else.

John So it wouldn't be a good message for the child if Dad was under Mum's control? Because the toddler wouldn't have to make that jump then, would he? He wouldn't have to realise that Mum wasn't God. If she was controlling Dad, he could continue to see her as God.

Robin That's right. I think the toddler has got to see that Mum isn't God as a first step to seeing that Dad isn't God, and that nobody else is either.

John I've never heard this before.

Robin Well I think it's a vital lesson, and perhaps the main

reason why the mother-dominated family doesn't seem to work too well for the children.

John What! Really?

Robin In fact almost all the families I've seen in child psychiatry, where the child was brought as a *problem*, were mother-dominated. Either that, *or* completely chaotic.

John This is astounding.

Robin Yes. Well, it was to me too when I noticed it. I was training in child psychiatry and I went to the senior social worker who allocated the cases after I'd seen about ten of them and complained they were all of this kind – could I have some of the other kind, please? She said not to worry; she'd been there ten years and they were *all* like that!

John Go on.

Robin Well, to put this in context, I have to say immediately that research on the *healthiest* families shows that the power in the family is *shared* between the two parents. They work together and make very conscious decisions about who's going to do what. But in all but those healthiest families, *if* one of them is to be the boss, it does seem more often to work better if it's the father rather than the mother.

John Better for the *children*, right?

Robin Oh, *yes*. I can't emphasise that enough. What couples do when there aren't any children is up to them, naturally.

John I am distracted by the sound of feminists sharpening barbs.

Robin Please! No one knows more than I do how sexist this sounds. It took me a long time to come to this view, but in the end I couldn't deny the evidence in front of me. But you've got to try to see the *whole* picture in these problem families. In the early days, we were certainly at fault because we used to blame it all on what we called 'castrating mothers'. Then, when we started seeing the fathers regularly, and seeing more clearly how the families operated, we realised that it was *just as much* due to the way the fathers opted out of responsibility.

John You mean the mothers had no option but to take over?

Robin Exactly. No option. But nowadays, looking at the whole thing more as a system, we can see it's no one's *fault*; it's just the way the system operates. Automatically. Mechanically.

John I am going to spell this out again just to embarrass you. In the healthiest families, the power is shared by agreement. In the *others* one parent or the other is usually more powerful. In your experience, where the mother is more powerful, the children are much more likely to have problems. And consequently you feel that, if there *has* to be a boss, it's better if it's the father. I want more evidence, please.

Robin Well I have to say . . .

John . . . Defending yourself desperately . . .

Robin No, not really. You see, it was the mothers who convinced me of all this.

John And the editorial board of *Spare Rib*?

Robin The mothers and the children. I resisted the idea.

John Brave chap.

Robin Really. For me the idea went against the grain. I believed in equality, discussion, shared decisions.

John Well of course that's how *really* healthy people work.

Robin Stop heckling and *listen*. Over and over again, where families came for help with problems with the children, mothers would say they longed for the father to take control. They still say that. And the brothers and sisters almost always agreed, and said that the father should be more strict.

John So sexism rules, OK?

Robin No, it was the *mothers* who decided the argument for me.

Let me tell you what just one of them said to me: 'It's something to do with having children. At first it's all right, and then the children come along, and you find you have so much to cope with, you are frightened because you have so many responsibilities to face, and . . . you need *authority* . . . you need authority, just a kind of injection now and again to enable you to *carry on*, to *cope* with the responsibility, to make you feel you are strong enough to carry on.'

John . . . Well . . . it's true, isn't it, sometimes you're struggling with a task and if someone says, 'Stop moaning, just get on with it,' it does give you a kind of strength. And, of course, if the husband is exerting some sort of authority, he's taking some sort of responsibility, isn't he, which *might* help her . . .

Robin Now later on she said something else equally interesting. She said: 'Suddenly you're faced with all that and you're petrified . . . and I think that by being *provocative* towards the male, and he being *aggressive* towards you . . . when he takes the strong part, he takes the responsibility, you draw strength from him in that way, it's automatic.'

John . . . 'Aggressive'?

Robin And I *then* asked her: 'So you would not see this aggression from the man as a hostile thing in those circumstances?' And she replied: 'No, certainly not.'

John Well, it sounds as though she's understood something that . . . well, I can't really get hold of it.

Robin No, but it's a message that I've heard again and again and again, and it seems that this kind of arrangement is needed *at this stage of development*. Maybe people can't understand it until they've actually got there and been through it.

John This woman changed her views *after* having a child?

Robin Yes. I asked her whether she would have rejected what she was now saying *before* she'd become a mother. She laughed and said she would have rejected it completely. As terribly sexist. This is why it's no use arguing with people about this; either they've discovered it or they haven't. Of course, it's *possible* that an *extremely* healthy person would never *need* to discover this.

John I suddenly think of the child being aggressive to force the parents to draw lines for him. What she says makes some sense if she needed her husband to help her to clarify *her* boundaries which had got fuzzy because she'd been so close to the child.

Robin That's what it seems to be about, yes. The mother has had to let her own boundaries go fuzzy to get back to the baby's level so they could get sufficiently close and involved, overlapping. When the baby turns into a toddler and starts trying to define his edges by provoking his mother, *she* may have trouble getting her clear edges back.

John But, presumably, this can happen the other way round too? Sometimes the man will lose his boundaries and need to have them defined by his wife.

Robin Oh certainly. There can't be many fathers who haven't had the experience of being left to look after the children and then finding themselves facing a furious wife when she returns to find the house in uproar and all the kids over-excited.

John With Dad behaving just like one of them. So she has to call him to order so that he can become a grown-up again.

Robin Do you remember that?

John Oh yes. Quite a bad feeling it is, too. Real shame.

Robin Well, that's because we feel we've been too childish, isn't it, and we know we need the rebuke.

John So in that case, Mother is redrawing Father's lines.

Robin And, of course, the father will need his mates to do this job for him too sometimes.

John How? By saying what sort of things? 'Oh, stop moaning, of course you feel left out, that's why God gave you such loving friends.'

Robin Yes. A mixture of encouragement and toughness. Keeping him up to the mark but supporting him, too.

John So you're saying that whoever's closest to the child may get his or her boundaries a bit blurred, and may therefore need someone further up the line of support to help to redraw them. And if *that* person starts getting a bit blurred too, he or she may need someone else further still from the child to redraw *his* or *her* boundaries. But as it's more likely that Mother will be closer to the child in the early stages, it's more likely that it will be Dad who will be redefining Mother's boundaries than vice versa.

Robin So I think it has nothing to do with sexism to suggest that they should play different roles in that parenting team at different times, for the child's benefit.

John In a sense they get the star role at different stages. It's interesting, isn't it, that the sexist implication more or less disappears if you see the parents operating *as a team*. I mean the whole point of a team is that it consists of different people of different abilities playing different roles, but with a common aim. It's no good if everyone wants to be goalscorer or goalkeeper. So the Dad/Mum relationship suddenly looks a bit more like Chairman of the Board and Managing Director. One more concerned with what's happening outside the business, the other more with the inside. And both equally necessary.

Robin Well as you'll see in some detail later on, the lessons the toddler is learning now are all about him being able to be part of a team.

John Considering others, learning the rules, accepting authority . . .

Robin Right. So if you've learnt these lessons and therefore see how teams *need* to work, you'll see that the parenting team can operate beautifully in this way without any implicit conflict. But anyone hearing this who's *not* made this jump themselves, won't be comfortable with being part of a team and will make the *assumption* that 'teamwork' must really be a power struggle. In that case they would see these views as sexist.

John That's a very ingenious argument. And circular too, I think. Never mind. I have another objection. All these jobs you've listed for Father at toddler stage, reclaiming Mum, drawing lines more firmly than Mum, helping the toddler to realise Mum isn't God, and giving him more accurate feedback than he might get from a loving Mum, all but the first, surely, could be done by someone other than the man. So what happens if there is no father?

Robin Well if the mother was *completely* alone . . . it might be very difficult indeed for the toddler to learn some of these important lessons. But there will almost always be grandparents or other relatives, good friends, neighbours, teachers, people who can be used by the mother – and by the child – to do these jobs. And this can work perfectly well, as long as the mother *accepts* that she will need help sometimes in redefining her boundaries in the way we've been talking about.

John So it really only needs another person who's not too emotionally entangled with the children. So it could well be another woman.

Robin Oh yes, often it's the grandmother. And, of course, a good grandmother is better than a bad father, but obviously a loving father is the ideal person for this job because of the other important parts he can play in the child's and the mother's lives.

Mr Wonderful . . . . . .

John So if the father plays his part, the parents will be able to draw clear lines. Which are necessary because the toddler needs the 'smack of firm government'. I've forgotten why.

Robin It's because, if you're allowed to bang on the walls your parents have set, you learn two things. First, if you've been able to bang on the walls and explore, your anger doesn't frighten you. You know you can control it so you can use it when you want to. So you can stand up for yourself and look after your needs. Second, because the walls are firm, you're also learning about other people's needs, the limitations set on your behaviour by the various aspects of society. So you'll get a map of the world that's accurate, *and* which has *you* clearly marked on it – the right size.

John OK. Well, if the toddler gets it right, what then?

Robin Well then he's getting the right balance between his own interests and everyone else's. So, quite frankly, life's not going to present him with too many big problems. He's learning the way the world works, he's finding his place in the world, and his right size in it, and how others see him. So he'll become gradually more independent, more self-sufficient, more free to move around and able to get what he needs because he knows what he has to do to get it. And that'll continue.

John And that's the lesson of the toddler stage.

Robin More or less. But there's another important way of looking at this. Remember it's all dependent upon the toddler being able to make the jump from being a pair with Mum

to being a threesome with Dad.

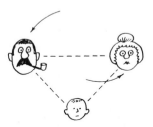

Becoming part of a team instead of somebody 'extra special' with a permanent, exclusive one-to-one relationship with Mother.

John So someone who's learned these lessons will be a good team member.

Robin Yes. They'll be able to join groups as and when they want, and they'll find their experiences in groups strengthen their resources.

John *Strengthen* them? You know, I find this hard to absorb. I think I immediately see groups as somehow *limiting*. Partly anyway. I suppose I didn't learn these lessons properly as a toddler.

Robin Neither did I. But remember you can always pick them up later, if you're open to them. That's what happened for me in the RAF during the war. To my surprise I discovered you didn't feel weak or humiliated when the NCOs gave you a tough time on parade, as I'd imagined. Instead, you felt a growing pride and confidence which made you feel really good. You were learning to be part of a highly disciplined team, yet *you* felt stronger. In fact, I think it was that experience that enabled me to understand the toddler stage when I went into child psychiatry later on!

John You mean where there's a kind of tough, aggressive containment – for your own welfare – you find more aggressive energy becoming available in yourself, that hadn't seemed to be there before.

Robin *Or* . . . had previously felt rather uncomfortable or frightening. The result is you feel closer to your full potential.

John Well, I always avoid things that I find difficult. Like climbing Everest or getting up in the morning. But if I simply can't get out of doing them . . . well, it's true when I have done them, I get a strange sense of achievement. And confidence. It won't seem so difficult next time. Except getting up in the morning.

Robin Well, the person who's got through this phase will see the demands that the team makes on him positively. Problems are there to be solved, not complained about. Being part of any large group gives you experiences that can make you stronger, sharper and more skilful.

John This is all very interesting to me because I know I've always had a subversive attitude towards larger groups, in other words, towards authority, and I suspect it's because my father, a very, very loving man, wasn't tough enough with me. He let me slide out of things too easily. But over the last few years it's been changing slowly, perhaps because I really have had to accept certain duties I couldn't craftily avoid. So whereas my sympathy used to be with the rebel, I now find that the soft option. It's all too easy and self-indulgent. In fact I'm beginning to develop a sneaking regard for the people who've got to get on with the job and take all the crap. But this business of attitude to authority is tricky. I imagine, ideally, you need to be free from compulsive needs to rebel *or* to conform, so you can make up your mind about any particular authority and whether it's being exercised well, or not. But so many people have an immediate impulse towards authority – that it's either 'good' or 'bad' – that in any particular case they aren't really free to choose which side they're on. It's automatic.

Robin I would see a rigid attitude to authority with a capital 'A' as essentially a childish attitude, whether the person is for or against it. Authority, hierarchy, organisation can be just ways of ordering things so you can get them done. *Everyone* can't go through a revolving door at the same time, and if a caterpillar moved all its legs at once it'd fall over. There has to be some arrangement, if the actions are at all complicated, or a lot of people are involved. It's like being able to take part in Scottish Reels. You lose the freedom of just doing your own thing and you have to take the trouble to learn the steps and fit into the pattern, but if you do, it's very enjoyable in a quite different way. And the music is not there just to boss you about.

John Yes it is. God, I used to hate them. I think they're designed to humiliate people. But then I'm only a toddler. However, I'd like to suggest to you that a *lot* of people are in this position of having a slightly vague and unresolved attitude towards authority. I mean, look at the extraordinary amount of media coverage there is every time John McEnroe has an argument with an umpire. It's essentially trivial and yet sometimes it's the second or third item on the television news. It must have such news value because it's an archetypal squabble between the 'rebel' and the 'authority figure'. And everyone seems to have *strong* views about it, siding vigorously with

McEnroe like you do, or equally vehemently with the umpire, as I do. The strength of the emotions are given away, aren't they? You only get excited about things you're not confident about, right?

Robin Yes, but don't forget that being healthy means having a balance between these two extremes of being a robot or a brat. I mean a balance on average, for a period of time. A lot of us have jobs or lives that push us strongly in one direction so it probably does us good if we balance things up when we are off duty. My job involves a lot of umpiring so I really enjoy watching McEnroe winding up the umpire and expressing my rebellious side for me. Your job as a comic gives you endless scope for undermining authority so I think McEnroe brings out the other side in you, the school prefect.

John But surely some people express the same side all the time.

Robin I think you'll find the two sides are always present, even if one emerges only in a hobby, or in fantasy or in dreams. In the healthy person both sides get expressed openly. But if this doesn't happen you'll either get someone who's always rebelling – a delinquent perhaps, who gets himself caught as a way of forcing external authority to provide a more healthy internal balance for him – or the complete opposite – someone who's rigid, obsessional and over-controlled, who outwardly toes the line and guards his tongue, but nevertheless drives everyone up the wall with his slowness and obstinacy while probably enjoying secret fantasies about taking a chainsaw to his boss.

John Or her boss. So even if we learn to tread the path between conformity and rebelliousness in the toddler stage, it's a path we need to make some effort to stay on afterwards.

Robin And that effort is the price of being healthy – or of political freedom.

John But something else strikes me. If you basically get these lessons right as a toddler, and so tread the path more easily . . . presumably when you get *authority* yourself, you exercise it better.

Robin I think that's the case. When the authority is exercised well, the person in charge takes time before reaching a decision, to collect all the information available and to listen to all the opinions of those below him. But then he or she takes the decision themselves. And once they've done that, they're prepared to *explain* it fully. Then they'll stick to it, be quite firm about carrying it out.

John I got fascinated by this while writing a film for Video Arts about decision-making. I came to see that if people were fully consulted, they would be prepared to go along with a decision that they *didn't* agree with, provided they felt their opinion had been taken really seriously, and provided the person in authority took the trouble to 'sell' the decision to them. So how would someone operate in authority if they *hadn't* learned these lessons?

Robin They'd either tend to be rather ineffectual, but occasionally act rashly to show they were decisive – and then probably have to climb down – or else they'd act in an authoritarian way while pretending they weren't. They wouldn't like the clash of opinions you get in real consultation, you see. So they'd only ask people who agreed with them. Anyone who didn't would be a 'saboteur'!

John And then they'd announce the decision and disappear without bothering to explain it. Sounds like three-quarters of British management and nine-tenths of the Government.

Robin Well maybe that's a *tiny* bit sweeping, John!

John Have you *heard* Heseltine's attempts to debate with the CND? Never mind . . . sorry, getting carried away. Just a little tantrum. Now if the toddler makes the jump from the twosome with Mum to the team with Mum and Dad, he gets a healthy, non-compulsive attitude to authority, becomes a good team member. He's getting correct feedback. So he's got himself the right size on his map.

Robin And, of course, as he's constantly redrawing that map every time he gets a new bit of information, that map is going to be changing the whole time. But because he's basically got it right, he's not going to have to make any enormous and very painful changes to it. If a bit of his behaviour *is* wrong, the error will be pointed out and the map will be slightly improved. And so his behaviour will fit the situation that he's in. He'll find it relatively easy to negotiate with others and to find acceptable compromises where there's conflict. And each time this happens, his map of others and of himself gets corrected and improved, more or less automatically, so he never stops learning how to cope with life and therefore how to be useful both to himself and to others – the team.

John When you say 'automatically', you mean there's no struggle, no effort?

Robin Well, there'll be a struggle each time there's a bigger correction to be made to the map – when he gets told off or heavily criticised. But because the map's basically right, the correction won't have to be too painfully large, as I said, and once it's corrected it'll guide him accurately, so no struggling is necessary – until there's another correction of course. So, he'll *respond accurately* to what the situation requires. That is, you can rely on him to show a lot of '*responsibility*'.

John It had never occurred to me that to be responsible means you can respond appropriately. OK, so if the toddler makes the jump from the twosome to the team of three, and thence into other teams, everybody loves him, he's perceived as likeable, and unselfish, and responsible, and yet he's fully aware of his own needs and nobody can push him about. In fact, he becomes Pat Wonderful.

Robin Why Pat?

John It's a non-sexist name.

Robin Oh, very good.

The outsider......

John Now tell me about Mr or Ms Unwonderful. The person who hasn't learned these lessons. What will they be like?

Robin What would you expect?

John . . . Well, they haven't made the jump from the twosome properly so they won't have separated enough from the mother.

Robin But they *have* separated to some extent. They're not clinging on, not sunk in depression. They've moved a bit in the direction of becoming independent.

John Agreed. But they haven't made it to the threesome. So they won't be good team members.

Robin That's right. That's why I think a good nickname for people like this is 'outsider'.

John Now wait a moment. Are these people 'outsiders' because they're too 'brattish' or too 'timid'?

Robin Both. The 'brattish' ones are more obvious, chucking their weight about and being obnoxious, but the timid ones can be just as difficult for the other team members in a subtler way.

John Quietly stubborn?

Robin Just not getting their jobs done properly, but for reasons that don't quite seem to be their fault.

John Losing orders by making customers fill out sixteen forms without making a mistake . . .

Robin Or helping others keep to the speed limit by not allowing them to pass.

John Right. Either way they don't fit in. They'll see the demands of a team negatively.

Robin Yes. They'll feel that really joining in would mean being controlled, being changed, cut down to size.

John Which it does.

Robin Though in a healthy way. Of course they don't see it like that. They'll feel they'd be losing something important.

John Whereas it's really something they'd be better off without. An illusion, a 'Big Ego'. A baby's ego, in fact, insufficiently shrunk.

Robin Yes. Because no one in their family has helped them to go through the shrinking earlier, by a combination of pressure and support. So they've got an unrealistic map of the world, with themselves the wrong size and in the wrong position.

John So they're much more likely to *miscalculate*. To offend people or invade Russia. A big ego makes them more vulnerable, weaker.

Robin That's right. It's always difficult to get across to such people that being 'cut down to size' by others actually will make them more competent, more able to get what they want. Because, of course, being 'cut down', limited, frustrated *is* painful; reducing the size of your 'ego' always is. But it makes us bigger people in the end. I think people know this instinctively, realise that soft, over-indulgent parents usually bring up children who are weak, who can't cope easily with the world, who have to hang on to a picture of themselves as someone special.

John But they *have* got further than the depressives.

Robin So to some extent they'll be wanting to mix and have the advantages of belonging to a group. So they have to find a compromise, where they can *appear* to be normal members of a group, accepting the authority and rules that go with that, while secretly preserving the fantasy that the world revolves around them.

John So how do outsiders keep reality from breaking in on their fantasy?

Robin By not putting themselves clearly on their own map. They keep fudging it, blurring the connections, keeping their pictures of themselves and their own importance separate from everything else. So their ideas about themselves and their ideas about others are not brought together.

John In other words, an 'outsider' has to keep himself outside his own map.

Robin That's why I like the word. So it's as if he keeps the picture of himself in a special file, and avoids putting it on the map he's making of everyone else.

John He avoids noticing anything that will show that his map doesn't fit reality, that he's not special.

Robin And of course he also avoids noticing that he's not noticing! So he expects others to keep rules, but he'll talk himself into believing that he's a special case. So he'll never really be a

part of a group, although he'll go through the motions. He may deceive some people in the group but most of them will feel he isn't committed. Instead of compromising, being prepared for a bit of give-and-take, and, above all perhaps, being willing to change himself when that's necessary – well, he'll always be trying to change everyone else instead.

John So that *he* doesn't have to change. That's fascinating, that he has to change other people because he can't bear to be changed himself. Presumably, if he – or she – has reached adulthood and his ego is still vastly oversized, there'd be so much pain attached to reducing it to a real size that he can never afford to relax for a moment for fear that a bit of reality is going to break through the defences and cause that illusion about himself to crumble. So he'd always have to be sending off signs to people not to say anything he's not going to like – or better, surround himself with an entourage he can rely on never to say anything that doesn't fit his map – anything *critical*.

Robin Right. He'll cajole, wheedle, pressurise, get 'difficult' all the time, to get his own way. He's always behaving like a puppet-master, tying strings on other people and trying to get them to dance to his tune, instead of learning to join in the big dance with everyone else..

John So people who *need* power, who spend their lives seeking power, are doing that so they can try to force other people to adjust to them. So they don't have to correct the overblown picture they've got of themselves.

Robin That's it.

John So a person with a good map, a realistic map, would *not* need to control other people?

Robin He'd be sure of his own identity so he wouldn't need to do so.

John But wait a minute. I haven't got all these implications yet because a lot of this is not a little startling. The power-seeker can't be a real member of the team because he can't take *and give*. So he can't be truly responsible, in your sense, because his *primary* concern is *always* the need to protect his own ego from reality, rather than to respond appropriately to a situation.

Robin He's also dependent on the group for his power.

John Not just in the sense of being dependent on them not to criticise him? Because he hasn't left Mother properly.

Robin In a way, I suppose. If you can do up your own buttons, you don't need to get Mum to do it for you. So you're separate, independent. But if you haven't got enough control of yourself to do something, you've got to control others and make them do it for you.

John Like the tycoon who needs a 'hatchet-man' to do the unpopular things. Or the chairman of the huge financial empire who, when he gets home, makes his wife confront the kids about pocket-money. So you have to control other people because you can't control yourself!

Robin That's right! If your 'ego' – your picture of yourself – is unrealistically big, you can't control yourself. So the outsider spends his whole life trying to control other people so that they won't be able to bring the truth about him to his attention, so that he'll never have to suffer having his 'ego' cut down to its real size.

The outsider's family. . . . . .

John Well, now you've told me about the 'outsiders', I want to get a clearer picture of the kind of family that he or she comes from. There seems to be a general principle that no child can learn the lessons of any of these developmental stages unless the parents have learned them and can pass them on. Not in his family, at least.

Robin I think that's self-evident.

John OK, so can I assume that the family of the child who can't make the jump from the twosome to the threesome are all 'outsiders' themselves?

Robin Yes. If the child is stuck, it must be because the parents are to some extent stuck at this stage themselves. So none of them will be very good at the give-and-take of real group involvement, and they'll all be trying to manipulate each other to some extent. There'll be a whole network of disguised power struggles going on the whole time. So the family's going to be a tangled skein of puppet strings all going from each member to the next.

John Yes, I can see that.

Robin But the trouble is this is rather more complicated than it sounds. Now we're talking about the whole family, we're talking about a complicated system, and it's really difficult to stretch our brains enough to see all the implications. Not just the chicken-and-egg situation between the generations, but also the circular, non-linear system that's in operation with everyone connected to and involved with everyone else, at the same time, controlling and being controlled.

John All right. But why do you mention it now? It's been true right from the beginning, hasn't it?

Robin Fair point. It's because the father comes into things more at the toddler stage so the circularity becomes more obvious.

John OK. Go on about the circularity of the family system then.

Robin The child's stuck because Dad's stuck. Which is why Mum chose him, because she was stuck because her parents were stuck. The toddler can't get unstuck until Mother gets unstuck by Dad getting unstuck enough to come in and unstick the toddler.

John I think I understand, so obviously I'm missing something.

Robin It's just that you need all your attention to hold all the thoughts and connections in your mind and you can only succeed now and again. So . . . a family of outsiders won't be hanging on to each other for dear life, like a depressive family. They'll believe in independence. Or at least they think they do.

John But in fact none of them has really made the jump from Mum.

Robin Not far enough to accept being really separate, no. So while they may approve of the idea of being separate and independent, in practice they can't cope with it so well as they think. So although they appear to be encouraging the toddler towards independence, they're also clinging together, but in a disguised way.

John So the toddler's getting contradictory messages.

Robin Yes. The toddler's hearing, 'You're a big girl now' or 'Big boys don't cry' or 'Why can't you manage on your own?' But then the very next minute it's, 'Oh I suppose I'll have to do it for you.'

John Telling them they can't cope after all, which helps to keep them dependent. 'Oh, you're hopeless. You can never look after yourself.'

Robin And if they do start doing something independent, it's 'Why don't you think about me, don't you love your Mummy?'

John Or more craftily, 'Oh you go off and have a good time, don't you worry about *us*.' So the toddler's placed in a pretty hopeless situation – a double-bind. So what the hell does he do?

Robin He's got to find how he can stay closely involved with the parents – dependent – while also appearing to take note of the orders to become more independent, separate, able to make up his own mind.

John I'm lost. How can he do both?

Robin Well, actually, in several ways. The most obvious one is to go on behaving like an ordinary toddler. That is to say, he continues to behave in a tantrumy, naughty, undisciplined kind of way, resisting authority, picking fights and exasperating the whole family.

John I'm sorry but I don't see how that solves it.

Robin Well, look. While you're arguing and struggling with another person, you're actually very close, and getting a lot of attention from them. And giving a lot of attention to them too.

John Ah! If you're fighting someone, you're involved with them!

Robin At the same time, the actual fighting keeps a safe distance between you, like a no-man's land in a battle. And it also partly feels, and also *looks to others*, as though you're behaving independently, moving apart from each other.

John The penny has dropped. And so the child provokes conflict to obey the contradictory order he's getting.

Robin *But* . . . remember it's a circular system. OK? They've all got the same problem. So if the toddler doesn't do something naughty, to start the argument, Mother will invent something to nag him about. And if the two of them are getting on well, Dad may find a reason to stir it up.

John They're all in the same double-bind so they've all got to be in a more or less permanent state of conflict with each other, because that's the best solution they can find to the dilemma.

Robin And it's usually a system that the family has operated by over many generations.

John As usual. And, of course, no one's aware of what's going on.

Robin No. But the parents usually agree on *one* thing, despite the fact that they are in a power struggle with each other.

John That *someone's* to blame!

Robin Although, of course, it's just a *system*. And the child often gets scapegoated.

John Fascinating. Can you give me an example? I mean a family you've actually seen?

Robin Well, there was a boy of 14 who was referred to me because he was always in conflict with his parents and his teachers – in other words he was still a toddler. So I saw him with the whole family – both parents and an elder brother and sister of 18 and 16. What came across very clearly was the way he forced the parents to focus on *him* all the time by provoking them and making them angry, while at the same time he could complain about them interfering with his life and tell them to get off his back. In this way he was getting a lot of attention, but also behaving as if he wanted to be independent.

John So he was solving his double-bind. What about the parents?

Robin Well, it was obvious that the father and mother didn't *really* feel at ease giving *each other* attention, and were more comfortable both concentrating on the boy. Like him, they would have felt embarrassed if they had treated him like an idolised baby, but they could hang on to their 'Mum and Dad' roles, and avoid having to cope with the more intimate,

'Husband and Wife' roles as long as he went on behaving like a difficult toddler. I kept noticing that every time I got them to look at each other and talk together, this boy would start shouting at them to leave him alone – which is exactly what they were doing at that moment of course – and they would immediately forget each other and both look at *him* instead.

John So you had to draw a few lines.

Robin While giving plenty of support, of course. And being very friendly to the children while also telling them to keep quiet and let their parents talk. One problem was that the parents were too ashamed to admit *their* need for attention while the children were there too, so after a couple of interviews I saw the parents as a couple, twice.

John So that was drawing another line between the parents and the children.

Robin Putting the generations in separate compartments. Also, of course, showing the parents how to draw lines themselves.

John Acting as a model for them.

Robin And reassuring the children that all was well and that the parents 'needed to give each other a bit of attention too, you know'. Once they were on their own they were able gradually to acknowledge that they both wanted more love and attention too, and I prescribed just that! More pleasure, three times a day, including sex! And I also told them to ignore the kids for a bit!

John They had a rule on their map stopping them from taking what they needed.

Robin Some rule that 'parents must be perfect' and not have needs themselves. So I tried to rewrite that one rule while being a 'supportive parent' to them. And I tried to break their rule in every way myself!

John How?

Robin Taking more interest in the parents than in the kids, showing exaggeratedly that *I* did what *I* needed, and *enjoyed* it and so on.

John And what happened?

Robin At the fifth interview, which was the last, I saw them all together again. The parents were sitting on the sofa together, really glowing. The boy's nose was somewhat out of joint, but his attempts to distract their attention on to him didn't work any longer. Later, I heard that he gradually settled down, but the symptoms he had been referred for had already more or less gone and he was working hard and fitting in at school.

John And you didn't really explain what their system had been, you just changed it, by drawing lines . . .

Robin Well, actually, at the last interview I did explain the family pattern to everyone and as they talked about it, they realised it went back over *four* generations! Each youngest child had been a similar problem at least back to a great-great-uncle.

John That was a family with a 'brattish' toddler. How does it work with a 'can't-say-boo-to-a-goose' toddler?

Robin Then the anger's been driven underground because the family can't cope with it.

John Yes, but I don't see how it works then. I mean, if the purpose of the anger is to keep everyone involved while keeping a distance, surely if you repress the anger you can't keep the distance.

Robin Yes you can. You can have *passive* rebellion, a 'sit-down strike' of some kind.

John Such as?

Robin A lot of different possibilities, but learning-difficulty is the most common form I've encountered, after the child has got to school at least. He stares at the blackboard, and frowns hard, sucks his pencil thoughtfully, but nothing goes in.

John Oh, I remember a boy like that when I was teaching. He put so much energy into looking as if he was struggling with the problem that he didn't have any left over for solving it. I remember that I could not teach him that the River Niger was in Nigeria and the River Congo was in the Belgian Congo. And when I asked him whether the Niger was in Nigeria or the

Belgian Congo he consistently got it wrong. I tried to reassure him. I told him I wasn't trying to trick him, and that I wanted him to get it right, but he just couldn't see the connections between the words, even when I'd pointed them out half a dozen times . . . I don't think I got angry, I was just kind of awed.

Robin Well you would have done if it had gone on for long. By the time I meet teachers, they're practically bursting, because the child looks so helpless and innocent that they feel guilty and inhibited about expressing their frustration and annoyance. In fact, their irritation is completely justified because this type of learning problem is a disguised version of anger, of rebellion against the parents, which can't be expressed directly at home.

John Because of the family taboo.

Robin That's right. So it's diverted on to the teachers at school where the fear of anger is not so strong. But it's still disguised.

John But don't the children do the same thing at home?

Robin Well, they're not in a classroom so it'll take different forms.

John You mean vagueness?

Robin Procrastination, slowness, being late, day-dreaming when they should be paying attention, going to do one thing and then forgetting what it is and getting involved with something else, and so on.

John Just 'not being there'.

Robin That's exactly it.

John So the child's getting a lot of attention from the parents but in the form of criticism, so there's distance, they're not getting too close; so the child's obeying the double message, 'grow up but don't grow up', and obeying the taboo too . . . but isn't there something else going on too? I'm sure I was vague as a boy and I think it was a crafty way of getting some space, a bit of privacy.

Robin Well, when you said 'not being there', you hit the nail on the head. They're not there, they're somewhere else where they can have a bit of freedom, have a life of their own, away from all the disguised clinging. Maybe the only way to get some freedom is to go off somewhere by themselves inside their own heads, while *outwardly* behaving as though they're completely under their parents' control.

John So why does the rebellion come out more at school? Because the taboo against anger isn't so strong?

Robin That's right. Their anger's less alarming to the teachers.

John But the child is still looking all innocent.

Robin And what he needs is quite simply to be confronted about his silent rebellion, just as the toddler, the naughty, healthy, disobedient toddler, needs to have lines drawn.

John This 'learning problem' kind of behaviour is a way of pushing to find the limits too?

Robin That's right.

John So if the teachers draw the lines firmly . . . tell the child to work, or else! . . .

Robin . . . then in my experience, the learning difficulty usually disappears.

John Really!?

Robin Yes. Once the teachers grasp what the child's really up to, and then read the riot act, get really angry about it – in other words treat him as though he's being overtly rebellious – with a bit of luck, the rebellion first turns into ordinary naughtiness, which the teachers recognise and know how to handle, and then gradually dissipates as it would with the naughty toddler who's handled firmly. Of course, what happens then is rather predictable.

John What?

Robin Well, the *parents* now start complaining that the child is more aggressive at home.

John He's being freed from the taboo.

Robin Exactly. And they can't tolerate this. That's one of the reasons why it's so important to try to see the family together and help *everyone* in it to cope with the fear of anger.

John So what does the child actually think he is doing? Does he know deep down that it is a kind of anger?

Robin I don't think so. Not until he gets a firm, containing kind of handling which treats his learning block *as* anger. After that's happened, the child seems to become aware that he *is* being defiant. Angry.

John Before he can do that, he needs to know that the people in charge of him aren't frightened of the anger, and can therefore help him to control it?

Robin That seems to be it. Once he realises that others can handle it, he's free to *feel* his anger and to stop pretending that it isn't there, he no longer has to disconnect it from the people towards whom he really feels it.

John What do you mean by 'disconnecting' it?

Robin It's quite hard to put that into words. It's not, as I say, that the feelings aren't *experienced* in some way. It's more that they are kept disconnected from one another so that the meaning of the feelings is lost. The different feelings – anger, fear, guilt and so on – are all present and correct but he can't see what they're all about because they're isolated, separated from each other – kept in separate compartments. And the 'cutting off' process is at the root of another group of mental disorders, the ones called obsessional neuroses.

Obsessional neuroses......

John What is behind an obsession? Is it where a person feels *compelled* to do or to think certain things?

Robin The person is constantly experiencing a struggle between different parts of himself, which he can't resolve one way or the other. And he doesn't really understand what the struggle is about.

John How is this different from the outsider?

Robin It's the same thing, only more extreme. And as with the other mental disorders, a vicious circle has developed where what starts as an attempt to *solve* a problem actually produces worse problems still. You see, what began as an attempt to keep himself off his own map, disconnected from other people, leads to *so much* disconnection that the different parts of himself aren't connected up either. So one part of himself, like his conscience, won't balance up and control another part, like his instincts, his impulses. Because of this, he's out of touch with himself. So he can't trust himself. He's always anxious that the disconnected bit or bits are going to fly out of control and land him in terrible trouble.

John What are the symptoms?

Robin Sometimes what just seems to be an excessive, inexplicable fear of doing something that will have harmful consequences, or of *having done* something harmful without realising it. That person will experience a need to keep checking he hasn't done it, reassuring himself he didn't do it when he wasn't watching himself, as it were. And naturally, he's watching himself the whole time. He'll know it's probably silly, and no one else will be able to understand why he's like this, either.

John What kinds of things does he worry he might do, or have done?

Robin Things that normally one's conscience protects one against. Particularly, violent feelings and sexual feelings. But it can be anything that would lead to social disapproval.

John But I understood obsessional thoughts, or compulsive actions, were like counting window panes, or always putting clothes on in a certain order.

Robin Well, I've started with the *more straightforward* kind of disconnection, where the person is at least aware with his mind – in his thoughts – what the feeling or impulse he's worried about really is, even though he's unplugged himself from the *feeling itself* to some extent. What I haven't yet said anything about is the vicious circle that can develop.

John Say about it now.

Robin What seems to happen is something like this: it's the lack of connection that is causing the excessive anxiety in the first place, but the person doesn't see it like that. So the more worried he becomes over the possibility of losing control and running amok, the more he tries to disconnect himself still further from his feelings. That is, whatever he was doing before to keep the different bits of himself in separate compartments, he'll now do even more.

John So he'll actually be making the problem worse.

Robin That's right. The attempt to disconnect, disguise or deaden the feelings doesn't work because it reduces the amount of real control the obsessional has, which makes him even more scared that what he's trying to avoid is going to happen. So he increases the attempt to disconnect and deaden, but the anxiety keeps catching up and increasing too. So he becomes more worried, more indecisive, more fearful of taking risks, more like a zombie. He's thinking, worrying, all the time, but other people will get the impression he lacks feelings – apart, of course, from the anxiety, which will break through in some form or other, often as thoughts he can't stop which express the dreaded loss of control in a disguised way.

John These are the strange obsessional thoughts?

Robin Yes. For example, a fear that something will go wrong with the gas or electricity, or that he's forgotten to lock the door, or that burglars will break in and damage the house, so he's always checking taps and locks and switches again and again and again. And even when he's just checked them he'll want to go and check them again. Or a fear that germs will get on to him so he's always washing his hands, or refusing to touch door knobs.

John These are all ways of expressing, *at the same time*, 'wrongful' feelings *and* his conscience's worry about them.

Robin If it's sexual feelings he fears will get out of control, that might express itself as a fear of getting VD, for instance. This expresses the sexual wish he's really feeling, as well as the obstacle his conscience is trained to put in the way of it. And a hand-washing compulsion would be like Lady Macbeth saying, 'Out, damned spot', expressing a murderous *feeling* he's guilty about.

John Though he's not really aware of either side of the conflict?

Robin That's how it seems to work. And to help a person like this to lose the symptoms, you have to support them very firmly while they get in touch with these feelings and accept them for what they are.

John I think I'm getting some grasp. It's a bit like a driver who's climbed into the back seat in case he has an accident, so that he can say it wasn't his fault because he wasn't holding the wheel! And these really awful, obsessional symptoms are one result of lack of firmness by the parents?

Robin Yes. Though I should say that it's thought by many psychiatrists – quite wrongly in my opinion – to be due to *excessive* firmness. All my experience points the other way, and encouraging parents to be more tough and confrontative quickly cures such symptoms in children who suffer from them. It's the same with adult obsessionals. If they're just allowed to free-associate, the shrink will die of boredom or old age while the treatment's still in progress.

Parental conflict......

John I want to know more about the outsider's family because another aspect has struck me. Since the parents are outsiders too, they're not good at give-and-take, so there's bound to be a permanent power struggle going on between them. They won't be able to agree on how to manage the child. So that's another reason why he's not getting clear lines drawn.

Robin That's right.

John So that'll give the child plenty of opportunities to play one parent off against the other, won't it?

Robin Yes, but putting it that way sounds as if we're blaming the child when it's just the way the system works. It may look as if he's manipulating the parents against each other, but that's because *they're* each trying to get him on *their* side.

John But they don't see it that way.

Robin No, they'll both feel they're standing up for what they believe in. Father may say Mother is too soft, and spoiling him; and Mother may say Dad is too harsh and hurtful. But if they can't agree, the *effect* is that the child is played off between them. So who's to blame him if he ends up joining in that game?

John It's the only one he knows, after all. But *sometimes* . . . he's not going to feel comfortable about all this parental conflict . . .

Robin That's right. So sometimes the kid ends up playing the power game a different way, trying to *help* things by being fair and siding with one parent and then the other, back and forth. Most kids want to love both their parents, after all.

John Trying to even things up.

Robin That's not the only tactic the child can try either. Our experience in *family* therapy is that most children make astonishing efforts to reduce the conflict between the parents and they come up with some brilliant solutions. Unconsciously, of course.

John But if the parents are *permanently* locked in a power struggle, what can they do?

Robin Well, basically the child can reduce the parents' conflict by becoming some kind of problem that the parents can agree about.

John Ah! If the child can become a *problem child*, he can force the parents to cooperate in trying to *stop* him being a 'problem child'.

Robin Or, even if he can't get the parents to cooperate, he may at least be able to limit their disagreement to the issue of how they should manage him. So their conflict becomes a 'limited war' fought in only that area of child management. Rather than an all-out, global confrontation which could end in divorce.

John . . . This suddenly seems very sad, doesn't it? That the child has to do this for the parents to help them become a more stable unit.

Robin I used to feel that too when I first started working with families. But now, for me, it's just a matter of mechanics, like diagnosing and fixing a motor where something has come loose. And, of course, now that there are so many new and effective ways of treating these problems, you know something can be done about it, *if* they can bear to face what's wrong. So that feeling of optimism balances the sadness you can't help feeling for them all.

John So how does it all work?

Robin Well, take the situation where the parents are quarrelling with each other all the time, and trying to get the child on their side. Look at these diagrams. First it's mother/child with father excluded.

And a couple of hours later, it may be father/child with mother out in the cold.

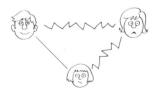

Now, if the child starts trying to solve this situation, to resolve the conflict by bringing the parents together, he can do it in one

of two ways. First, he can be a brat – a toddler. He becomes so obnoxious and impossible that the parents get so angry with him that they forget how angry they are with each other.

Or he can achieve the same kind of effect but in a completely different way. He can develop some nervous or medical problem, which worries the parents so much that they unite to look after him and try and get him better. Or, of course, use some illness that already exists – asthma, for instance – for the same purpose.

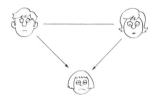

John Fascinating. Both ways it brings the parents together. In the first case by acting as a kind of lightning conductor for all the negative, rejecting, critical feelings, and in the second by attracting all the caring feelings. But now, *wait a minute* . . . you said the child sometimes plays the parents off *against* each other . . . but these ways are how it tries to bring them *together*.

Robin It sounds contradictory, I know, but it's not.

John You mean children do *both*, according to the situation?

Robin Exactly. These two ways of behaving are just two components in the complicated family system, which is regulating the closeness, or the distance, between people in the family. And every family has a tradition – and I mean a *habit* rather than an attitude people are aware of – about the normal distance there should be between a husband and wife. They'll be comfortable with that habitual distance – it'll be 'familiar' – and it will feel wrong either to be 'too close' and 'lovey-dovey' on the one hand, or on the other, too independent and seeming they might go off and leave the children. So as they get either too far apart, or too close for comfort, the child, as part of the system, will be giving little touches on the tiller to keep the distance right. Automatically, I mean, as part of the way the system operates.

John I'm beginning to see about 'circularity', and how hard it is to hold all the connections in your head! All right, those are ways the child can respond to the parents' power struggle. Now let's look at this from the point of view of the *mental map*. If the parents aren't able to compromise . . . the child will be getting *two* different maps – one from each parent.

Robin Yes. Maps which contradict each other to some extent. And because children want to love, and be loyal to, *both* parents, then if the parents can't agree, the only solution is to take both parents' attitudes on board and to keep them in separate mental compartments.

John So the child ends up taking the parental conflict *inside* himself.

Robin Right.

John And then he will have to try to operate according to two contradictory maps. This is not a recipe for peace of mind.

Robin No, it's likely to lead to neurosis unless the child, or the adult with this problem, is helped to become more aware of the two maps, and the conflict between them, and helped to bring them together. But you may be intrigued to know that this kind of two-map conflict can also lead *some* people to be highly creative.

John I know that neurosis and creativity are supposed to go together. In fact I've observed it a thousand times. But why do you think *some* two-map people become creative while some don't?

Robin What seems to make the difference is the attitude of the person towards their internal conflict. If they accept it passively, deny it in the sense of avoiding becoming aware of it in order to cope, then they're likely to have neurotic problems. Where it's led to high creativity, though, the person seems to have grappled with it, admitted it to some extent and struggled to find a way of marrying the two conflicting maps.

John The neurotic might not be able to admit there were family problems, whereas the 'artist' will?

Robin I think that's got something in it. But certainly the struggle to unify the two maps seems to force people to think in unusual, original ways, to be able to create something new.

John But creative people, who *are* struggling with the problem, can still show neurotic symptoms?

Robin Oh yes. The conflicted background will make them vulnerable. But the creativity is helping to resolve the problems.

John Does this mean neurosis *produces* creativity?

Robin No. The conflicting maps can produce either creativity or neurosis. Or a combination where the creativity is tending to cancel out the neurosis.

She's been creative all day! Should we call a doctor?

John I have at least two friends who are worried that if they underwent therapy their creativity would suffer. You wouldn't agree.

Robin Well, I've never found that. My experience, and that of other therapists, is that creative people become more creative. Have you?

John I *think* so. I don't think that whatever creativity I've got has necessarily increased, but I feel I've been freed to use it more widely; with less constraints, as it were. Enough auto-biography. I want to get back to rows. I can see how outsider parents are going to give the child two maps, because of their constant conflict. Whereas if there's a healthy relationship, the parents will agree about the handling of the child, so he'll get one consistent map. Yet even healthy parents don't agree about *everything*.

Robin It wouldn't be good for the child if they did!

John Because . . .

Robin Because we all have to cope with conflict in our lives. So we need to learn how to handle it in our families. Luckily, in any couple, the partners are bound to be at least a bit different because they've grown up in different families. So they'll disagree, at least at first, though perhaps less as time goes on, about the way to bring up the children. But if they've got through the outsider phase and learned to be part of a team, they'll be willing to listen to each other and argue until they hammer out a compromise.

John So healthy parents don't see conflict as unhealthy! So they can, for example, accept the tantrums of the toddler in a way that helps the child develop naturally and pass through to the next stage of life. And also, he will eventually get one agreed message from them on which he can base his map.

Robin Yes, *but* . . . he gets something else as well: the idea that it's natural to be different, and healthy to disagree, but *also* that it's best of all if you can put different ideas together and struggle over them a bit until some middle ground is agreed on. So the child isn't just getting a consistent map of the whole, he's also getting an example, right there before his eyes, of how to find a solution, if your map disagrees with someone else's.

John He learns by example.

Robin Which is always the most powerful way. Children learn much more, and more deeply, from what you do than from what you say. So if parents tell a child he should stand up for himself but they don't dare to stand up to each other – well, he's obviously getting a bad model, a model that contradicts what they're saying, and that child may have trouble holding his own in a group or showing enough independence and initiative to be a valuable team member. He's more likely to be a conformist, or even an obsessional kind of character.

John So it's good for parents to be able to fight?

Robin Absolutely. As long as they also love each other, and can get together and work out a compromise most of the time, at least about where they are going to draw the line for the children. Also, the *ability* to be open about aggressive feelings seems to be connected with feeling at ease with sexual passion too. So when couples are not frightened of conflict it helps them, the marriage . . . and the children, too.

Afterthought:
Healthier by the Dozen

John We've talked a lot about teams and giving and taking and fitting in with others, but mainly in the context of the first child. What's the effect on the family of the arrival of a second baby?

Robin From the parents' point of view it's usually a very different story. For one thing, the big jump has already been made from the first intimacy as a couple, where they could concentrate their attentions on each other, to being a family where they both have to get together to look after someone else. Now they're just moving from being a small family to being a bigger family.

John The basic principles are the same, so they can apply what they learned with the first child to handling the arrival of the second?

Robin Yes. So, other things being equal, it'll be a lot easier to know what to expect and to meet the child's needs. With the first child, it's a new world for the parents, and their ignorance is bound to arouse a certain amount of worry that they're making mistakes. But with the second, they'll feel like old hands. They'll know that most of the anxieties they went through the first time were groundless, and they'll handle the simple problems confidently, without needing guidance from books or other people. In fact, I always advise people they should have had the second child first!

John Yes, but even so it can't be as easy to look after two as after one.

Robin No, I just mean that looked at *separately*, the second child is likely to be an easier proposition for the parents than the first. But having two of them now is still 'double trouble'. And that's not just because there are two mouths to feed and two bottoms to wipe. There are also the new relationships between all these family members to cope with.

John You mean that by the time the second baby arrives, the first one's moved on a couple of stages, so they'll need different kinds of care?

Robin So the parents are going to be concerned about dividing their attention between the two children in the way that's most helpful to both. One way, if parents can cooperate well, is for the father to take over more of the needs of the older child so as to leave the mother more available for the baby. Couples will share more of these tasks nowadays, of course, but I've already explained why this kind of division of the roles makes sense when children are young.

John But suppose the parents have difficulty *sharing*?

Robin Then there are several possibilities. In the *outsider* family the power struggles can become even more complicated as the children get older, as there are so many more kinds of alliances possible. In the *clinging, depressive* family, the mother often pairs off with one child and the father with another, not as a cooperative arrangement but at the cost of their relationship as a couple. Instead of a marriage partnership, there are really two couples, each composed of a parent and a child. Families with *fuzzy* boundaries, or where there is a lot of projection, will tend to divide the children up into 'good' and 'bad', with the 'good' one idealised and the 'bad' one scapegoated. And both will come to behave accordingly, to fulfil the prediction.

John All right, now let's look at the bigger family from the children's point of view. What's it like to be an eldest or youngest or in the middle?

Robin There's a great range of possibilities, even for 'eldests' and 'youngests', depending on such things as the sex of the other child or children, and even the *parents'* positions in their *own* family order. But there are some general differences which are fairly obvious. For example, the eldest inevitably gets a lot of parental attention. This is nice in one way, because it means more gravy at the start, more encouragement and help. The negative side is that there's also more expectation, more pressure, and though that makes for achievement and success, it also loads the eldest with the parents' ambitions, which he may end up trying to achieve for them instead of living his own life. And, of course, it's a terrible come-down for the eldest when the second child arrives.

John You were an eldest, weren't you? Do you remember that?

Robin I was the eldest of five boys. And I certainly do remember it. There's a feeling of sunshine and bliss in connection with the first four years, until the brother next to me arrived, and then it's as if the bomb went off, and after that for a long time the general feeling is grey and dismal. Like many eldest children, I'm sure I was 'spoiled' at first, then resented the new arrival even more because of that, and got myself in everyone's bad books as a result. I also think my family had a fear of jealousy over several generations, so my parents had it behind the screen. Therefore they tried to stop me being jealous by giving in to me, when they would have done more good by drawing firm lines within which I could learn to cope and gradually get over it.

John So was jealousy a bit of a problem amongst you and your brothers?

Robin Absolutely. Jealous squabbles were always bursting out between us, and our parents could never find a way of handling it successfully. 'We can't understand why they're all so jealous,' they'd say to people. 'We try to be fair.' And they were. But because jealousy frightened and worried them so much, we never got the chance of *being* properly jealous, finishing it, going through it, and letting the feeling find its normal, natural place in our personalities. Still, I've learned from this, and nowadays, when families I see professionally complain of jealousy in their children despite the fact that they always cut the cake equally with a ruler and give everyone penicillin when only one child has a sore throat, I know what to do. I usually tell them that, though they are such a nice, successful family in many ways, they're obviously *not very good at being jealous* and need more *practice* before they come to see me next time.

John So in a very approving way, you encourage them to become more aware of jealousy so they can let it emerge from behind the screen.

Robin Yes. It helps if you make a game of it, make it all slightly hilarious. And start with Dad – tell Mum to give him one less potato than everyone else, at Sunday lunch, and suggest everyone should gloat a bit. He'll usually be happy to take the lead like that in order to set everyone else a good example, if it's suggested, and if it's then his job to decide who should be the second victim.

John The parents don't mind you suggesting that they might be jealous too?

Robin Not if you put it this way – that it will help the *children* if they give *them* a chance to be jealous, so they can face up to it and learn to handle it. But of course, you're also giving the same message to the parents too, indirectly. You're also trying to give *them* an opportunity to bring jealousy out from behind *their* screens and feel more at ease about normal competitiveness towards each other. You see, the children are usually expressing openly the natural rivalry the parents feel but are trying to avoid facing in themselves.

John The parents' *natural* rivalry?

Robin About each other's differences, advantages, as male and female, father and mother. It may also reflect some rivalry they felt for brothers and sisters in the families they grew up in. If the parents learn to feel relaxed about their own competitiveness towards each other, a lot of the children's quarrelling disappears by itself.

John I was an only child, and I can see that I missed out on a lot of lessons you learn from having to deal with the natural rivalry with brothers and sisters. So I'm sure I had competitiveness and envy behind the screen to some extent and it was only when I came into your group that I began to see them more clearly.

Robin What else do you think you missed as an 'only'?

John Oh, the rough and tumble. I was more fragile than my friends – which can be made worse because parents of only children have to put all their concern and worry into you, instead of sharing it around on your brothers and sisters.

Robin And the child can pick up that attitude himself.

John Then again, because you're the only one, I think you get the idea that you're a bit 'special'. Perhaps that's why I find that I share some of the 'outsider' attitudes you've described. And finally, because your parents have only you, it's harder to escape and become independent of them. I lived in the States for eighteen months after Cambridge and, to my shame, hardly wrote home at all. But I think that was my clumsy and unconscious way of finally severing the umbilical cord.

Robin Well, only children are apt to find it even more difficult to get free of their parents' involvements than eldests do.

John How do 'onlys' compare with 'eldests' in other ways?

Robin Only children are found to be more aggressive and less anxious than eldest children, probably because they haven't had to go through the trauma of being the 'one-and-only' and then finding themselves suddenly dethroned.

John And what about youngest children?

Robin Well they have all the disadvantages of remaining the baby, because the parental apron strings can't be moved down to the next little stranger. But like the eldest and the only child, they get a lot of special interest and support from the parents; but unlike the 'eldests' and the 'onlys', they get support from older brothers and sisters too. *Middle* children can get rather left out, and spend their childhood wearing elder children's shrunken socks, but they're usually better at fitting in and getting on with other children than either eldests or youngests. But remember, all the children can get together and form a team to outwit the parents and escape from any undue possessiveness. They can divide and conquer, and escape control and surveillance by causing confusion, providing alibis for each other, or giving the parents too many leads to follow,

like outlaws riding away in different directions knowing that the sheriff's posse can't follow them all at once.

John As they'll all be pooling healthy input they've each received from outside the family, that teamwork should protect them a bit from taking on the parents' problems.

Robin It does. One of the best ways of growing up reasonably healthy in a difficult family is to make sure you have a lot of brothers and sisters. There's a positive spin-off back to the parents too. One of the nicest family interviews I can remember was with a family where the parents, who had first come as a couple, were among the most wild, violent and uncontrollable pairs of partners I'd encountered. I couldn't handle them on my own, so my wife shared the task, but they ran rings round us. So we got their seven adolescent and young adult children to come too – that made a circle of eleven in the room – and we were astonished to find how normal and nice they all were, by comparison with the parents. They even made it possible for the parents to talk about their sexual relationship constructively for the first time since we'd begun seeing them.

John The *children* helped them . . . how?

Robin It was mainly the older daughters talking to the father. One daughter in particular was very good. 'I don't want to upset you, Daddy,' she said, 'and I hope you won't mind what I'm going to say . . .' He told her to go ahead, and sat quiet and attentive. So she continued, 'The trouble is, Daddy, you don't understand *women* very well. All that shouting and bad language, it's *not the way to go about it*. You've got to be *nice* to them . . .' And so on. He took it all in thoughtfully, nodding away, and we began to make some progress. Of course, the other children were backing her up. It would have been more difficult in a small family.

John It sounds like an argument for democracy, doesn't it? The more opinions that are being expressed, the better chance you have of picking the ones that are helpful to you. As an only child, I received only my parents' attitudes, and I don't think it was till I got into your group and had a *new* family experience, with you and Prue as temporary parents and the rest of the group as brothers and sisters, that I was able to get free of certain Weston-super-Mare attitudes that weren't working for me. Perhaps if I'd had brothers and sisters, there would have been a better debate at an earlier stage!

5 What are You Two <u>Doing</u> in There?

A matter of life and death . . . . . .

John We've dealt with sorting out boundaries, becoming independent and joining teams. What's the next key idea?

Robin Sex. Everything you always wanted to know about it, but were too worried you ought to know already to ask. Like why we need two sexes; how men and women are different, and *whether* they are; why incest isn't a good idea; how the female is the human prototype, and the male an adaptation; how homosexuality seems to develop; why Oedipus killed his father so he wouldn't have to grow up; and why all the recent developments in sex therapy work so well.

John And all this carnal knowledge comes now because it's the next stage the child has to deal with?

Robin Yes. Because the toddler's becoming aware of his sexual identity.

John All right. Would you please explain something first? I have heard several hundred thousand dirty jokes in my life, and only seven of them were funny. But provided the punch line includes a four-letter word, everyone falls about. I used to think this was because I was more embarrassed about sex than they were. Now I'm sure it's the other way round. But why are we *all* embarrassed about it?

Robin I think it's because it can arouse such overwhelming, mind-blowing emotions. We're uncomfortable about its sheer power.

John And the dirty jokes are a way of defusing that power – of pretending that these emotions aren't *really* very strong, because 'we can all laugh at them, can't we?'

Robin I think that's probably right.

John So why do you think the idea of sex is so powerful?

Robin I think there are a lot of reasons, which we all know but somehow manage to forget most of the time. For instance, it's the source of our very existence! We wouldn't even be alive if our parents hadn't bestowed their favours on each other.

John The thought of Daddy and Mummy mating can be quite a strain on the imagination, can't it? Let alone the notion that our life once hinged on it.

Robin And once you start thinking of that, you're only just round the corner from the thought that one day you *won't* be here.

John Which I suppose might lead us into questions about what we're here for, which we normally prefer to avoid.

Robin So all those thoughts are a little uncomfortable. Then there's the fact that the sexual experience itself is about the most positive, powerful and moving experience we can have, short of the religious ecstasy which most of us will never know.

John 'The earth moved.'

Robin And earthquakes may be exciting, but they're a little unsettling too. And another source of discomfort is that sex is exciting and fulfilling only to the extent that we can lose control and give ourselves over to the experience. We have to 'let go'.

John So we're not sure what might happen? We might find out something about ourselves we didn't know if we allowed ourselves to get too lost in the experience?

Robin Yes. Even chatting about sex can arouse a tingle of that danger in the background of our thoughts. Then again there's another aspect – that it's so hugely important in the structure of our lives. For example, our security in childhood depends so much on the quality of the sexual relationship between our parents. It's such a cement to the marriage, and the marriage is the foundation of the family we're so dependent on when we're young. I believe children sense this even though they don't quite know what it's all about, because if the parents are happy and have that glow that comes from a good sexual relationship, you notice the children glow too.

John And even when we're adult, it can be a bit alarming to think our marriages may depend on something so explosive and unpredictable. I think that's why it's always been such a cast-iron ingredient of farce. Everybody senses deep down how powerful and disruptive the sexual urge can be, so the farce writer can get his characters into ridiculously dangerous situations quite credibly.

Robin And, of course, the more we try to pretend sex *isn't* important, and try to repress it, the more powerful and uncontrollable it is when it does burst to the surface. So it would be surprising really if we didn't feel a little in awe of the power of sex – and so try to cover it up with humour.

John But none of this explains why it's so much *more* difficult for *children and their parents* to talk about sex together than it is to discuss it with people who are not in their family.

Robin Well, this is such a universal experience that I think that most people, including those in my profession, take it for granted and don't really ask why. I believe that it's because sex is such a powerful force – perhaps *the* most powerful force – pushing children towards growing up, becoming truly independent and leaving home. It can be a very bitter-sweet realisation for parents to become aware of their children as sexual beings who will one day go off and marry someone else; and also for children to be aware that they'll never have the intimate closeness with their parents which the parents have with each other. And this is especially so when the children reach sexual maturity and each parent and child is most aware of how attractive and nice the other is.

John With the parting coming ever closer.

Robin And that parting can remind them of another one – that the parent is likely to die before the child. These are all very uncomfortable, saddening thoughts, and reasons why sexual discussion in families can be so awkward.

John But many parents do talk very freely with their children nowadays about sex.

Robin Yes, but if you pay attention to their manner, you'll find that they're usually leaning over backwards against the same discomfort. The 'facts' may be talked about a lot, but the 'feelings' are being shoved under the carpet. And it's the feelings that really count.

John You once said in our group that you thought that the embarrassment parents feel about disappearing into the bedroom and closing the door to keep the kids out wasn't primarily sexual – it was about separation, parting, even when the children were very young.

Robin Yes. If you enquire into the embarrassment most parents feel about shutting the children out, and even more about making a noise while having intercourse that the children may overhear, people can never really explain it, even to their own satisfaction. It's disproportionate. It only began to make sense to me, and then to the parents I discussed it with, when I realised that the worry was about *excluding the children*; and then I understood that for the children, being excluded and feeling jealous of their parents' special intimacy and pleasure, was a powerful force pushing them to turn their interest away from the parents towards the outside world, where their own similar fulfilment can only be found.

John So if we exclude our children and make them face this painful fact, we guarantee that they will ultimately leave us for someone else.

Robin Which is as it should be, and the best gift we can give them. But we find it difficult, and shrink from it, just the same. And finally, there's yet another powerful reason for awkwardness. It's that, for the children to be pushed towards maturity, *there needs to be 'the right amount' of sexual feeling between the parents and the children.*

John How do you mean?

Robin Well, not too much, of course, but also not *too little*. The parents have to walk a tightrope between, on the one hand, a cold, frigid, non-sexual atmosphere, and on the other, an atmosphere where there is a bit too much sexual feeling around.

John To put it crudely, between frigidity at one extreme and incest at the other?

He said he was going to marry his mother, and now it looks as if he'll have to.

Robin That's right. All the family members sense, deep down, the need to get this balance right, so it's no wonder there's a general feeling in families that sexuality is a bit of a minefield.

John This is an impressive list you're producing. In fact I'm beginning to feel quite relaxed about my inhibitions. But there's one aspect you haven't mentioned – how fundamentally absurd the sex act is. I mean if you had to describe the process in court to a Chief Justice, he wouldn't believe a word of it, would he? He'd think you had gone insane. 'And then you did *what*?'

Robin I sometimes find myself thinking that the whole hilarious ritual was designed to make us aware of our lowly position in the scheme of things, and to stop us getting too big-headed. You know the old religious idea that we are part men and part Gods – that in our imagination we can soar to the height of the Gods. Well, nothing reminds us of our earthly limitations so much as the contemplation of us 'humping' each other.

John I like the thought that all that frantic bliss-seeking is just a cosmic banana skin. Now, all this beating about the bush ... I know it's traditional before talking about sex, but have we done enough?

Robin I don't think we can put it off any longer.

Why two sexes? ......

Robin So ... sex. Well, the point is there are *two of them*.

John So far so good.

Robin That's because it takes two to make something new.

John You mean a virgin birth would produce a child that was like a clone of the mother.

Robin Yes, if we could bud off babies as some primitive plants and animals do, they'd be genetically identical to us. But in humans, the chromosomes are half from the mother in the egg and half from the father in the sperm. Which is why it's always a new combination genetically.

John What's a chromosome?

Robin Didn't you do *any* biology?

John Yes, but the teacher was a former rugby international and he didn't know either.

Robin Well it's like a tiny, microscopic string of beads, where every bead is carrying some instructions for making the new individual. In *each* human cell you find twenty-three pairs of these chromosomes, which carry the whole programme for the design and maintenance of that person.

John So every cell has a kind of 'instruction booklet' for making the new baby. But why 'pairs'?

Robin They need to be in pairs so that when each cell splits in two, each of the two new cells gets a set. Now the point is that *one* pair of chromosomes is strikingly different in males and females. The normal female cell has two similar long chromosomes, called X chromosomes, and the normal male has a long X chromosome and a shorter one, called a Y chromosome. Now, when the sex cells are made – the sperm in the man and the egg in the woman – they each get only one half of the *pair* of chromosomes that are standard in all the other cells.

John Get on with it.

Robin The worst is nearly over. So when an egg from the mother gets together with a seed from the father to make a baby cell, the mother's egg is bound to have an X; but the father's seed may have an X *or* a Y.

John So the father's cell determines the sex of the baby?

Robin Right. Now right at the beginning, when the baby is inside the mother and still very tiny, it has the equipment to make both types of sexual organs. But if there's no Y chromosome present, the male parts disappear, and the female parts grow to form a womb and a vagina.

John If the male chromosome happens to be an X, you'll get an XX combination – a girl.

Robin And if the male chromosome is a Y, the presence of the Y in all the baby's cells switches the development on to the male track. Then, instead of the female parts growing, the testicles grow instead. Next, these testicles produce chemicals which cause the female equipment to be absorbed and the male parts to grow – so you get a penis instead.

John I'd never realised that the female was the prototype. The baby cell grows in the female direction *unless* it's switched on to the other track by the Y chromosome?

Robin Right. But once the Y chromosome has 'pulled the points', they can't be switched again. The direction is set.

John Can this simple little XX or XY plan go wrong?

Robin Very occasionally. A baby *can* have only one X when you get a definite female but she can't have babies herself. Or it's possible to get two Xs and a Y, XXY, when you get male sexual parts but with very small testes and some breast development. And there can be males with an X and two Ys who tend to be abnormal in many respects. There are even some conditions where a tumour makes extra sex hormones, or the hormones don't work properly, or where the mother is given some medicine during pregnancy which has an unintentional hormonal effect, so the switching mechanism goes a bit wrong at a later stage. But these are very rare.

John So, *physically* speaking, you're one or the other. And psychologically?

Milestones of psychological development ......

Robin Let's start with a quick run-through of the milestones of sexual psychology in a child's development, beginning with the toddler.

John To what extent does the toddler know what sex he is?

Robin Well it's during this stage that the child begins sorting this out. But at the start, and for some time, he seems to want to be both and to believe he can be. So growing up means he's got to renounce the other gender.

John Well that must be a pretty huge step for him in terms of his ego getting shrunk. When does this happen?

Robin At about two and a half, children are getting interested in the differences between boys and girls and by three*ish* the core gender identity is firmly established.

John Wash your mouth out.

Robin I'm sorry. It means a deep and relatively unalterable sense of which sex one really belongs to. Let's just say . . . our sexual identity.

John So does that mean that about the age of three you can identify a more 'boyish' or 'girlish' way of behaving?

Robin Well, that's been developing all the time, partly through inborn differences and partly through the fact that parents tend to treat boys and girls differently from the start – and as everyone knows, it's extraordinarily difficult to tell those two influences apart. The child's sexual identity – that is, what he makes of all these differences himself – is something else again, and takes time for the child to sort out. But by about the age of four, children begin dividing into groups according to sex, and getting a lot of fun and enjoyment and excitement over showing off their private parts too.

John Which indicates a certain pride in their new sexual identity.

Robin It looks like that. Another thing you notice is that this developing interest in the sexual apparatus and in how babies are made, and in marriage, is usually accompanied by a romantic, admiring and really quite touching attitude from the little boy towards his mother, or the little girl towards her father. They'll be very affectionate, indeed quite possessive, and often show jealousy towards the parent of the *same* sex. With the result that the child interrupts and tries to separate the parents if they pay too much attention to each other; or he may find excuses to come into the parents' bedroom at night and prevent them from being together in private.

John How long does that go on?

Robin Well, provided that the parents have resisted it, very kindly but very firmly, and have shut the bedroom door, the child will have got over it, more or less, by about the age of six. Then the romantic feelings go underground, and don't really surface again until the sex hormones begin to trigger the adolescent stage.

John The child will have had to cope with a lot of jealousy and nasty feelings of exclusion . . .

Robin Yes he will. But that's all necessary, because if the child goes through this *now* he will avoid certain problems later on.

John Which might arise if he was allowed to separate the parents?

Robin Right. So by six, the child has given up his attempt to disrupt the marriage. And after that we get the period known as 'latency' which lasts up to about twelve.

John But how latent is that? They don't really lose interest at all, do they?

Robin Oh, certainly not! They learn to *hide* their interest, like adults do, and it remains a lively subject of conversation among themselves. But the *feelings* that create that first 'eternal triangle' with the parents fade, and free their energy for other interests and activities.

John Perfecting foul language and learning about ways you can torture people, or make them envious.

Robin All those natural, healthy pursuits, yes. *But* of course when adolescence begins – 'puberty' – the sex glands start producing chemicals which stimulate all sorts of changes in the bodies.

John Girls start earlier than boys, don't they?

Robin Yes, the ovaries start producing an egg every month and she begins to get periods somewhere between ten and sixteen, with an average age around thirteen. The hormones cause her to take on a more womanly shape, with the hips widening, the breasts growing, and so on, to prepare her body to be able to bear children. The whole process is spread over three or four years in the girl.

John Whereas, in the boy . . .

Robin Well, in the boy, equivalent changes begin later and take four or five years to complete. The testicles begin producing the male sex hormone and the boy's chest gets bigger, together with the muscles generally, and the genitals too of course. The voice deepens, and the body hair grows. The testicles produce sperm in readiness for fathering children, and he knows this because he starts getting nocturnal emissions.

John I thought that was French late-night television.

Robin 'Wet dreams' to you. Unless the build-up of sperm is removed by masturbation before the overflow occurs.

John And very nice too. What age are we talking about here?

Robin Any time between about eleven and sixteen is quite normal for wet dreams to begin, but fourteen is about average.

John So what's happening psychologically?

Robin One effect of the sex hormones is to stimulate sexual feelings and thoughts, which can be quite disturbing to young people who aren't expecting this, or don't know why it's happening. Another effect is to programme both sexes to be turned on by the new shape they're seeing when they look at the people on the other team, as if they've suddenly been given a recognition chart.

John Till now, they've been staying separate and occasionally reviling each other.

Robin Yes, but now they start being drawn together. First they play it safe by mixing only in large groups, usually still keeping the safe distance by teasing and pushing each other off their bicycles; but just occasionally showing shy and hesitant signs of affection before hastily retreating to the safety of the crowd again. But gradually the groups get smaller, until they're down to foursomes, and finally to pairs.

John Well it looks to me as though psychological sexual development breaks up into four main stages. The stage up to around two and a half, when the child is settled in its sexual identity; the stage from about three till six, where the child goes through and gets over the romantic attachment to the parent of the opposite sex; then the stage from six to twelvish, the 'latency' phase, when interest in sex seems to be comparable to interest in a lot of other things; and then the phase of adolescence when the hormones are rushing around stirring up fifty-seven varieties of new thoughts and feelings.

Robin That'll do. Now let's go right back and work through it all in proper detail.

The toddler learns his sex ......

John You said that at the start of the toddler phase, the children seem to believe they can be both sexes.

Robin That's right. They still want everything their own way.

John They're at the 'outsider' stage, so having to fit in to the male team or the female team will feel like a limitation, being 'cut down to size' too much?

Robin Yes. So they don't like surrendering to the idea of not having what the opposite sex has got. But of course they have to. The little girl has to give up the idea that she can have a penis and the little boy has to abandon hope of ever having babies. But this comes very hard at first.

John So what helps the child to do this?

Robin The example of the parents is much the most important influence.

John Not what they say, of course, but how they behave.

Robin That's the key thing. The child learns his sexual identity by modelling himself on the parent of the same sex. But of course it's all much clearer if he can learn about the opposite sex at the same time, and compare them.

John So he needs *both* parents to be able to do this properly.

Robin Or at least two persons of opposite sexes taking an active part in his life.

John But what *sort* of models should he be getting?

Robin Well, that was quite simple till recently, wasn't it? Fathers just had to be manly and mothers womanly and everyone knew what that meant. But now, with the sex roles changing from the traditional pattern, we'll have to cope with quite a lot of confusion for some while.

John What do you think will be the outcome?

Robin My guess is that a lot of the traditional pattern will remain, or even return in the case of people who have tried to change it drastically, but that most of the good changes will stay. So most men and women will be wanting equality, and quite a bit of sharing, *but also* definite, clear differences from each other in a psychological sense.

John So how does all this correspond with what the child needs, if he's to accept his sexual identity happily?

Robin Well, the research on what makes for health, happiness and confidence in the sexual role suggests that the parents who help their children most in these respects show quite a bit of *overlap* in their sexual roles – they share a good many similarities in what they are and what they do. But they also enjoy, and believe in, being *different* from each other in many respects as well.

John So a unisex arrangement between the parents is not good for the children.

Robin It seems to lead to confusion in the child. The child needs parents who share some activities and interests, and at least *some* of his care. But the child also needs them to *be* different, and stand for different things, and to respect and enjoy and admire each other's differences. You need *two* landmarks to get a bearing and find out where you are – and you need them to be a certain distance apart.

John So you are saying that, for instance, the father makes his sons masculine by setting a very masculine model by the way he behaves?

Robin No. It's very interesting that the evidence in fact suggests that fathers can't *make* their sons masculine simply by setting a very masculine model themselves. Nor by just putting pressure on them to behave in that way, either. In fact this can have the opposite effect! It's where the fathers are masculine *and also* *loving*, supportive, and engaged sometimes in the day-to-day care of their children that they produce sons and daughters both sexually confident.

John And the mothers?

Robin The same story. If they're positive towards their own femininity, and their daughters' femininity, *and also* enjoy the masculinity of their husbands and their sons, they help their children to grow up with a happy acceptance of their sexual identity.

John It sounds as if the father's presence is vital at times, but that it isn't essential for him to be there as regularly as the mother.

Robin It seems that's true, yes. The amount of time he's present is less important than the part he plays when he is there. But a lot of evidence shows that *absence* of the father in the early years often causes difficulty in developing a comfortable sexual identity, especially in boys.

John Because then the daughters will at least have a model of what they should develop *into*, even if they lack one for the opposite sex ... but the boys won't have a model at all – except the sexual role they *shouldn't* follow?

Robin Yes, but it's more than just that. There's another reason, which is that the development of the male is more complicated than the development of the female. It's as though something 'extra' has to happen, for the boy, which doesn't have to happen for the girl.

John As in the baby stage, where the extra Y chromosome had to come in and 'switch the points' to produce a boy?

Robin Yes, it's a psychological echo of that idea. Have a look at this diagram of what's happening up to the age of about one and a quarter. Because both male and female children start life inside the mother, and only she has breasts that can feed them, all children normally start with an attachment to the *mother* – so I've put them on one side of a metaphorical river. The father, on the other side, is at first a more distant figure for the children. He's minding the shop, as it were, supporting the whole operation. So at this stage the children are mainly influenced by the mother and *both* modelling themselves on her.

John So if that situation continued, the boy wouldn't get the male influence he'd need.

Robin Right. So to become psychologically male, he's got to 'cross the bridge' to be with his *father*.

John Whereas the girl can stay where she is with her mother?

Robin Yes. Of course she can always play around on the bridge, cross a little way, or even go quite far for a time and be a real tomboy. But everyone is expecting her to end up on the same bank she started on, with her mother, and that first intense attachment to her mother will be helping her to end up there.

John So crossing the bridge is the 'something extra' the boy has to do?

Robin Yes. And that of course means struggling against that powerful mother-tie.

John So what helps him to get free of that attachment and cross over?

Robin He needs two forces to break that primary tie. *One*, he needs his mother to help him cope with moving away from her, because there's an emotional umbilical cord joining them, and if the mother won't let go of her end, it'll be very difficult for him to get free. And *two*, he needs his father to love him and want him as a fellow male.

John If he gets help from them both, how long does the crossing take?

Robin He needs to be across by about two and a half. Indeed, it's hard to *reverse* the process after about one and a half. But both sexes go on getting used to, and learning about, the roles they're expected to play on their sides of the river for some years after that.

John So by about three and a half the boy is across on the father's side. That means he feels confident and happy about being male.

Robin So he turns round, faces his Mum and starts flirting with her, just as the little girl, on the other side, is flirting with her Dad.

From now up to the age of about five is the period I mentioned earlier, when the children have a romantic affair with the opposite-sex parent.

John This is the Oedipus complex?

Robin Yes, though there are several other aspects to that too. There's the jealousy of the same-sex parent, plus the fear that he or she will take revenge on the child for trying to steal their marriage partner.

John Now during this time when the boy has been crossing the bridge, what's been the influence of the father on the *girl*?

Robin Well the girl needs to separate from the mother too. So all the fatherly jobs we've talked about, laying down guidelines, firmness, encouraging exploration, and of course 'reclaiming' his wife, are helping the girl to become more independent of her mother. So although she stays on the same bank, she'll move apart from her, precisely because she has her own identity to discover.

The male ego ......

Robin This river-and-bridge metaphor helps us to understand better some other puzzling behaviour too. For example, men are usually more uncomfortable about expressing the need to be looked after and supported by a woman than women are about asking for that from a man.

John ... Because men are frightened that they'll be pulled back across the bridge?

Robin That's it. They associate these needs with being on the mother's side of the river as young children. So some men are scared that if they ever allowed themselves to be mothered, they might not be able to get back across to the male side again!

John Mothering could turn them into *permanent* babies?

Robin Yes, or into females. So they have a great fear of this power they *feel* women have over them – which is in fact proportional to their deep hidden need to be mothered. So they often end up adopting a macho position, showing a scornful and denigrating attitude towards women, just to avoid the danger of getting too close emotionally.

John In case they might suddenly reveal their needs and fall into Mummy's power for good.

Robin Yes, and this kind of male insecurity is made ever greater because it has to be handled in the face of the traditional demand on him to be hunter, the protector who'll look after everybody else.

John But hang on. Given enough stress, all men need to be looked after. Why is mothering frightening to some and not to others?

Robin It all depends on whether or not the man can admit the occasional desire to be supported and babied. If he can, he will have the measure of it. He will have experienced it, so he knows he can control it; he knows it won't overwhelm him. Also, he has learned that after a time, when the need is satisfied, it'll disappear like any other appetite, and he can go back to being 'a man' again. So he's not frightened of admitting the need, and can feel secure in his male identity despite it.

John Being able to acknowledge the need gives him a more secure sexual identity?

Robin And being secure allows him to acknowledge the need – it's a self-perpetuating circle.

John Whereas if he *can't* admit the need, if he's *denied* it . . . ?

Robin Well, then, because he's hiding his desire, he's out of touch with it. He's never experienced it. Nevertheless he senses its power, which is the greater because it's never been satisfied ... so he's terrified that if it ever surfaced he wouldn't be able to control it and get back to being a responsible adult again.

John Catch 22 again. He's not admitting it because of his fear that he can't control it, but he can't get the confidence that he can control it unless he admits it. So he's insecure sexually?

Robin Even if he's not 'macho', he'll need to keep women at a distance. They're a threat to him because they could reveal the hidden need.

John Meanwhile, back at the bridge ... if *women* require support, mothering, then there's not the same problem because that's all associated with the side of the river they're on anyway.

Robin And there's no warrior image acting as a taboo against asking for support either. So women are more able to take it for granted and are therefore more secure in their female identity. In fact, when I see men and women at their most natural and open, as they're able to be in the privacy of a doctor's consulting room, I'm constantly impressed by how much stronger women appear to be than men. *On the surface* many of them may seem less confident; but *basically* they have their feet on the ground much more firmly.

John People used to ask me why we wrote so few funny parts for women in 'Monty Python' and the only answer I could give was that I didn't know so much about women, but from what I did know they didn't seem to me anything like as silly as men.

Robin That's right! They're not keeping up acts in the same way, they don't live in dreams of status and power and achievement to the extent that men do. And because they don't take that stuff very seriously, they're not so fragile, their egos aren't so delicate. And because of that, incidentally, because they're closer to reality, they're much more responsive to treatment.

John What about the feminists? Some of them are caught up in male-style power struggles and the need to achieve, aren't they?

Robin Yes, the kind of militant feminist who is rivalling the traditional male role *is* less confident than other women in this fundamental sense – those that *I've* seen at least.

John Are we suddenly talking about power and status and achievement because they're really just a kind of substitute for real sexual self-confidence?

Robin Yes. When you look into it closely, they're usually an outward display that a man uses to reassure himself – and those around him too, he hopes – against a deep inner fear that he's not adequate in his male sexuality.

John Perhaps that's why so much of the posturing of powerful people is so funny – we're intuitively aware of the vulnerability underneath.

Robin And there's another interesting point about this male vulnerability. It's astonishing how considerate and protective women are towards it. They'll go to extraordinary lengths – often at great cost to themselves – to avoid putting a man in a position where he has to face up to this kind of weakness.

John What kind of weakness exactly? Just admitting that he *does* have the need to be mothered sometimes?

Robin Yes, if *in his own eyes* that would make him feel inadequate. So he's put up a façade to hide this, which women are loathe to attack. I've noticed this particularly when working with female colleagues. When seeing a couple or family, they'd often let the husband get away with murder and then tell me afterwards how angry he'd made them feel. I'd say, 'Why didn't you tell him? It would have done him good.' And they'd usually reply, 'Oh, I *couldn't*, it would be like *castrating* him.'

John Although he really *needed* to have his weakness – due to his *fear* of his desire to be mothered – pointed out to him before he could do anything about it?

Robin Yes.

John And these were trained therapists?

Robin Yes. Even doing this work, where they have to help people face the truth, at first they find it terribly difficult to put a man to the test. It's as if they've been trained from birth to avoid it. Even the support of the women's movement doesn't seem to have freed most women from that inhibition about testing the man's ability to stay on the other bank of this river. After all, if the poor fellow's balls fell off, metaphorically speaking, we'd know what the trouble was and could help him glue them back on more securely. And if they didn't, that would be reassuring to everyone. It's astonishing – this womanly need to protect the male ego seems to be one of the most deeply ingrained inhibitions of all.

The variety of possibilities ......

John You said that if women cross the bridge, they're in trouble. But why should a woman do that at all?

Robin Well, if her mother is very cold and offers her nothing, and her father offers her more, she may cross part or all of the way. If she ends up completely on the wrong side, she'll become a trans-sexual.

John Which means?

Robin She feels as if she's really a man. Psychologically speaking, she's *become* a man. She wants to behave and be treated as such, so she may want to have a sex change.

John And male trans-sexuals?

Robin These are boys who've got stuck on Mother's side of the bridge, identify completely with her, and think that they are *really* female.

John So why haven't they got even as far as putting a foot on the bridge over to the father?

Robin Well, that's because they typically have mothers who have given them a blissful infant experience but prolonged it far past the time when they should be helping the child to separate, because the mother doesn't want him to grow apart.

John And the father isn't offering the boy anything to coax him across?

Robin No. They're usually nonentities who are hardly even there. So if these boys aren't helped across by two and a half or so, when the sexual identity is getting fixed, change becomes increasingly unlikely, even with treatment. They may become quite uninterested in becoming male psychologically and also want a sex-change operation.

John All right. Now what about the people who are on the bridge – who've started to cross but haven't reached the other side? Are they homosexual?

Robin Yes, I would see homosexuals as strung out along our bridge at different distances across it.

John So the mothers have let them go to some extent?

Robin Well, typically, the male homosexuals have rather powerful, possessive mothers.

John But less possessive than trans-sexuals' mothers?

Robin Less completely identified with the child, anyway. Also, from the studies I've seen, I have the impression they're women who provide the boy with a less gratifying, positive experience too. So there's less incentive to stay.

John And the boy's father?

Robin He's most commonly reported as providing little of the kind of influence that normally encourages a boy to get across to his side, either because he's absent, distant, ineffectual, *or* because he's harsh and unloving. Nevertheless, homosexual males are far enough across to have accepted a male identity. Perhaps partly because the tie to the mother is also threatening.

John Why is it threatening?

Robin For the same reason that women can be a threat to males who have reached the other side – they're frightened they'll be attracted back to the mother's side permanently. But of course this fear is even greater for gay males because they haven't even got across to the father's side. And also, since they haven't therefore had a close relationship with the father, there's a greater fear of his sexual jealousy if they rival him.

John So as the gay male hasn't reached the father's side, he can never turn round, flirt with his mother and go through the Oedipus story.

Robin No, he remains on the bridge, facing towards the father; or rather the father-he-wanted-and-needed-but-never-got. So his attachment stays on males instead of returning in a sexual form to his mother and hence to females generally.

John Are you suggesting that the gay male is essentially continuing to look for a loving father who'll give him what he lacked?

Robin That's the basic idea – although, of course, it's much more complicated than that for many reasons. But in my experience, I'd say the gay male is someone who *hasn't* had a normal homosexual – that is, 'same-sex' – warm, loving relationship with his father.

John A *homosexual* relationship with his father . . . ?

Robin Well, I don't mean playing with each other's genitals. But I do mean *physical*, certainly, like romping and cuddling and rough-housing, in the way that male football players exchange obvious physical embraces when someone scores the crucial goal.

John Or indeed any goal. So someone who's had a father who's loved him in this warm, physical, horse-play kind of way will be more likely to have found his way right across the bridge?

Robin And, incidentally, will also have gained strength and authority from the father by accepting his authority, as we said. So he'll be more likely to feel *competent* to take on the *responsibility* of a wife and family. The gay male hasn't usually got over this hurdle about authority and spends his life going through the *motions* of doing so by perpetually seeking the *symbol* of the father's authority and strength, in the form of other men's penises, rather than the real thing – the authority and responsibility itself.

John That's an amazing idea. You mean you think that gay males like other men's penises because they symbolise something that they don't feel they have quite enough of.

Robin Yes. The penis stands for the father's love and warmth, his loving authority and strength, and, through that, the feeling that this authority and strength has been taken in, possessed. So symbols of that – other men's penises – are collected instead. And as they're *not* the thing they symbolise, the person is never satisfied, never has enough, often goes from one partner to another.

But, of course, I'm talking about men in a particular position on the bridge – the ones in the middle, who've settled for that position and given up trying to get across. Those who get nearer the father's bank may find that a relationship with another man of a deep, emotional kind gives them something they didn't get from their father, and they're able, through that, to get right across to join the men's team. That deep bond to another man may be accompanied by physical sex too; but very often it isn't, and is more like a fatherly relationship.

John So if gay men and women are stretched out across the bridge in different positions and some of them are stuck nearer the male side, and others nearer the female side . . . they can pair off in male and female roles and have some of the experience of being different, and complementing each other, that 'straight' couples do.

Robin I think that's true, although let's not push the bridge metaphor too far. It's only expressing one aspect of it all.

John All right. Now we've hardly mentioned gay females.

Robin No. It's interesting that in the literature there's much less about them than has been written about male homosexuals. It's as though it's regarded as more normal, less necessary to investigate.

John How about in feminist writings?

Robin Well, they'll tend to regard it as even more normal than psychiatrists do. Certainly the professional contact I've had suggests to me that female gayness is somehow more natural, loving and supportive than one usually sees among male gays. So they don't often seek treatment for it. It seems to be, often, a stage in growing up for many women.

John But, like the men, they haven't flirted with the opposite-sex parent – they're still facing the same-sex parent.

Robin Yes, and the same principle applies – they usually seem to have missed out on, and are searching for, an intimate, loving, physical relationship with their mothers.

John All right. So to sum up, sticking to the bridge metaphor, we've got the feminine girls on the mother's side but a bit separate from her; the masculine boys on the father's side; the male trans-sexuals still haven't left the mother's side at all; the female trans-sexuals have crossed right over to the father's side; and the homosexuals are stretched out right the way across the bridge. Let me ask one last question. I thought it was now generally accepted that very few people's psychological make-up is 100 per cent heterosexual. So would it not be more accurate to suggest that most people are *on the bridge*; in other words have *some*, although perhaps very mild, homosexual inclinations?

Robin Yes, well, this is where the metaphor becomes somewhat misleading. But to make it useable a bit longer, let's say that, under some circumstances, we *can* return to an earlier stage of our development, even though we may *prefer* to operate in terms of a later stage. For instance, it's not uncommon for men who are isolated from women for a long time – in prison, or at sea, or boarding school – to have sex with other men because there's no alternative, even though they are heterosexual when there are women available. But you're right, all these *feelings* will be there somewhere in normal people.

John But they don't feel they want to act on them.

Robin Either that, or they may be unaware of them, because they've put them behind the screen.

Sexual politics ......

John Now when I look at this bridge of yours, I see people who are physically male *and* physically female stretched out across the bridge in *all* positions and on *both* banks. Any individual's position is supposed to indicate his or her *psychological* sexual identity. But what are the psychological differences between 'maleness' and 'femaleness'?

Robin The trouble is, that question is extraordinarily difficult to answer. Ordinarily we're all aware of very striking differences between men and women, aren't we? But when you begin to try to measure them, to define exactly what the differences are, they keep disappearing. In any case, any given finding only applies to the *average* man or the *average* woman.

John Any particular woman may be more interested in astrophysics or sailing round the world than any particular man.

Robin The overlap is huge, much more than people expect. In fact the psychological differences between people of the same sex are bigger than the average differences between men and women, on almost everything that's been measured.

John So some differences *have* been established?

Robin Well even those aren't very well proven.

John Wait a moment. Are we talking about inborn differences or the ones due to conditioning?

Robin Well, again, there's a tremendous difficulty in establishing whether any given difference is inborn or entirely due to the different ways boys and girls are treated as they grow up. Obviously, if all the boys in a school learn science and mechanics and the girls learn sewing and cookery, it won't be altogether surprising if boys enjoy, and are good at, mending motorcycles and girls are better at making cakes and sewing on buttons. And the different expectations and influences that push boys and girls in opposite directions are so universal, and so powerful, right from the moment of birth when the physical difference is known, that it's very hard to tease out what real, inborn differences there may be.

John Do you think any have been established?

Robin Yes, but again, don't forget they are only *average* differences. But several definite inborn ones have been described by Corinne Hutt, an expert on this subject in Britain in whom I have a lot of confidence. She cites, for example, a higher energy consumption base-level and activity-level in boys, and also greater capacity for dealing with visual and spatial tasks. Girls, on the other hand, develop more quickly in most respects – intellectually, physically and socially – and they score better in being able to handle language, and to communicate. And males are in general more aggressive than females. A very thorough review of the literature by two American researchers, Maccoby and Jacklin, agrees with most of that, but suggests that even the difference in respect of visual, spatial and language skills seems stronger where women are subjugated and weaker where both sexes are allowed independence, so there's even doubt there about how much it's inborn.

John What about any difference in aggression?

Robin That's the best-established and most widely noted difference. And it *is* clearly connected with physical causes. For instance, an increase in male sex hormone leads to more vigorous, out-going, aggressive play in boys, while increase in the female sex hormone – and both sexes have male *and* female-type hormones, incidentally – makes a boy more docile, quiet and less vigorous and less aggressive. But even here, there's a big element of circular argument because, for instance, it's been found in some animals that male sex hormone increases if there's a receptive female available, and it falls if the animal is defeated in a fight, or if it's under stress.

John You mean if both sexes have both hormones, and the *balance* between the hormones is affected by what's going on in the *environment*, we're heading back towards Square One again?

Robin It's not as straightforward as it seems, at least.

John But whether it's inborn or not, men are more aggressive on the whole, aren't they? That's why they tend to dominate, hold more powerful positions, and get more of the gravy.

Robin Yes, so it's not surprising that the women's movement pays a lot of attention to helping women to be more assertive. But again, don't forget that this is an average difference. The most aggressive females are *much* more aggressive than the least aggressive males ... it's appallingly difficult to get it straight. After I'd been studying it for a while, I began to realise that in every book I consulted the argument was circular, tautologous. Men were masculine because they did masculine things, and masculine things, of course, were what men did.

John Unless women did them.

Robin And *vice versa*. Sometimes you think you're beginning to find an answer, and then it'll just vanish.

John So basically, you're pig-ignorant in an *extremely* well-informed way. Well, don't worry, economists manage to live with that.

Robin But the trouble is we *need* to know because we're all in the midst of working out new relationships between men and women. The 'Me Tarzan, you Jane' arrangement is no longer acceptable to a lot of people, but we haven't yet settled on a better way that works for both sexes – and for the *children*. So both sides seem to me to be taking up tough negotiating positions for fear the other will gain advantage if they don't. And the evidence that's quoted by each side tends to be very biased and unreliable.

John People are distorting the evidence to suit their points of view?

Robin Yes, though I don't think it's usually deliberate, wilful. It's more a matter of people seeing what they want to see, noticing what will support their beliefs and prejudices. There's the same kind of selective blindness and wishful thinking operating in this area of sexual differences as there is in the subject of severe mental disorder, like autism and schizophrenia. So some people see basic differences between men and women, and others don't see them at all. And this applies to what at first looks like very careful research, because the attitudes you start with influence what you choose to measure and how you measure it, and in the end the conclusions you reach depend on the way the findings are interpreted. Because of this, in judging the results and opinions of 'experts', you first have to weigh up how open and unbiased they are about the subject, by reading a lot of their writings and watching for signs of some *emotional* position they're taking in the matter. So even when the evidence looks very strong, it can be hiding difficulties.

John You think that evidence about what causes sexual differences of a psychological kind is especially unreliable at the moment.

Robin That's usually the case in science when the findings have major political and social implications. About the only thing I now feel completely sure of is that both the hard-line traditional and the extreme feminist positions are wrong and that the answer's going to be somewhere in between – but just where we won't know for some time.

John But seeing couples and families every day, you must have some sort of gut reaction even if you can't prove it scientifically.

Robin Well, the most interesting single idea I've come across is something we've already discussed – Guttman's concept of the 'parental emergency'.

John That's the idea that the arrival of the children pushes the parents into different roles by creating a kind of emergency.

Robin Yes, so that it's the *needs* of the children that cause the separation in those sexual roles. Because, as we've seen, a baby needs a caretaker who's very close emotionally, who enjoys being tender and nurturing in a consistent way *over quite long periods*. Well, anyone who's tuning in to the baby like this will, to some extent, lose contact with the harsh reality of the outside world. Obviously under primitive conditions that would be rather risky unless there was a second caretaker to deal with external needs and dangers, someone who could look after the first caretaker. This second caretaker role would require very different qualities that were good for fighting and getting food – such as physical strength, aggressiveness and ability to plan. So since the baby grows in the female and suckles at the female's breasts, it would have made complete sense for the female to take on the first caretaking role and the male to take on the second.

John So in the past men and women came to be trained for these different roles from early childhood so that they would be ready to spring to action stations when the babies arrived. And all this got fed through and became a habit of society that's been transmitted over centuries. But this is more or less what the women's libbers believe, is it not?

Robin They do imply it's a kind of *arrangement* – that to a considerable extent we're trained in our different roles, which is correct. But they avoid looking at the very obvious *purpose* it served towards the survival and welfare of children, under past conditions at least. And where the feminists are quite wrong is in imagining that this is all due to a wicked male conspiracy. The men are trained into their roles *every bit* as much as the women are conditioned into theirs; the reason the system's so durable is that they've *both* been trained to keep each other where they are.

John Just as a family system works to counteract any change that one member may try to make. Hence the insistence in family therapy on the need to treat the family as a *system*, and not to pick on one member and blame him or her, when he or she is no more and no less responsible for the system than anyone else. In fact, perhaps the more militant libbers should remember the point you keep making, that blaming any one member makes it far harder to put the family system right!

Robin So the way the system we call society has worked in this respect is that the men have kept the women down – because they're trained to do that – and the women have kept the men *up* so the men *could* keep them down – because they're trained to do *that*. It's circular, chicken-and-egg.

John Which explains your observation earlier about how difficult most women find it to undermine men when it comes to the crunch. But I'm glad you make this point about it being a system because there is a line of female argument that I've encountered which goes something like this:

Woman You, man-creature, have done something I do not care for.
Man And you, female-being, did something that did not delight me.
Woman But, man-creature, you are big and strong and powerful, and therefore what you do you freely choose to do. Whereas I, a female-being, am weak and oppressed and down-trodden, so I have no free choice. What I do is what I have to do, my spontaneous and necessary reaction to outside events. For this reason I cannot be held responsible.
Man So I am responsible for what I do, but you are not responsible for what you do.
Woman Why has it taken so long for you to understand this?

Robin But men are no better. Think of the hen-pecked husband who's always provoking his wife to nag him, and then implying he can't help his inadequacy but that she should be able to make allowances for *him*.

John Agreed. So we need to view society as a system and not join in the paranoid confrontation between two groups using rival conspiracy theories. But to get back to the 'parental emergency' idea, if you look at the sex differences as arising out of the need to bring up children, it certainly explains why girl and boy babies are so similar at first, and then how the two sexes gradually grow apart as they grow older.

Robin Even splitting into separate groups as though they're in different training camps! And it's certainly true that men and women seem to be at their *most* different, and often find it hardest to communicate, when they're raising a young family. Even after they've felt very close only a short time before the children arrive.

John But what happens as the children get older and start leaving? If Guttman's right, the differences should get less.

Robin That's what happens. Indeed, by their late fifties, some couples may even cross over!

John What!?

Robin Haven't you noticed? In their fifties and sixties women often become more active, outgoing, assertive and ambitious than they've ever been before; while men tend to become gentler, more relaxed, more sensitive and emotional, more interested in nature, gardening and things like that. So the sexes first get more like each other and then may 'cross over' so that any previous conflict due to their different sexual roles is actually reversed. The woman may have been complaining all her life that the man wouldn't share her feelings and emotional interests. Then finally he does so and she doesn't want that any more – she's too busy running for mayor or concentrating on her Open University courses – while the man, who used to criticise her for being so bound up with the house, wishes she'd stay at home with him.

John It's strange that I've observed that, and yet it never really penetrated my alleged consciousness before. Perhaps I was screening it out because it didn't fit in with my received ideas. So Guttman's idea holds up rather well, doesn't it?

Robin And it ought to please the women's movement because it shows that the roles *are* extremely flexible, even though there may be an important biological, inborn element.

John So to sum up, there's no really clear evidence or definition yet of what it means to be female, or to be male, psychologically speaking.

Robin Not in absolute terms, no.

John Well, can I ask you this? What guidance would you give on this burning issue of sexual roles to people who *are* living together about how they *should* be behaving towards each other until such time as you psychiatrists are able to make your bloody minds up?

Robin I'm glad you asked me that. All we *can* do is what comes naturally, and try to keep an open mind. Luckily, that seems to be the *ideal* formula for good relationships between couples anyway. That way we really *look at* each other. And that gives us the best chance of understanding each other and of helping each other to grow into interesting, complete individuals rather than stereotypes.

The Oedipus complex . . . . . .

John So to get back to the toddler . . . by the age of three, if everything's going normally, a boy will have crossed right over the bridge to the father's side, while the girl's stayed behind on the mother's bank. And provided they're clearly on one side or the other, you say they'll have accepted their male or female sexual identity – even if no one can quite define what that is.

Robin Well at least they'll have absorbed all the guidance they're getting, mainly from their parents, about how boys and girls are *expected* to behave. And this guidance is, of course, conveyed automatically, without anyone being very aware of it, by the way they're picked up, dressed, handled, talked to, played with, from the toys they're given, and so on. Plus whatever biological differences there may be!

John They have a strong sense of belonging to one team or the other . . .

Robin And the sense of belonging is reinforced not just by your own team expecting you to be like them, but also by the other lot emphasising how different they are.

John So now they are on opposite banks they can turn round and face across the river towards the parent of the opposite sex.

Robin That's right. So now they're in the Oedipal phase, which

lasts from about three till about six.

John Now in the myth, Oedipus kills his Dad and marries his Mum without realising that that's who they are.

Robin And then suffers such guilt and horror when he discovers, that he blinds himself.

John So this early situation comedy is relevant because Oedipus fancied his mother?

Robin Yes. Because little boys are now going through a very romantic phase with their Mums. And they're not only affectionate but also quite possessive, and frequently show jealousy towards their fathers.

John They'd like to get rid of them, as Oedipus did. And is the same thing happening the other way round between the little girl and her father?

Robin Yes.

John And it was Freud who first pointed out that this was going on?

Robin Well, he was struck by how *important* this little drama seemed to be in the history of all the patients who came to him – and also that there seemed to be a universal tendency to forget about it, indeed even to *deny* that anything of this kind ever happened.

John Presumably people might be embarrassed by what they might feel were the incestual implications; so even if they didn't deny what was happening, at least they'd try to play down the importance of this stage.

Robin Yes, and one mustn't underestimate how important this phase seems to be for the child. The feelings are very powerful, and the child not only becomes possessive and jealous, but at times may feel quite worried by the force of these emotions. Children sense that they're trying to steal the parent of the opposite sex away from the spouse. And, not surprisingly, they're also experiencing powerful fears that the same-sex parent will be equally jealous in return.

John The 'castration complex' is the child's fear that the same-sex parent will punish him for stealing the other parent? A punishment to fit the crime . . .

Robin Freud, and his followers, made a lot of that, and it's certainly one very prominent way in which fear of the parent's jealousy and reprisal shows itself. But it is really *only one* expression of a general fear of losing the same-sex parent's love and support; which would of course be a devastating worry for a child of this age.

John So the child's in a very difficult, rather frightening position, isn't he, trying to steal one parent but being frightened of the other's revenge. What does he need to resolve this dilemma?

Robin Well, fortunately, it's simple enough. He only needs his parents to get on well and to put their own relationship first – above all, to have a good sexual relationship. If this is the case, they'll resist the child's attempt to interfere with their relationship *kindly but firmly*. They'll shut the bedroom door. Which will be a tremendous *reassurance* for the child because then he will realise he's *not* going to succeed in stealing the opposite-sex parent away. The child senses that this would wreck the marriage relationship on which his emotional security depends so completely.

John So the child will be brought up against jealousy, and his feelings of exclusion.

Robin And that's a painful frustration, of course, though it's necessary. But those feelings will be soothed to the extent that the child feels loved and cherished in other ways. To sum up, the child needs to suffer a defeat of his hopes of conquest – but a *benevolent, loving defeat* where the same-sex parent doesn't react with as much jealousy as the child fears, but, on the contrary, offers continuing love and support.

John So what the child needs to know *above all* is that the parents' marriage is 'safe', that their first love is for *each other*.

Robin Exactly. And the best way they can get that message to the child is to behave naturally and to show their feelings for each other openly. And provided they're doing that, then the more the parents respond enjoyably to the child's romantic feelings, the more they're helping the child to gain confidence in his sexuality, so that this can bloom at a later stage.

John So by about the age of six, the child will have learned, to his great relief, that his attempts to interfere with the marriage have failed!

Robin And then he will have decided that 'if you can't beat them you might as well join them' and that the best alternative for a boy who can't marry his Mum is to learn to be like Dad, and at least share a bit of her admiration by identifying with him and becoming like him; and for a girl, it's to imitate her mother because that's obviously the way to attract a nice, attractive fellow like Dad. In these ways, the child is pointed towards adulthood and given a powerful incentive to learn as much as possible at school and to be successful socially, in the playground, on the sports field and everywhere else. In other words, he can move on to the next stage.

John Now if the child doesn't get the reassuring message that the marriage is safe, it could be for two reasons. Either it really isn't; or it *is*, but the parents *aren't* making that clear.

Robin Yes, and it's important to mention this second possibility because it explains why it's the very permissive, indulgent parents, who are frightened to make the child feel excluded or to express even the slightest feelings of jealousy that they might feel towards him, who have children who often develop really intense fears in this phase.

John Which manifest themselves how?

Robin They're usually well concealed from everyone else, but they show themselves symbolically in the child's play, and often in phobias or nightmares, which are expressions of this conflict between love and jealousy in a disguised form.

John So if the parents are frightened to exclude the child, then the child will become unusually afraid that he could break up the happy home.

Robin And this can also happen if the parents feel they can't shut the bedroom door; in other words, if they're hiding their sexual feelings for each other from the child so completely that, although the marriage is fine, the child suspects it isn't, and imagines – horror! – that he's won.

John I see. Now, supposing the marriage *isn't* fine . . . ?

Robin Well then there's the danger that they may be competing for the child's affection.

John Responding *too* warmly to his romantic behaviour?

Robin Yes, and that will put the child in the position of maximum anxiety, because he can feel that he's succeeding in breaking up the marriage. He imagines he's won, *even* though the problems in the marriage are really nothing to do with himself.

John So what happens to a child who's suffering this anxiety about pulling the parent away from his or her partner?

Robin Well the prospect of breaking his parents' marriage up is so frightening that he will become scared of his developing sexual awareness – which seems to be causing all these problems. So he may, so to speak, cut the telephone wires between his brain and his sexual feelings, leading to frigidity or impotence in adulthood.

John Do you mean impotence in a literal or metaphorical sense?

Robin Both. And in the metaphorical, or psychological sense, impotence means a pervasive fear of success generally.

John Not just sexual success?

Robin No, absolutely anything that the person might see as success; or even anything they think other people might see as success.

John Because he or she was successful in interfering with the parents' marriage, they're scared any other kind of success would have disastrous consequences too?

Robin That's right. In a sense, because the parents haven't excluded them firmly enough, they stay *stuck in this Oedipal phase*; which also means they may go on repeating the same sexual pattern over and over again.

John The pattern of competing with someone of the same sex for possession of someone of the opposite sex?

Robin So you find men who are attracted only by married women but who can't sustain the relationship if it threatens to become more than an affair.

John They *need* the husband to protect them from a *full* relationship?

Robin Exactly as women who repeatedly get involved with married men need the wives. This way they guarantee they don't have to face up to a real, *full* relationship, which they're not prepared for. Because they never went through this stage properly as children, because the parents let them interfere with their marriage.

John Or let them *think* they were interfering with it.

Robin That's right. So even if the parents' relationship was reasonably good, you can get similar though less severe problems if the parents hide their sexual feelings from the children, as we've said, or if they were just embarrassed and shy about sex in general. Either way the children can get the *impression* that they're being allowed to interfere in the marriage, and can get stuck with a bit of the same problem.

John At best, the kids will be getting a feeling that sex is 'not quite nice'.

Robin Yes. One of the things that the child has got to learn in this phase is to *enjoy* the romantic, sexually tinged feelings he's experiencing. He needs to feel at ease with them, secure in the knowledge that they're not going to harm the marriage. Now if the parents become very embarrassed by this, that may cause the child to switch off the sexual feelings. Then, in adulthood, it may be hard for him to switch them on again when he falls in love. By finding his little girl attractive when she flirts with him, though keeping a proper boundary, the father is increasing her sexual confidence; and exactly the same is going on between the mother and her sons.

John The 'flirting' is safe because it's clear the real sex goes on behind the bedroom door. But how much should the children know about what's going on behind that door?

Robin Well, the details of what the parents are up to are not the child's business. But it's in fact good for them to *know* that the parents do make love, and that they enjoy it, and that it makes them happy.

John Which sends the child two separate messages. One, sex is good. Two, it's not available from Mum or Dad.

Robin And that means that the sexual feelings act as a kind of carrot to the donkey, motivating the child to grow up and find a partner of his own with whom he can eventually enjoy it too.

John So prudishness removes the carrot completely and then the donkey's got no reason to go forward ...

Robin And incest, whether technical or, a million times more commonly, the situation where a parent offers a child a closer emotional relationship than the other parent receives ... allows the donkey to *eat* the carrot. Once again, the urge to go forward, to grow up, is reduced.

John So prudishness and incest *both* stop the child growing up. Perhaps because the parents don't really want to grow up either. They want everyone to be together always.

Robin Yes. I think that's exactly what incest is really about. And, again, we're not just talking about *technical* incest. We're talking about the situation where the parents don't have a good sexual relationship, are not fully satisfied by each other, and are allowing their sexual feelings to be displaced on to the children, even though in *very disguised and unconscious ways.*

John OK. So if the parents lovingly but firmly resist the toddler's attempts to disrupt their relationship, and also show the child that they're enjoying each other sexually, the child's going to pass successfully through this Oedipal phase by about the age of six. So that brings him to the third of the four stages of sexual development, the 'latency' phase.

Latency – an interlude ......

Robin Freud called this stage the 'latency' period to indicate that sexual feelings and interest went underground. But more careful studies of what children do and talk about during this time have shown that the interest actually continues quite strongly.

John I thought you said that sex stopped being such a central issue and simply became as important as a number of other subjects.

Robin It's the romantic attachment to the parent which fades at this point, so the emotions connected with it don't predominate in the same way. Also, they've learned the rules so that they keep their sexual interest to themselves to fit in with the grown-up's *belief* that they're not interested. But the curiosity about it all continues, and there's quite a lot of experimenting going on between them in a harmless, and probably quite useful, sort of way.

John What sort of experimenting, and how common is it?

Robin It varies greatly, depending on social class, urban or rural location, and so on. But one study in a fairly conservative mid-Western American suburb showed, for example, that more than half the boys of age eleven had masturbated and the same number had taken part in sex-play with girls. Over a quarter of them had engaged in homosexual play and a similar number had tried sexual intercourse.

John Some sort of homosexual play around this age is quite normal?

Robin Oh yes, erotic play between children of the same sex is very common round about the age of twelve or so. Actually, I don't really like using the word 'homosexual' here because it doesn't mean they're more likely to become gay later on – they're just practising on someone like themselves, as a first step to approaching the opposite sex later.

John It's just a bit of field research to flesh out the theory.

Robin But of course they get a lot of the theory wrong, especially about the facts of intercourse, so clear information from Mum or Dad can relieve a lot of anxiety.

John I suppose the act of telling them is a clear indication from the parents that they regard sex as something good, that they approve of, at the right time and place.

Robin Exactly. That's something the children don't get if the parents leave it all to the school to do this job. The children will find out anyway, sooner or later, but if the parents *don't* play their part they *haven't given it their blessing*; so sex can become more of a hole-and-corner affair – however well the facts are presented by others.

John And how long does this latency period last?

Robin Up to about age twelve.

John Next . . . adolescence.

The crisis of adolescence . . . . . .

John So we now move on to the fourth stage – adolescence, which you described as a kind of re-run of a lot of the things that were happening between the ages of three and six, during the Oedipal phase.

Robin As far as the parents are concerned, all that hassle has *seemed* to go underground for about six years. Even if the child's been very interested, those feelings will have been concealed from the parents. But once he gets to puberty – the start of adolescence – it's as if the child can't keep those feelings under wraps any longer because they're getting multiplied and made much more intense by the chemical changes now going on. So out they burst.

John So the child's now beginning to experience real sexual feelings for the first time.

Robin Yes, and they're very new and powerful – even at times alarming – feelings which the teenager will feel quite shy and awkward about. So the natural urge to flirt and experiment with this growing attractiveness will usually be tried out at first on the parent of the opposite sex, where it feels most safe, provided the relationship is reasonably good.

John It's like the Oedipal business, flirting with the opposite-sex parent and getting jealous of the other one?

Robin Yes, but the big difference is that this time it's much more tricky and uncomfortable for the *parents*. They're no longer little kids comically play-acting being Mum's knight in shining armour, or Dad's Marilyn Monroe. This time they're people who've nearly grown up and are giving off real, powerful, sexual vibes that the parents may not have had beamed at them for quite some time.

John The child is becoming genuinely sexually aroused and physically attractive.

Robin So the parents are in the hot seat!

John But they should try to respond as before – that is, naturally and with enjoyment, but drawing the line clearly so that the behaviour never gets really sexual?

Robin Thats right. But it's not so easy to get the balance right all the time. One of the big troubles is that because teenagers are nervous about it all, they'll tend to blow hot and cold; they give the come-on and then back off suddenly, as if they're about to be molested by someone in a dirty mac!

John I can see how tricky it must be. I mean if the parents don't respond at all, or just get frightfully embarrassed and British and awkward, it might seem like rejection to the children, so they're going to be put off and stop flirting to avoid being rebuffed again. Which will mean that they won't be learning to be confident about their sexuality. Whereas if the parents do respond a bit, the young people may withdraw because they suddenly get a bit scared of what's going on, of the possible effect their sexuality could have.

Robin And if the teenagers do switch off and become very awkward and prickly, they can leave the parents wondering if they've done something wrong and feeling awkward and inhibited too. Of course, the teenagers aren't really *aware* of what's going on or of the signals they're sending.

John It must be very difficult for the parents, with the young people being very friendly one moment and cold and rejecting the next.

Robin It is! They often end up feeling as though *whatever* they do is wrong. Of course, they'll be getting it right *part* of the time anyway, managing to find the right balance, enjoying a bit of teasing and warmth and flirting, while making sure it doesn't go too far. But what they really need to accept is that they *are* going to be put in the wrong some of the time . . . and they need for the children's sake to be able to accept that and carry on naturally without worrying about it.

John Not shut off *their* natural feelings just because the adolescent has switched off.

Robin That's the vital thing. This practising with sexual behaviour is very important for teenagers, but it's worrying for them if they feel that they're able to *control* their parents' sexuality too much, in either direction.

John Turn them on too much, or turn them off too easily.

Robin That's right. It's too heavy a responsibility for teenagers to cope with. So if they sense they really have this power to control their parents' response, they may get scared and switch off their sexuality completely, to make things 'safe'; and then acquire an automatic habit of doing this.

John This rings a very loud bell. A few years ago I had a relationship with a marvellous girl, but there were always difficulties with the sex. It would start perfectly all right but suddenly she would switch off, and I always got blamed for having done something or having not done something – although for the life of me I couldn't see what I was supposed to have got wrong. Unfortunately, we never solved this and drifted apart, but when I saw her some time later, she said that she'd gone into therapy for a time and had traced her behaviour back to her teenage relationship with her father. He was the best kind of very straight, very upright, professional-type person, and they would start flirting a bit and all of a sudden ... he'd actually realise he'd got a sexual feeling towards his daughter ... and that meant *incest*!! Shock, horror!! So he'd switch right off just as she was beginning to rather enjoy the buzz. Which made her feel terrible, as though she'd done something very wrong. So to protect herself, she had to learn to switch off before he did. What was happening in *our* relationship was a kind of re-run of this, with her switching off each time she reached a certain point because unconsciously she was scared that I was about to do so.

Robin That's a perfect example of the effect it can have in later life. How is she now – do you know?

John She told me not long ago that once she began to see what was happening, she started slowly to be able to stop switching herself off. But it took her quite a time to get real control over it because the conditioning had gone so deep. I must say, talking about this is a bit worrying because it's all making me realise what a narrow line the parents have to tread, and my daughter is just twelve and extremely pretty. Help?

Robin Don't worry. She'll *cue* you. I mean, she'll make you aware of what she needs. She'll practise exercising her charms on you, as and when she needs to, and when she's had enough, or you go over the limit for her in your response, she'll withdraw for the moment until she's ready to use you to practise on again. All you have to do is relax and enjoy it, and don't either get embarrassed when she puts the eye on you, or get upset when she tunes you out after she's had enough. It's the idea of the *landmark* again: don't alter your natural response to protect yourself, but keep still, or rather keep your own course. Then she can use you for target practice. In any case these difficulties for the parents are made much easier if they've got a good sexual relationship going on in their marriage, and if they make that obvious to the teenagers. Then they'll have no need to worry if they sometimes get a slight turn-on when they realise how attractive their offspring are becoming – in fact, a slight buzz of that sort can then be reassuring to everybody that things are proceeding normally.

John Because everybody knows that the real sex is locked away firmly behind the parents' bedroom door.

Robin Right. Remember that the young people's anxiety that they may be able to switch on or switch off the parents' sexual feelings too easily is also due to a healthy desire not to harm *both* parents by upsetting the marriage. The more it's clear that the marriage is healthy, sexy and thriving, the more the teenagers can relax and enjoy getting in a bit of flirting practice.

John Yes, but isn't there something else going on here that makes life harder for everyone? The parents are entering middle age round about now, beginning to sense the decline of their own sexual drives and attractiveness. Several women have told me that they feel their sexuality wasn't encouraged to blossom when they were young because their mothers were jealous of them and discouraged them – indeed attacked them – if they started looking attractive or behaving too sexily.

Robin Well, once again, the parents are unlikely to feel more than a mild, passing jealousy if their own sexual relationship is still really satisfying. And also, they'll be less likely to feel seriously jealous if *they* had plenty of experience with the opposite sex in *their* teens, before they settled down to marriage. But of course the change, over the past generation, to the present climate of sexual freedom means that young people are having a much easier, more enjoyable time, much more openly than their parents did. Which may make it harder for the parents to tolerate the envy that adolescent affairs naturally stir up in them. And, of course, if things aren't right with the marriage, that'll be emphasised if the young people are always

on the 'phone to lovers, or coming home in the small hours, or taking three hours to say goodnight on the doorstep.

John And if the parents *are* very jealous, it might force the teenagers to switch their sexuality right off to avoid all the nasty feelings it's arousing from the parents.

Robin Yes. So it's very important that the parents should try to be aware of this jealousy, and take it into account when deciding how strictly to lay down the law, what time the young people have got to be in, what the house rules are about girlfriends and boyfriends.

John Of course the house rules won't just be about sex. So what about guidelines the parents may be setting in other areas?

Drawing the lines for adolescents ......

John You describe the adolescent phase as in many ways a re-run of the toddler phase. Well during *that*, it's vital for the parents to draw clear and firm lines for the children. How much does that apply to adolescents?

Robin It's terribly important for adolescents to feel that their parents' attitudes are stable and firm. They're getting ready for even greater independence – independence from the family.

Instead of needing Dad's support to loosen the attachment to Mum, they now need support from *outside* the family – especially from their friends – to loosen the attachment to *both* parents. They're trying to establish their new, *separate* identity and to get confidence in it. And one very healthy way they do that is to rebel a bit.

John So they need something to rebel *against*? Clear lines they can test their strength on?

Robin Just like the toddlers, and for similar reasons.

John So the parents are also giving them *security* by drawing lines?

Robin Absolutely. One mustn't forget how insecure and changeable teenagers can be. One minute they're full of confidence, demanding freedom and independence and resenting all parental constraint; and the next minute collapsing into uncertainty, helplessness and demands for reassurance and support. In a sense they're grown-ups one moment and children the next. It's a very unsettling time, so they need firm, stable guidelines.

John It sounds as though the parents may feel they've been through it all before.

Robin Actually they'll be lucky if they *have*! If they didn't draw clear enough lines at the toddler stage, it'll be much more difficult now that the children are bigger and stronger. But it will need to be done, even if life is rather hair-raising for a time!

John So apart from firm house rules, what can the parents do to foster the children's independence?

Robin By encouraging their interests and activities outside the home. And *in* the house, by giving them areas where they can exercise their freedom without undue constraint – for example their bedrooms. Each teenager more or less declares a state of UDI by making his or her bedroom unmistakeably different from the rest of the house. And that's all right. But out in the common areas of the house, which they have to share with parents and brothers and sisters, it's important for the parents to insist on reasonably considerate social behaviour – leaving the bathroom fit for others, helping with the housework, for instance.

John I remember your once saying, 'Hell hath no fury like a teenage girl who's not forced to help with the washing up'.

Robin '. . . by her *father*'. You forgot that bit. At a certain stage in therapy, it's the passive father, who 'only wants a quiet life', who gets the torrent of blistering scorn and reproach poured over him by his teenage daughters. 'And *what's more*,' they'll shout as they reach the final count on the indictment, the capital offence, '*you don't EVEN make us do the washing up!*'

John So the teenagers actually want house rules. At the very least it gives them something to complain about.

Robin And to struggle against, even if only mildly. You see, at this point, the teenagers' personalities are not necessarily very well defined, so it's hard for them to be really independent in a positive way. To some extent they have to learn about themselves in fundamentally *negative* ways. At the start, anyway.

John So they can learn independence more by *not* doing what the parents want, or doing what the parents *don't* want, than they do by doing what they themselves want.

Robin At the start, anyway. Because they may not be quite clear about what they *do* want, what kind of a person they are. The sense of identity isn't yet clear. And also, you don't develop your muscles by relaxing or taking the line of least resistance, do you? You struggle against some resistance – lift heavy weights, push against an obstacle. It's the same with willpower, strength of character, confidence.

John So they need something to push against to help them become more independent. Perhaps that's why all those teenage revolutionaries go on about the 'importance of the struggle'. It's helping them to grow up.

Robin Naughty! So if the parents can accept that the struggle is necessary to *help* the children, they'll hold the lines firmly and give them something to push against. Of course, they *should* adjust the lines from time to time because as the kids get older and more independent, it's good that they should be given more space. But it's important for the parents not to get too caught up in the details of the struggle and think that the arguments are necessarily *resolvable* at that moment, or become anxious that they're doing something wrong and try desperately to put it 'right'. If they do adjust to the young people's demands, to try to please them, to make them happy, they'll not only end up feeling even more inadequate and in the wrong, they'll actually be providing the wrong response. The whole point of the operation is that the teenager is looking for something to struggle against. So if the parents keep giving in, the teenager has to embark on a desperate search for some behaviour that *will* get a reaction, and the conflict will be escalated until the parents *do* make a stand, or the children burn the house down.

John It's fascinating to realise that you have to stand back and see what the behaviour's about, instead of getting involved in the details of each disagreement. So what about house rules on 'dress'?

Robin Well, some parents may decide to give them more freedom, some parents less. But it would be extremely bad for the teenagers if the parents made no rules at all, or on the other hand demanded that the children dressed *exactly* as they did. It's amusing too because just before adolescence children are easily embarrassed, at school prize-giving or sports day, if their parents are not dressed in the most sober and conformist way. I remember my daughter ticking me off for wearing a tie with three stripes rather than two. But the moment adolescence is reached, the kids love trying to embarrass the adults by dressing in as outlandish a way as they can get away with.

John So to help teenagers, the parents need to stand their ground.

Robin Yes. They have to be landmarks against which the children can define and measure themselves, taking what they like and rejecting what they don't. And, of course, the first requirement of a landmark is that you must know where it is.

John So the parents should *express* their views clearly and not mind if the children disagree; indeed, accept that they *won't* agree a lot of the time, and will probably be regarded by them basically as tyrannical, fascist lunatics.

Robin Exactly. If the parents can accept this role, and just enjoy their own lives, they probably won't have a 'teenage' problem at all. Studies of ordinary families have shown that about 85 per cent of teenagers like their parents, and respect and get on well with them. Their lively exploratory behaviour isn't seen by the parents as a 'problem' at all.

John Well, in that case, haven't you been rather over-emphasising this 'struggle' business?

Robin I think all parents might be reassured to know that some conflict is quite normal, because it *always* comes as a bit of a surprise. Most people will sometimes have doubts about whether they're handling it wrongly by standing firm. Even those parents who have been influenced by prevailing ideas about permissiveness may be persuaded to stand firmer if they realise that some conflict is absolutely necessary.

John You've given a lot of reasons why you don't approve of permissiveness in the general sense of the word, that is, of parents not offering children clear guidelines ... but in the *sexual* sense, you're not against it, are you?

Robin How do you mean?

Fantasies ......

John I get the impression that you think it's a good idea for young people to pair off with lots of different partners, so that they can get plenty of experience, both emotionally and, if they want, sexually.

Robin Yes I do, provided that doesn't go against that person's religion, or the moral code they want to follow.

John Why do you think it's beneficial?

Robin It gives them a more solid basis for their marriage later on.

John That's your professional experience?

Robin Yes. I regularly meet the situation where married people, in middle age, who have missed out in adolescence, and had very few boyfriends or girlfriends, get embroiled in extra-marital affairs of a very unrealistic, adolescent kind. Or, worse, spend most of the time in fantasies about how much happier they would be with someone else.

John Do they feel that they are getting old and have missed out on having some fun, or what?

Robin It's simply that they haven't had the experience of different affairs, so they glamorise them. They've never faced the reality of relationships, so they cling on to the idea that the grass in the next field might be greener. So whether they actually *are* unfaithful, or just *think about* being unfaithful all the time, they are always comparing the spouse with some perfect fantasy and – surprise! – the marriage doesn't come up to the fantasy standard.

John Their expectations of the marriage are unrealistic?

Robin Impossible, yes. But they haven't *found that out*. Whereas people who've played the field and had a reasonable amount of experience have realised that it isn't easy to achieve a good sexual adjustment, and that it depends enormously on how good the whole relationship is. They've found out that you have to work at it, and so they're more likely to put their interest and energy into their marriage rather than into dreams of other partners.

John Why do you say that the fantasy of infidelity is 'worse' than actual infidelity?

Robin Because the fantasy ruins the existing marriage without giving the person who's indulging in it the opportunity of discovering the *real complications* of extra-marital affairs.

John You mean they never really discover how difficult it is to run two relationships, how true to life French farce really is.

Robin More than that. They never get the chance to discover that the same problems that they're having with their wife or husband are eventually going to turn up in their affair too.

John Whereas if they're actually having an affair, they may find this out?

Robin And then they may decide that the existing marriage is not so bad after all.

John But supposing the existing marriage really is terrible?

Robin Ah, well, *then* the relief given by the fantasy may make it just bearable enough to drag on. Whereas in reality it may be better if they both got out of it while they still have time to build something better.

John I'm glad to hear you say this about fantasies, because they've always struck me as basically harmful, since they give us a bum steer when we're making decisions about our lives. I'm not talking about playful fantasies, which can be indulged or let go as you want, but about fantasies springing from the ludicrous concept of Romantic Love. I can't think of a single 'romantic' notion that doesn't – in the long run – make people less happy than they could be. It's as though someone made a list of the characteristics of depressives and sanctified them – it's wonderful to cling; it's highly moral to be dependent; it's ignoble to get emotional support from more than one source; the most fulfilling emotion of all is the anticipation of loss; missing someone makes you feel really alive; and suffering, in general, guarantees that life *is* ultimately worthwhile. Yet my kind of talk is not popular. People are proud of being romantic. 'I'm a bit of a romantic, I'm afraid,' they say, smiling with that bizarre sense of moral and spiritual superiority. And they can get pretty cross if you ask them to explain why self-inflicted misery is so self-improving. Especially women, who seem surprisingly attached to the *ideas* of romance despite the fact that they're much more clear-sighted – and decisive – in their relationships than men.

Robin I don't think there's that much difference between men and women over the amount they live in fantasy – in fact, I think, if anything, men live further away from reality, but dress it up with serious names like 'politics', 'philosophy' and the like. In the past, at least, women used to encourage this to keep them out of the kitchen so they could get on with more vital things.

John So the best thing to do with illusions is to get rid of them.

Robin No, not necessarily. I think people should be left to make their own choice about that. I *personally* prefer the idea of getting rid of illusions, and living closer to reality, but I don't recommend it for everybody. In professional work of the kind I do, certainly the patients who get the greatest benefit are the ones who want to get rid of illusions, but it's a painful process . . .

John Losing an illusion can be as painful as losing something real?

Robin Yes. And not everyone can bear that, or wants to bear that. So I just help them to face and change their illusions *only* so much as is absolutely necessary for them to get what they've come for; but *not* more. You mustn't destroy an illusion until the person is close to having something better available, in reality, to take its place.

John So when you approve of the idea of young people experimenting a bit, this is because you feel that they will learn from it, get rid of some of their fantasies about relationships, find out more about themselves and their needs and about the opposite sex; and that all this will give them a much better chance later on of choosing a partner with whom they can create a long and successful marriage.

Robin Absolutely. If I accept that sexual freedom before marriage is a good thing, it's because I believe in the importance of a stable marriage for the family, and because I value fidelity and commitment. Couples are more likely to *choose* these values if they've discovered that shallow, transient affairs bring lesser rewards. Pleasant though the latter can be, they simply don't compare with a full, committed relationship. But people are more likely to accept this if they've found it out for themselves rather than if they're told to take it on trust.

Curing sexual problems ......

John So, we've been through the stages of sexual development, right up to the threshold of marriage. To summarise: our awareness of our sexual identity takes time to develop and is normally settled by about the age of two and a half or three, with the child taking up a clear position on the male or female bank; then comes the Oedipal phase – the first love affair with the parent of the opposite sex, between about three and six; and then six years of comparative latency, where interest is maintained but at a less obvious level; and then there's adolescence, when the hormones stir everything up and the Oedipal phase is repeated, this time with a *real* sexual buzz; after that, the young people can go off and start getting the experience that they need if they're to choose a really suitable marriage partner. So let's get on to the question of what can be done if any of this has gone wrong.

Robin Well, it largely depends at what point the problem has arisen in the developmental cycle. The later it's arisen, the more we can do. For example, nowadays the outlook for sexual problems like impotence, frigidity or premature ejaculation has been completely transformed by new methods that can help most cases in a matter of *weeks*, where in the past even years of therapy might not have produced much change.

We've come to you doctors because of my problem with premature — whoops...

John But supposing the problem has arisen *before* the Oedipal phase. In other words, if it's to do with the person's sexual identity.

Robin Well, that's often very hard to do anything about. And with most trans-sexuals and the majority of homosexuals, a psychiatrist wouldn't even be asked to try to alter the deviation itself, because they have dealt with it by adjusting to it, accepting it. So the question of change doesn't really arise.

John But changes are *possible*?

Robin Oh, yes. But where this does happen, it can be very slow, arduous and often painful work, because what has to change is in the very foundations of the personality. It may affect *everything*; so a change in sexual identity can demand a change in almost everything about that person. In other words, it requires a major rebuilding job. So obviously each person has to decide whether it's worth the struggle and suffering. For many, it probably isn't, and for some it may even be dangerous to try. Anyway, I think it's the psychiatrist's job to respect the views and vulnerabilities of each individual patient. Patients often sense what's best for them better than the psychiatrist does. So if such a person seeks therapy for some other matter, we can often do a lot to help them improve their lives and enjoy themselves more, while respecting their wish to stay as they are sexually.

John I notice you use the word 'deviation'.

Robin The original word was 'perversion', of course, but that collected a lot of negative associations at a time when there were strong legal sanctions against anything except ordinary sex within marriage. So 'deviation' is now used instead.

John But many homosexuals object even to the word 'deviation'. They prefer the word 'variation', to suggest that one sexual orientation is as 'normal' as another.

Robin I don't disagree in the least with their right to believe that themselves and to advocate their ideas – provided they accept the same rules about not harming others, like everybody else. But as you can see from the way that I've explained the stages of sexual development – and the explanation not only makes sense of all my clinical and personal experience but also enables us to help people to change their behaviour and function more effectively – I think that these different sexual orientations can best be explained and understood by comparison with normal development. I've chosen that way of viewing them because it is useful to me, it works, it makes sense of things. But if other people prefer to think deviations come from nowhere, with no explanation – and of course that attitude is understandable if they don't want to change – then I'm quite happy about that. The scheme of development I'm describing doesn't imply any *moral* attitude of blame, and there's no suggestion that people *ought* to be different from the way they are.

John So it's difficult to treat problems of sexual identity even if the patient wants to change, because that person's personality has been built upon the identity he or she has, so that major dismantling and rebuilding would be necessary. But how about problems that have arisen at a later stage in development?

Robin Well, let's take frigidity, impotence and premature ejaculation, which are generally called sexual 'dysfunctions'. These problems have arisen *after* the sexual identity stage has been satisfactorily negotiated. With the deviations, the train's gone off onto the *wrong* track. With the dysfunctions, the train is on the right track, but it has met a *red signal* and stopped. So the therapist has to change the signal to green.

John So the person got this red light against letting their sexuality develop during the Oedipal stage?

Robin Yes. Take frigidity. If the father gets too easily embarrassed by the little girl's romantic feelings for him, and sends off embarrassed, frightened, negative responses, *she* will start thinking that these new feelings she's getting are *'wrong'*. So she'll try to switch them off. So later on, when she's grown up, she may have got into the habit of switching them off to such an extent she can't switch them on again.

John The same could have happened if the father had come on too *strongly*?

Robin Yes, again she would have had to switch the feelings off to feel safe. Or this might come about because a strong prohibition against showing sexual feelings came from *outside* the home, from a very strict community attitude. Or sometimes, though more rarely, because there's been an actual trauma, something nasty in the woodshed.

John And impotence could arise in the same ways, except that it would be the mother who gave the wrong response to the boy?

Robin That's right. But it's important to add that *any* man can experience *temporary* impotence – that's the inability to get an erection, or the tendency to lose it during love-play or intercourse – if he's under stress, or unwell, or under the influence of certain drugs or of alcohol; or even if he's particularly *anxious* that things *shouldn't* go wrong – as, for instance, when he's having intercourse with a lover or wife for the first time. Now, if that does happen, a vicious circle can develop with increasing worry about performance leading to worse performance, and more failure leading to still more worry. That can eventually lead to impotence of a more persistent kind, unless an understanding woman, or therapy, or just good luck, breaks the vicious circle.

John But you say that the prospects for curing frigidity and impotence, whatever the cause, are very good.

Robin Yes. And the easiest cases – and fortunately they're much the most common – are due to these vicious circles of failure and anxiety, started off by some unusual circumstances affecting a man who was functioning normally before. Of course, it may be *more* likely for that to happen if the chap was a bit inhibited or shy about sex already, for the kinds of reason we've mentioned. Of course the same principles can operate to make a woman frigid.

John Now what about premature ejaculation? Is that just another attempt to switch off, to avoid sex by ending it before it's really started?

Robin No, I don't think it's anything to do with that. Mind you, there are several different theories about why the new cures work so effectively. But the fundamental idea that makes sense of them all is that men who 'come' too quickly, before the partner is ready, are *not* in fact *over*-sensitive to the pleasure, but the *reverse*. They can't control themselves because they're not as fully aware as they should be of the physical pleasure that's building up during love-play and intercourse, in the sexual parts and the penis particularly. So the situation is a bit like the image we've used before – the man is like the driver of a car who has taken his hands off the steering wheel and climbed into the back seat – the car being his penis and the steering wheel being his connection with it, his *awareness* of the *sensation* in the penis. So the excitement gets out of control and runs away with him, just as a car would do in those circumstances.

John You mean the 'excitement' isn't properly connected to the *physical sensations* of pleasure? He needs to feel the pleasure more if he's to be able to control himself?

Robin Exactly. So you can see why the old-fashioned sex manuals actually made the problem worse. They usually recommended ways he could *reduce* his excitement by thinking of other things – reciting the multiplication table, things like that. So if he was already in the back seat of the car, this put him in the boot!

John Why would the man have disconnected himself from the physical feelings in the first place?

Robin He would probably have turned his attention away from his sexual sensations because of the kind of anxious family responses we've talked about. So in childhood, he's got the idea that it is 'not quite nice' to have a healthy, lusty sexual appetite and to enjoy feeling really randy and 'turned on'.

John Well now, you said that in the last ten years, treatment for these 'dysfunctions' has become amazingly effective. Why was there such a sudden improvement?

Robin It really started with the work of Masters and Johnson in the States. Instead of treating only the partner who was supposed to have the difficulty, they saw both members of the couple at the same time; and the two therapists worked together as a couple too; so sometimes there would be all four of them there. And then, instead of just *talking* about what might have *caused* the problem – childhood experience, and so on – the therapists gave them *advice* and *tasks* to carry out. In other words, they guided the couple supportively but firmly back towards *trying again and not worrying if they failed at first.*

John They didn't concentrate on the causes, they just got the couple to practise?

Robin Right. It was tremendously effective. And others have found the same.

John What sort of advice and 'tasks' do you have to give?

Robin Well, if a couple have been suffering from the effects of frigidity, or impotence, and they're both very uptight and lacking in confidence that it'll ever work again, you have first to gain the couple's confidence and get them talking together again. Then, you advise that they should put off attempting full sexual intercourse for the time being, while they just get used to enjoying each other's bodies in a simple way.

John By ruling out intercourse, you'd reduce their anxiety about failure. So what sort of 'tasks' would you give?

Robin You might suggest that the couple should take it in turns just to touch and massage each other for half an hour or so, in ways that each one enjoyed, but staying clear of the sexual parts of the body. While each person is being touched by the partner, he or she would just be asked to 'relax and enjoy it', while telling the partner what they find most pleasurable, so they can cooperate in making it as enjoyable as possible.

John This is a 'behaviour therapy' principle, isn't it? Starting with something easy that doesn't arouse much worry, then moving on towards the target a step at a time, always stopping if the anxiety starts building up.

Robin That's it. So by agreeing to avoid intercourse for a time, and even to keep clear of the sexual parts, the couple remove their anxiety about 'performance'. Then they can go back to 'getting to know each other' again; they can make a fresh start. And given the encouragement to be tender, and gentle, and sensitive to each other, the couple will usually find themselves opening up and sometimes almost falling in love all over again.

John And they work gradually towards full intercourse?

Robin Yes, by slow degrees, as they feel ready. For instance, if the original problem had been impotence in the man, the first step, after they felt at ease with non-sexual touching, would be for the woman to play with the man's genitals, just teasing and pleasuring him, without *any* expectation that he will get an erection, or minding if he doesn't. Of course, with all the pressure off, the machinery usually soon begins to work again, and the fact that she's leading him on, but isn't in any hurry to finish him off, may result in his feeling unusually eager. When he's really feeling confident again, they'll try penetration, but again without expecting he'll keep the erection, and if there's a setback they go back to an earlier stage of the process so there's

I think we're ready now, Doctor, if you'd just move out of the way.

We wouldn't want you to get hurt.

no discouragement or chance of that vicious circle starting again. Usually, within a few weeks at most, sex is working normally again and the enjoyment and satisfaction they're getting reinforces the cure.

John Supposing the couple 'jump the gun' and try intercourse before they're advised to?

Robin It doesn't matter. If it works – and often it does because the 'tasks' have made them so turned on they just can't wait – the process is just speeded up. If it *doesn't*, the limits you've set let them off any feeling of failure – they can just feel they've been enjoyably rebellious and delinquent instead!

John You say other therapists have found these methods effective. Have they varied them much?

Robin Oh a lot. But the one thing *all* these new techniques have in common is that they focus on *immediate experience*.

John The couple's attention is directed to what they're feeling?

Robin Yes, to their here-and-now experience with each other, so that they can begin to connect up with the sexual feelings and sensations they've learned early on to tune out, and to feel them more and more vividly and deeply. And the principle which makes this possible is the demand that patients should actually *do* certain tasks; that they should *try* to change things.

John And no time is spent trying to work out what's caused the problem?

Robin Well, *now* many therapists are beginning to *combine* these new methods with the more traditional psychoanalytic techniques that give an understanding of the causes. And we're finding that this enables us to help even more of the dysfunctional problems.

John All right. Now, if problems of sexual identity arise during the toddler phase, and the 'dysfunctions' during the Oedipal phase or later . . . where do masochism, sadism and fetishism fit in?

Robin Well, here again, the people have got a bit stuck in their sexual development. They may have got as far as being reasonably sure about their sexual identity. But they haven't got far enough to be able to have a loving, trusting relationship with the opposite sex where they can be totally relaxed and natural. So they can't completely let themselves go in the sexual act. There's an element of fear and distrust that gets in the way. So the peculiar form of sexual satisfaction the person prefers is the *nearest* they can get to enjoying normal sex, *while at the same time protecting themselves* against that fear.

John A fear of what?

Robin Essentially, that some advantage will be taken of them if they allow themselves to be completely open, and vulnerable, in the way that's necessary if sex is to be really satisfying. Their experience in early life has left them with a mistrust of close relationships, a fear of love or involvement. So they're looking for a kind of sex that avoids that, which is hedged about with special conditions in order to get some of the pleasure without so much of the risk.

John But sado-masochism isn't that unusual in mild forms, is it? A lot of couples exchange 'love-bites' or get a bit rough when they get excited, don't they?

Robin Oh yes. A bit of teasing and biting and dominating and being dominated is a turn-on for most couples, at some stage at least. As long as it adds to the enjoyment of everything else, it's perfectly normal. It becomes abnormal only if they can't trust each other, and give themselves freely; in other words, when it's used as a *substitute* for love and commitment, as a way of separating sexual excitement off from the emotional closeness that normally goes with it.

John   It's abnormal because it's sex without love?

Robin   Yes. It's without love even in the sense of *feeling* for the other person as a *human being*. Systematically inflicting real pain, as a condition of enjoying sex, usually has two purposes. The first is that it gives the *illusion of being very close* and intimate, as real lovers are when they entrust themselves to each other, willingly put themselves in each other's power by allowing their feeling of love to sweep them away and control them. But in fact, sado-masochism puts *a vast distance* between the partners. As far as the sadist is concerned, the partner is an object, a thing, to be exploited and used without feeling, concern or compassion. The pain inflicted on the victim is a second-hand substitute for the love and involvement the sadist desires but can't risk since this would put him in the victim's power. And on the other side, the masochistic victim is *also* protected against real involvement, love and commitment. Because the fear and the pain force the masochist to shrink away, which puts a safe emotional distance between the sadist and themselves. In this way they are *both* protected from closeness and giving, so they *can* then tolerate some degree of attraction due to the sexual excitement.

John This principle of protecting oneself from involvement would apply right across the spectrum of sado-masochistic practices?

Robin Yes. I believe so.

John From the infliction of serious pain at one extreme, to, at the other end of the spectrum . . . what?

Robin Well, it's present in a rather feeble form in the man who tries to shock women by exposing himself, or the Peeping Tom who takes advantage without even making his presence known. And incidentally, most pornography is based on the same principle – the attempt to separate sex completely from love, and to avoid any feelings of tenderness or warmth accompanying the sexual stimulation.

John So what sadism, masochism, fetishism, voyeurism, exhibitionism and pornographyism all have in common is the fear of involvement.

Robin Because the person can't cope with sex *and* love together. They fear that will put them in the other person's power – which it *will*, of course, that's what love is all about! But they can't face this because they've had a bad experience of that power being misused by someone they loved in their childhood.

John So, in a way, the perversion is protecting their sexuality against *further* danger?

Robin That's right. The sexuality was threatened early in life, so to hang on to it, they had to *hide* it to keep it safe. They had to disguise it so that people wouldn't recognise it; or to conceal it somewhere that would be avoided by the person who was threatening it. In other words, the loving sexuality's been locked away where people can't find it. So it can be expressed only in a distorted form that doesn't risk the loving feelings people exploited in childhood.

John And that problem is then made even more difficult because society condemns this 'safe' way of expressing their sexual feelings.

Robin So naturally they tend to treat it as a guilty secret. Of course they hang on to it because it's the only sex they can really have. So they practise it only as much as they dare.

John Do they seek help for it?

Robin Only some do. And if they do come to therapy wanting to change, they tend *not* to want to examine what it is that they're trying to change *from*, because they feel guilty and ashamed about it. But of course if we want to *change*, we have to start from where we are *now*!

John You mean they're wanting to find 'normal' sexuality, while trying to forget where they locked it away.

Robin Yes. It's like the man who drops a key and then goes looking for it under a lamp-post fifty yards away because the light's better there. And this is exactly why simply encouraging them to *try* to have more normal forms of sexual satisfaction is so useless. If we can start where the sex *is*, and free it, it can escape and turn into something more natural, more connected with all the other normal feelings that can then help to control it. So the beginning of the treatment has always got to be a search to find where the sex has got locked away; and when it's found, one has to help the patient to learn to accept it in that form, and even to enjoy the fantasies that trouble him.

John Enjoy them? They came to get rid of them!

Robin It sounds strange, I know. And I don't mean that you encourage the person to inflict his fantasies on other people. But whatever the deviant impulse or fantasy may be, that's where the real, true, loving sexuality is hidden. And if he avoids facing that squarely out of shame or guilt, he'll never find the good thing that's hidden there. Whereas, if you support him in letting himself *feel* the turn-on that's connected with the deviant feeling, gradually the deeper hidden feelings will be released too. Once they start being freed, they'll flow along the normal channels, so eventually real loving sex becomes possible for that person.

John Do the new Masters-and-Johnson-type methods help with these problems too?

Robin Not directly. As I said, these sorts of deviations are somewhere in between the problems of sexual identity, like trans-sexualism and homosexuality, and the 'dysfunctions' like impotence and frigidity. They may be more easy to change than homosexuality, if the person really wants to, but they're much more difficult than those for which you've just got to change the signal from red to green. They'll normally need a year, maybe several years, of regular therapy of an analytic kind.

Our own worst enemies . . . . . .

John When you think of all the people who have trouble getting a *normal* sex life together – despite the fact that nowadays this is widely approved and encouraged – you realise how appallingly difficult it must be for people who've got some form of 'deviancy' and have to cope with the fact that even what they *can* do is disapproved of and felt to be shameful.

Robin And, of course, these disapproving attitudes harm society itself.

John In what way?

Robin Well think of the huge contribution that can be made by homosexuals and others with deviant life-styles. Where there's intolerance and rejection of deviancy, they're driven underground, pushed into a kind of 'outlaw' status where they have no alternative but to identify with others in their minority group, in *self-defence against* society as a whole. They're more or less forced into a hostile attitude to the society that's hostile to them.

John They'll be forced into rejecting everything 'normal' instead of feeling free to take what's good.

Robin And that doesn't help them *or* society. And the same applies with equal force the other way round. Take homosexuality again. If there's a powerful taboo against it, people can get very frightened that some normal aspect of their *own* behaviour might be 'homosexual'.

John Because, as you've said, most people have homosexual aspects, in the sense that they can experience feelings of enjoyment of the attractiveness of the people of their own sex?

Robin But if they're not at ease with feelings like that, they'll try to squash them, repress them and stick them behind the screen.

John Then they'll be terrified even to touch people to express affection, for fear it's a signal that they're beating on the closet door.

Robin But much more than that. Since there's the same basic *energy* powering both the homosexual and the heterosexual feelings, by putting a tighter rein on one set of feelings they're putting a tighter rein on *all* their sexual energy at the same time. That'll mean they won't be able to let go and enjoy themselves with the *opposite* sex, as much as someone can who's at ease with *all* his or her natural feelings.

John I had exactly this experience. I'd been with a girl for some time and we had a very good sex relationship. But one day we discovered we were being bothered by very similar feelings. She was working with a girl who had suddenly started to flirt with her, and it made her very uncomfortable. And I said that at the gym where I worked out there were several good-looking and desperately fit young men who were always showing off by throwing the weights around effortlessly, and they *irritated* me. So the girl and I vowed that we would try to enjoy these situations. So she went off and found she could quite enjoy flirting back at the other girl, found it didn't make her too uncomfortable at all; I went back to the gym and, gritting my teeth, tried to take pleasure in these virile young men. I felt acutely uncomfortable for a time, mostly from fear I was turning into an old queen, and then, hey presto, yes, they *were* good to look at! I *could* enjoy them and not feel too British and irritated about their slight narcissism. And within days the girl and I noticed a quite dramatic increase in energy and enjoyment in our love-making. Some part of our sexual energy that must have been tied up by this fear was now released.

Robin This is the whole point about real loving sex. You need to give yourselves completely up to the experience, putting yourselves totally in each other's hands, while it's happening. You have to be completely free, abandoned, neither trying to control yourself nor seeking to control the partner, but just responding to each other in a mounting chain-reaction of enjoyment and love. You *can't* do that if you're *guarding yourself* against some reaction you fear from the partner. And you also can't do it if you're worried that *you* might show some feeling, or do something, that you believe is out of line. Of course, this applies not only to homosexuality but to feelings right the way across the spectrum. You see, ideally we don't lose touch with the earlier stages of our development completely as we grow up, and one of the nicest things about sex is that all these stages can get expressed in love-making. So it doesn't matter what turns a couple on. They might enjoy playing domination and submission games, or babying and cosseting each other, or being aggressive Rabelaisian toddlers or turning the tables and playing each other's usual roles. If it's all play within a basically loving relationship, it's great. It means that all the different needs of the personality are getting expressed, and that not only gives an opportunity to make up for important experiences that were

missed in childhood stages of growth, but it also frees our
energies for the maximum enjoyment of sex, of each other, and
of life.

John The idea of '*play*' seems to be important here. Somehow, if
it's play, it's easier to be freer, to let go and take risks, isn't it?

Robin Yes. But don't forget that the essence of 'play' is that it
needs a *boundary*. That is, a time and a place, so you know
where it begins . . . and where it ends and the rules change back
to everyday life. People can feel safe to let themselves go completely only if they know there's the protection of a boundary. If
there is one, then you can let all the other barriers down,
abandon yourselves completely, and allow yourselves to fuse.

John And feel able to get out again when you want to?

Robin That's it. Research suggests that this ability to move in
and out of intimacy, without feeling uncomfortable about being
very close sometimes, and without minding being very far apart
at other times, is a key ingredient in the most healthy families.
And I believe it is the main thing to aim at to make a marriage
richer. But you can only let yourself 'fuse' if you're confident
your boundaries will re-form afterwards.

John You mean there can be a fear of getting so close that you
can't get your separateness back later.

Robin Yes. Problems like this come when people haven't
completed the stages of growth their families should help them
with, because then they are stuck; they can't leave their fathers
and mothers properly. So either they stay attached to them
instead of to the spouse; or, if they do get away and put a
physical distance between themselves and their families, they
nevertheless bring all those unfinished feelings about the parents
with them, and re-run them with the spouse or the children, as
if they *were* the parents.

John Which brings us full circle back to the principle you stated
right at the beginning – that the reason partners choose each
other is . . . '*unfinished business*'.

Robin That's the key to it. But we've got to 'finish' it if we're to
grow up and become separate persons – and that means we
have to *leave our parents in the sense that we don't hang about
waiting for them to give us something more*. We don't have to reject
them or lose their friendship and support. In fact, though actual
incest is forbidden, there's no rule at all against choosing a
partner who's as attractive or nice or sexy or loving as your

Mum or your Dad, or your brother or sister, or Gran and Grandpa – or all of them together if you want.

John That's a remarkably liberating thought.

Robin I think it is too. In fact, you don't fully realise how much your choice of partner is influenced by early affections for people in your family, *until* you realise it's perfectly all right to choose a partner in that way, and that you aren't breaking any rules by doing so.

John You know, this suddenly puts a new light on things. A lot of problems in marriage might be quite unnecessary. I mean, people might be switched off sexually because they don't *realise* it's all right to enjoy with the partner the *good* feelings they had about people in their family. If the reason for the attraction to the partner was hidden behind the screen, the relationship might *feel* incestuous and therefore uncomfortable, even though it isn't incestuous at all.

Robin That's absolutely right. If you look into marital and sexual problems, you see that *many* of them are due to the feeling that sex with the partner is incestuous, *because* of that resemblance. Of course it *isn't* incestuous; that idea's just due to a confusion, a muddle. But people are more likely to be muddled about it if their parents were awkward and uncomfortable about sex. So you can see why good sex between the parents would make the muddle less likely to occur in the first place because it would be quite clear where the sex really was. That's another reason why the sexual relationship between the parents is a vital basis for the security of the children, and why parents are doing everyone else a good turn, as well as themselves, by making sure they have a good time in bed as well as out of it.

John So it's the same principle for sex as it is for all the other problems that were unsettled with our parents – if we can get them out from behind our screens, we can solve them with our marriage partners. In other words, as long as we realise what's *really* going on.

Robin Isn't it comical ... all the problems that cause us most headaches are imaginary! You know, when patients are almost ready to leave therapy, and have finally understood how they're creating all their problems themselves without realising it – they almost always ask me why I didn't tell them that *before*. Of course, the truth is that I've been telling them exactly that at almost every meeting since they started to see me, and they've been furious with me for saying it!

John And at this point, if I remember rightly, you laugh at them.

Robin And then, if they laugh at themselves as well, because the whole business is so ridiculous, they're ready to leave.

Further Reading

Those interested in the ideas expressed here about the way families and marriages operate may like to look at *One Flesh: Separate Persons* (Constable, London, 1976), my introductory text on family therapy, which is written to be understandable to the layman. I have developed the ideas further in chapters in two more recent books. One of these, the *Handbook of Family Therapy* (Ed. A. Gurman and D. Kniskern, Brunner/Mazel, New York, 1981), is the definitive textbook on the subject, with contributions covering all the main schools of thought. The other, *Family Therapy: Complementary Frameworks of Theory and Practice* (Ed. A. Bentovim, G. G. Barnes and A. Cooklin, Academic Press, London, 1982), presents some British views. *Foundations of Family Therapy* by L. Hoffman (Basic Books, New York, 1981) is a brilliant, readable, though intellectually demanding account of modern ideas about the family as a 'system'. *Marriage and Marital Therapy* (Ed. T. Paolino and B. McCrady, Brunner/Mazel, New York, 1978) is an excellent, definitive text on the marital aspects.

The basic ideas of Freud, as well as Jung, Adler and Janet, are developed with wonderful clarity against their historical and social context in *The Discovery of the Unconscious* by H. Ellenberger (Allen Lane, The Penguin Press, London, 1970). Our Chapter Two depends heavily on the ideas of Melanie Klein, founder of the 'English School of Psychoanalysis', which are most clearly outlined in *Introduction to the Work of Melanie Klein* by H. Segal (second edition, Hogarth Press, London, 1973). *Playing and Reality* by D. Winnicott (Tavistock, London, 1971) is a good introduction to the idea of 'transitional objects'.

The application of ethological concepts, including attachment behaviour, to human interaction is most readably described in *The Place of Attachment in Human Behaviour* (Ed. C. Murray Parkes and J. Stevenson-Hinde, Tavistock, London, 1982). Excellent popular accounts of human development are provided in *A Child's Journey* by J. Segal and H. Yahraes (Penguin Education, Harmondsworth, 1981), *Child Alive* by R. Lewin (Temple Smith, London, 1975) and (two psychoanalytic views) *Secrets in the Family* by L. Pincus and C. Dare (Faber and Faber, London and Boston, 1978) and *Childhood and Society* by E. Erikson (Penguin, Harmondsworth, 1960).

It is more difficult to know what to advise in regard to mental disorder. *The Empty Fortress* by B. Bettelheim (Collier Macmillan, London, 1967) is a fascinating study of autism, which fits well with much of my experience and ideas, but it needs to be complemented by the opposing view, set out in *Psychoses of Uncertain Aetiology* (Ed. J. and L. Wing, Cambridge University Press, Cambridge, 1982), an authoritative, professional work which is nevertheless clear and concise, and brings together the most up-to-date research on autism, schizophrenia and depressive illnesses. *Schizophrenia and Madness* by A. Croyden Smith (George Allen & Unwin, London, 1982) is a more popular and more balanced account. R. Laing's *The Divided Self* (Tavistock, London, 1960) and J. Foudraine's *Not Made of Wood* (Quartet Books, London, 1971) are sensitive descriptions of the inner experience of psychotic and near-psychotic individuals. H. Dicks's *Licenced Mass Murder* (Basic Books, New York, 1972) is a study of the psychology of the Nazi SS by the pioneer of marital therapy who later became official psychiatrist at the Nuremberg War Crimes trial.

I do not know a popular book on depression that I can recommend, but an excellent, comprehensive, professional text is the *Handbook of Affective Disorders* (Ed. E. Paykel, Churchill Livingstone, London, 1982), which includes good accounts of the psychological and family aspects. The American College of Psychiatrists has produced good, brief, professional but readable overviews in *Schizophrenia: Biological and Psychological Perspectives* and *Depression: Clinical, Biological and Psychological Perspectives* (Ed. G. Usdin, Brunner/Mazel, New York, 1975 and 1977).

Two excellent accounts of available information about gender and sexual role development are *Males and Females* by C. Hutt (Penguin, Harmondsworth, 1972) and *The Psychology of Sex Differences* by E. Maccoby and C. Jacklin (Stanford University Press, Stanford, 1974).

A splendid account for the layman of sexual development is W. Gadpaille's *The Cycles of Sex* (Charles Scribner's Sons, New York, 1975). *The Sexual Relationship* by D. Scharff (Routledge & Kegan Paul, London, 1982), at a more professional level but very clear and readable, puts it in the context of the marriage and family and covers both behavioural and psychoanalytic approaches to sex therapy. Recent advances in sex therapy are more fully described in H. Kaplan's *The New Sex Therapy* and *Disorders of Sexual Desire* (Bailliere Tyndall, London, 1974 and 1980).

An overview of the research on healthy families is given in *Normal Family Processes* (Ed. F. Walsh, Guildford Press, New York and London, 1982). The Timberlawn research on exceptionally healthy ('optimal') families is described professionally (but very readably) by J. Lewis *et al.* in *No Single Thread: Psychological Health in Family Systems* (Brunner/Mazel, New York, 1976) and in a popular account by J. Lewis, *How's Your Family?* (Brunner/Mazel, New York, 1979). *Adaptation to Life* by G. Vaillant (Little, Brown, Boston and Toronto, 1977) is a fascinating study of healthy individuals followed over thirty years, from adolescence to late middle age.

Different types of psychotherapy are well described for the layman in *A Complete Guide to Therapy* by J. Kovel (Pantheon Books, New York, 1976) and a most readable, authoritative text is *Introduction to Psychotherapy* by D. Brown and J. Pedder (Tavistock, London, 1979).

Robin Skynner